Brigadier General
William Haines Lytle

Brigadier General William Haines Lytle
The Union's Poet-Soldier

BRYAN W. LANE

McFarland & Company, Inc., Publishers
Jefferson, North Carolina

ISBN (print) 978-1-4766-9709-3
ISBN (ebook) 978-1-4766-5572-7

LIBRARY OF CONGRESS CATALOGING DATA ARE AVAILABLE

Library of Congress Control Number 2025043390

© 2026 Bryan W. Lane. All rights reserved

No part of this book may be reproduced or transmitted in any form or by any means, electronic or mechanical, including photocopying or recording, or by any information storage and retrieval system, without permission in writing from the publisher.

Front cover image: stylized artwork showing Lytle on horseback, sword drawn, leading his troops in battle. He was, in fact, holding his sword when he was shot from his horse (from the collection of Virginius Cornick Hall, Jr.).

Printed in the United States of America

McFarland & Company, Inc., Publishers
Box 611, Jefferson, North Carolina 28640
www.mcfarlandpub.com

To Connie and Virginius,
and all who hear the past whisper

Table of Contents

Preface 1

Introduction 5

Chapter 1. Lytle's Roots 9

Chapter 2. Our Dear Boy 16

Chapter 3. The Mantle Falls 22

Chapter 4. Volunteers 30

Chapter 5. The Folly and the Beauty 35

Chapter 6. Tensions Mount 40

Chapter 7. Antony and Cleopatra 45

Chapter 8. On the Eve of War 51

Chapter 9. Clear the Way 54

Chapter 10. The First Fall: Carnifex Ferry 64

Chapter 11. Recovery and Reunion 71

Chapter 12. Lytle Moves South 77

Chapter 13. Hope 86

Chapter 14. The Second Fall: Perryville 93

Chapter 15. The General and Mrs. Lytle 105

Chapter 16. A Cross, a Speech, and a Bridge 115

Chapter 17. John Brown's Body 123

Chapter 18. Old Pete Arrives 132

Chapter 19. The Third Fall: Chickamauga	135
Chapter 20. The Rain on the Tent	148
Chapter 21. She Remembered	154
Chapter 22. The Funeral	158
Epilogue	162
Appendix: The Speech at Bridgeport	171
Chapter Notes	177
Bibliography	193
Index	201

Preface

This book began with a trip to the local library. I had gone there to research another Civil War general, and decided to check out a book by Glenn Tucker, *Chickamauga: Bloody Battle in the West*. That is when I first learned of William Haines Lytle. His story fascinated me, and I wanted to know more. Unfortunately, there was not much information out there about him.

Over the years, more information has surfaced about the Union's poet-soldier. Dr. Ruth Carter's excellent book *For Honor Glory and Union: The Mexican and Civil War Letters of Brig. Gen. William Haines Lytle* provides details about Lytle's family but not as much information about the Civil War battles and campaigns in which he fought. Other authors have produced fine histories of those battles and campaigns but shed little light on his life otherwise. I decided to try to fill this gap by researching his life and writing this biography.

This book is not a complete history of the American Civil War or antebellum politics in Ohio. There are other references for that information. This is also not a hagiography. Lytle had his share of problems. This is a biography of William Haines Lytle, presented with the good and the bad details of his life.

Past events do not change but our interpretations and understanding of them do. Even for the people who were there and experienced the events, their memories could and often did change over time. Details are forgotten, created, or garbled, and descriptions of the original event are distorted. Add in later "interpretations," and at some point, we find ourselves wondering: what exactly happened?

Nobody reading this book has firsthand knowledge of the American Civil War. Therefore, we are left with the written and photographic (and sketched) records of those who experienced it. That is why, for this book, I attempted to use firsthand contemporaneous accounts whenever possible such as letters, journals, diaries, and newspaper accounts. Even contemporaneous newspaper accounts can be wrong. (Think of the "news" we get today and how differing versions of events are presented based on what news provider you choose.) But the accounts written by war correspondents of the battles they witnessed are often compelling records.

As an example of a contemporaneous version being wrong, after the Battle of Carnifex Ferry, a Cincinnati newspaper published the names of the soldiers of the Tenth Ohio killed in that fight. Comparing that list, however, to the names of those shown as killed at the battle on the official roster of the Tenth Ohio, you see that in some cases the names are not even close. Then consider the intentional distortions. After Carnifex Ferry, Lytle's officious brigade commander, Henry Benham, praised Lytle in his official report of the battle but in a letter home wrote disparagingly of the colonel from Cincinnati.

One thing, though, that became clear as I researched Lytle is that he was an extraordinary person. Of course, his family members loved him, but there seemed to be an almost universal agreement that he was a charming, talented gentleman. Even his enemies admired his eloquence, talent, and style.

To learn more about him I spent time in Cincinnati, working with a descendant of Lytle's sister's family. That relative, Mr. Virginius Cornick Hall, Jr., opened his home, shared family stories, and allowed me to see priceless Lytle family heirlooms. I saw the bust that sculptor Hiram Powers made of Lytle's father. I even held the piece of wood in my hand that Lytle's mother brought back from George Washington's tomb. These were very personal connections to times, places, and people that are long gone.

Mr. Hall and I went to Lytle Park where his family's great mansion once stood. We went to Spring Grove Cemetery and found the two places where Lytle had been interred. The first spot is quiet and removed from most of the visitors of that beautiful cemetery, and the second, more famous final resting place, is the one with the lovely monument near the entrance to the grounds.

The Cincinnati Museum Center houses the Lytle Papers. I spent many hours there poring over Lytle family letters. Anne Shepherd, Mickey DeVries, Christine Engels, David Conzett and Arabeth Balasko were all very kind and helpful to me. Dr. Allen Bernard, Mr. Jeff Suess, and Ms. Bonnie Speeg of Cincinnati were all generous to me with their time and input. The Filson Historical Society in Louisville, Kentucky, houses journals and letters of Lytle's Civil War aide and friend, Alfred Pirtle. I enjoyed reading Pirtle's accounts of Lytle, written from the vantage point of a friend and fellow soldier. Jennie Cole, Hannah Costelle, and Hailey Brangers of the Filson were very kind and helpful. Thanks also to Lynn Niedermeier from Western Kentucky for access to their special collections.

Lytle's service for the Union spanned nearly three autumns. He fought in three battles and was wounded in each one, the last time mortally. I visited each battlefield and worked with local experts to retrace his steps. Terry Lowry, author of *September Blood: The Battle of Carnifex Ferry*, shared his valuable time with me to help me understand the battle and Lytle's role in it. At Carnifex Ferry I met Rick Proctor. He shared his knowledge of the battle and showed me the "muddy, slushy" road the Tenth took to their first battle and where they emerged from the dense woods into the clearing where they came under fire. As I stepped into the open space there was a distant, sharp peal of thunder. The sound rolled over the hills and fields, and just for a split second, the thought crossed my mind, "the skirmishers are at it."

At Perryville the pristine nature of the park makes it easier to "see" how things might have been. Chuck Lott, a Perryville historian and guide, shared a day with me and we drove past where the Russell House was, down to Doctors Creek, then back up to the ridge where the Tenth stood and fought. We walked behind the Bottom farm along the fence line where the Kentucky and Ohio troops of Lytle's Seventeenth Brigade stood against the Confederate onslaught. We also walked in the cornfield where Lytle struggled to rally a rear guard and then fell and was captured. Bryan Bush, the park manager of Perryville, reviewed my book and offered excellent suggestions for improvements.

At Bridgeport, Alabama, there is a walking bridge across the Tennessee River where the Civil War bridge once stood. There is a small museum at Bridgeport and the railroad tracks that carried Lytle's remains back to the North are still there. I stood alone on the bluff and imagined Lytle watching the great fire the night the Rebels torched the bridge on the south side of Long Island.

At Chickamauga, James Ogden III, the battlefield historian, shared his time and helped me understand the movements of Lytle's troops on that terrible September day when Lytle gave his life for his country. He also pointed out where the camp of the Tenth Ohio was established after the battle. This helped me to visualize the night Lytle's friend, Alfred Pirtle, visited Lytle's remains and heard the rain on the tent.

Thank you to Elizabeth Foxwell and the fine people at McFarland who believed in this book project. I would also like to recognize and thank my friend Randy Duncan. He has been editor, encourager, and critic, and he supplied terrific photos. I also want to thank my wife Connie who encouraged and allowed me to continue this project. Thank you.

If I may, I would like to share a story that is not specifically related to this book. It is more about for whom this book is intended. Several years ago, my wife and I took our boys to the "historic triangle." None of them were too excited about it, frankly, but I wanted the boys to see Jamestown, Williamsburg, and Yorktown. It was hot that summer. We were worn out from walking around and our last stop was Yorktown. Our car was parked near Redoubt 9. I started the car to cool it off, and as I stood outside waiting for the boys to climb into the vehicle, I noticed there was another car parked near us.

Beside that car stood what I would describe as an "older" couple and their adult daughter. She was wearing a dress. Maybe they had just come from some other engagement or maybe she considered this grassy, silent field to be a sacred place, worthy of her respect. She told them she wanted to walk up to Redoubt 10. They said they would stay at the car and wait for her. Then she walked, alone, to the Redoubt. I wanted to follow her and tell her, I get it. I hear the past whisper, too.

This book is for the lady at Yorktown and the parents who take their children to these historic sites. And the children who grow up and take their children, as my parents did for me and we have tried to do for our children. American history is important. The people who gave their lives for our country deserve to be remembered. William Haines Lytle deserves to be remembered.

Introduction

Robert Sparks Walker grew up around Chattanooga, Tennessee. He was a poet, journalist, naturalist, and Pulitzer Prize–nominated author. One of his books, published in 1941, was about Lookout Mountain. Chapter Eight of that book is titled "The Heart of a Soldier." It is about William Haines Lytle. Walker said he chose to tell the story of Lytle in the chapter "to illustrate the heart of a soldier who falls in battle and the reaction of his death in the hearts of his foes." Mr. Walker included a few of Lytle's poems as well as the speech at Bridgeport. (The inclusion of that speech by the "Yankee general" led to Walker's book being banned by the Georgia library committee established by Governor Eugene Talmadge.)[1]

This book you are reading is about the heart and life of William Haines Lytle, a soldier who was also a poet, lawyer, orator, and politician. It is also about the reactions to his life and death in the hearts of his friends and foes.

William Haines Lytle was born into a prominent family in Cincinnati whose influence was already beginning to wane when he entered the world. His grandfather, who could boast of friendships with Andrew Jackson and other distinguished people of his day such as Arthur St. Clair, Henry Clay, and Simon Kenton, was a rough and tumble frontiersman with a fondness for education and music. Lytle's father was much more refined and cultured than the grandfather. He was a well-known orator (earning the nickname "Orator Bob"), politician and lawyer. Lytle's cultured, refined, and intelligent mother came from a family with important connections to politics and wealth in New Jersey and New York. William Haines Lytle seemed to combine the best of all his progenitors.

Besides his several vocations, he liked to travel and enjoy life and noticed and enjoyed beauty in all its forms. He was charming, funny, talented, and intelligent. However, he could also be unfocused, petty, and vain. He had a drinking problem that plagued him throughout his life and likely cost him a timelier promotion during the Civil War.

His mother called him Will or Willie. His sisters and other family members called him Will. His sisters also called him "Bub" and "Bubby." His friends called him Bill or Billy and his Civil War troops knew him as "Old Bill." Some of the Confederate generals had known his father so they referred to him as "Bob Lytle's son." His devoted Civil War aide and friend, Alfred Pirtle, simply called him "the General."

Lytle was well educated. He graduated from Cincinnati College before studying law under the tutelage of his lawyer uncle. He served in the Mexican War although his regiment arrived in Mexico as the war was ending. Returning home to Cincinnati, he set up shop in a law firm with his uncle and practiced law until being elected to serve in the Ohio House of Representatives. Like his father, William Haines Lytle was a gifted speaker and this ability helped him win friends and influence political enemies. After an unremarkable time in office Lytle continued to be in demand as a speaker for other candidates and on behalf of his beloved Democratic Party. He participated in community events, had a circle of devoted friends, and was a loving older brother to his two sisters.

In his spare time, he wrote poetry. One of his poems was published to great acclaim and earned praise from around the country. Soon other poems were published but he did not focus his energies and talents on writing, or politics, or the law, and he was often distracted by pretty women, partying with his friends, and traveling.

When the American Civil War began Lytle was serving in the Ohio state militia as a major general. He resigned that position to become the colonel of the Tenth Ohio Volunteer Infantry regiment. His considerable talents and energies were finally focused by the requirements of leading his men during the war. Lytle cared deeply for his men and could almost always be found at the front. That is how he ended up being wounded three times.

He was funny, heroic, and sometimes sad. He traveled, read, wrote, spoke, lived, fought, and died well. As well known and highly regarded as he was in his lifetime, Lytle was concerned that he would be forgotten. In his poem "When the Long Shadows" he ends the piece with a haunting question that echoes down through the years: "In the wide world, will none remember me?" Many people did and do remember Lytle. Others may not remember him, but they are familiar with his work as evidenced by the story of Mr. Lucas McIntosh Dargan.

Mr. Dargan, a native of South Carolina, began reading poetry in high school because his teacher required her students to read, remember and recite great poems. During World War II he served in the United States Navy and often recalled his favorite poems in the darkness of the early watch. After the war he married, and he and his wife were the proud parents of four daughters. He went to work as a forester and figured he planted a million trees in his lifetime. In November 2016, the then–99-year-old Mr. Dargan lay in a hospital bed in the McLeod Regional Medical Center in Florence, South Carolina. He was dying.

His daughters and their families took turns spending the night at the hospital with Mr. Dargan because his body was shutting down. One night it was the turn of his son-in-law, Steve Zeitlin. Thinking Mr. Dargan had fallen asleep, Steve took out his laptop to get some work done when he heard a familiar, raspy drawl. Mr. Dargan was reciting a poem.

> I am dying, Egypt, dying!
> Ebbs the crimson life-tide fast,
> And the dark Plutonian shadows
> Gather on the evening blast....

Mr. Dargan said he remembered the poem but not the name of the poet. A quick internet search revealed that the poem was by someone named William Haines Lytle. The two men talked quietly in the dark for a while, Lytle's words still fresh on their minds. Then Mr. Dargan went to sleep.[2]

This is the story of the man who wrote that poem, the Union's poet-soldier, William Haines Lytle.

Chapter 1

LYTLE'S ROOTS

Near the central business district of downtown Cincinnati, a small, weathered sign identifies a plot of land as Lytle Park. Trees and flowers beautify the two-acre setting. People walk along the short trail with their friends or dogs or by themselves. Interstate 71 runs beneath the park grounds and just down the rise to the south is the original superhighway of the region, the Ohio River. The National Park Service says the river took its name from the Iroquois word "O-Y-O," meaning "the great river." The French, misunderstanding the Iroquois meaning, or perhaps adding their own editorial comment, would later call it *"La Belle Rivière"* (*"the* Beautiful River").[1] It is difficult to imagine now, among the tall buildings and indifferent passersby, how important this small plot used to be. But this is where the old Lytle mansion once stood, and this is where William Haines Lytle was born on November 2, 1826.

His grandfather, also named William, built the house in 1809 at a cost of $2,900. Builders used 215,000 bricks for the mansion, and another 75,000 bricks for the outbuildings. The home stood at Symmes (now Third) and Lawrence streets and originally faced Symmes (Third) Street and the river (south). (The photos we see of the mansion today were taken after the entrance was moved to the Lawrence Street side in 1867.)[2] The front gates were flanked by pillars. A broad walk, shaded by trees, led to the front door which opened to a hall 50 feet long and 12 feet wide.[3] The Lytle mansion was home to Cincinnati's first piano and, at one time, the largest personal library in town. It was also the scene of many parties and dinners involving politicians and the elite of the Queen City.[4] Over the years such prominent people as Andrew Jackson, Henry Clay, and Daniel Webster enjoyed the hospitality of the Lytles.[5]

W.H. Lytle's great-grandfather, Captain William Lytle, moved his family in April 1780 from Carlisle, Pennsylvania, to Kentucky to claim bounty land earned for his service during the French and Indian War. The captain, whose Irish-born father had come to the New World years before, was born October 15, 1728, near Carlisle, Pennsylvania. He had been commissioned captain of an independent company of foot near Fort Hamilton in the Tuscarora Valley, April 9, 1750, by Lieutenant Governor Robert Morris and served the Crown loyally and well in the French and Indian War, and later at Fort Pitt for three years.[6]

Accompanied by his wife, Mary Steele Lytle, along with their sons and daughters, Lytle sought a new beginning in the wilderness. They, along with other settlers, left Pittsburgh and journeyed down the Ohio River. His son William (W.H. Lytle's grandfather) was nine years old at the time of the trip (born September 1, 1770) and would later write about his adventures.[7] The settlers traveled in modified flatboats called arks or Kentucky boats (protective walls were added to shelter them from Native American arrows and bullets) down the Ohio River and landed at Beargrass, Kentucky, near the Falls of the Ohio. They would later move to near what would become Danville, Kentucky, in 1781 before moving in 1784 to Lexington.[8]

Zadok Cramer, a printer and bookbinder in Pittsburgh, accumulated stories and journals from river travelers and published an early travel guide. Although his book was published more than twenty years after the Lytles' trip, we can get an idea of river travel from his publication. Regarding Ohio River travel, Cramer advised, "On shoving off at Pittsburgh, if the water should be high, your boat will require but little attention, otherwise than keeping her bow foremost and giving her headway by the application of the oars." He did warn that the wind could be a problem but the trip from Pittsburgh to the Falls of the Ohio should take between ten and 15 days.[9]

When the Lytles began their journey down the Ohio River in April 1780, the American Revolutionary War was still undecided. The important Battle of Kings Mountain would not be fought until October of that year. The French and Indian War had ended only 17 years before and just five years prior to this journey; much of the land that would become Kentucky was still largely unsettled by Europeans. A man named Richard Henderson, along with other investors, and quite against the wishes of the English government, coerced a group of Cherokees to convey the territory to Henderson's group, the Transylvania Company, in March 1775. One of the Cherokee leaders, a man named Dragging Canoe, vehemently opposed this transaction and uttered a phrase that would live on past his lifetime. Whether it was a warning or a threat, or a recitation of Native American history for the area, Dragging Canoe pointed toward Kentucky and said the English would find the area to be a "dark and bloody ground."

As settlers made their way into the newly opened territory, they indeed found it to be dark and bloody as Native Americans including

Chapter 1. Lytle's Roots 11

Kentucky boats added protective sides to shield the temporary mariners from Indian attacks. In fact, as they floated down the Ohio River, the right side of the river was known as "the Indian side." "Sketch of a flat-bottom boat, such as are used to descend the Ohio and the Mississippi" (Library of Congress).

tribes from north of the Ohio raided their settlements. In June 1780, not long after the Lytles and the rest of their group had settled in Kentucky, the British led a coalition force of Native American warriors from different tribes across the Ohio with the intent of wiping out the Kentucky settlements. After initial successes the British and Native American force retreated back across the Beautiful River, leaving behind dead and wounded settlers and taking away hundreds of prisoners. The Lytles were not among the casualties.[10]

Even after the American Revolution ended, the frontier was a dangerous place. Beginning at the age of 16, Lytle's grandfather joined raiding parties against Native American villages north of the Ohio River and earned a reputation as a fearless warrior.[11] This was the time of Daniel Boone, Simon Kenton, and George Rogers Clark, and Lytle's grandfather was one of those fighters who participated in and witnessed the horrors of frontier war. Besides the terror of Indian warfare, there were constant threats from disease, wild animals, and criminals like Samuel Mason and his gang, and a duo now known as America's first serial killers, the Harpe brothers, who terrorized the western settlements until they were finally hunted down and killed. But when the immediate threat of fighting with Native Americans died down, William Lytle joined with his friend Nathaniel Massie and the two worked as surveyors. Massie was a speculator in western lands and helped Lytle accumulate wealth. After amassing what he felt were sufficient funds, Lytle married Philadelphian Eliza Noel Stall on February 28, 1798.[12]

Connections were as important then as they are today, and it is worth noting that Eliza's sisters married men who would also become prominent Cincinnatians. Frances Stall married Arthur St. Clair, Jr., and Mary Stall was the first wife of Samuel W. Davies, mayor of Cincinnati from 1833 to 1843.[13]

While surveying north of the Ohio River, Lytle began to make plans to move there. After 20 years in Kentucky, William Lytle and his wife moved across the river in February 1801. They founded Lytletown, which was later renamed Williamsburg, in Clermont County in what would become the state of Ohio.[14] The following year they built a house overlooking the East Fork of the Little Miami River, not far from the center of the town. Lytle named his farm "Harmony Hill" and opened his land office near the house.[15] William and Eliza would be the parents of five children: John, William Henry, Robert Todd, Eliza Ann and Edward Hiley. Four of the five children would die in early adulthood from consumption. William Haines Lytle's father, Robert Todd Lytle, was born September 19, 1804, in Williamsburg.[16]

William Lytle served as major general of the Seventh Division of the Ohio militia, held various government posts, surveyed, bought and sold horses, and ran a mill.[17] As a result of his rank in the militia he would be known for the rest of his life as "the General." He helped found Port Clinton, Ohio, and was always on the lookout for business opportunities. These efforts sometimes angered others, including in one case his sister, Jane, who, in response to a dispute over money, told him she didn't want anything to do with his "win dig fortune."[18]

In January 1806 William Lytle bought eight and one quarter acres in Cincinnati (formerly Losantiville), 30 miles west of Williamsburg. This property, from what would become Fifth to Third Street, and east and west from Broadway to Pike, included an area called the "Peach Grove." A former owner of the property, Dr. Richard Allison, had planted a small grove of peach trees there, inspiring the nickname. Lytle improved the lot and added more plants and trees and on March 10, 1808, received 101 engrafted apple trees, 11 pear trees, six cherry trees, 12 plum trees and two "quinch" trees. (Early settlers believed the boiled seed of quince trees produced an astringent that made hair curl.) William Lytle would ultimately add more than 250 trees to his property. In time the Lytle land nurtured maple, sycamore, and oak trees with linden trees in the front yard. There was a cornfield on the lot and the field extended to Deer Creek. Beyond that was forest.[19]

William Lytle became a leader in many local organizations and was an early and generous contributor to the new Cincinnati College. Although the Lytles were Presbyterians (they would later change to Episcopalian due to political disagreements), William Lytle also donated 200 acres of land he had earned as a surveyor to the local Catholic church for their use in Brown County.[20] With all his success, prominence and philanthropy, William Lytle was no stranger to failure. For example, Lytle attempted to build a canal near his Portland, Kentucky, property. The attempt was a disaster.[21] Ensuing legal battles, however, that even involved Henry Clay, left him broken and bewildered. As legal matters arose, his brother-in-law, John Rowan, "handled" them. His price was more and more of William Lytle's land in payment.[22]

Surveyors and speculators like William Lytle would often accept a percentage of the land surveyed as payment. As a result, he had grown rich in land but poor in cash. Mismanaged surveys also caused Lytle and his customers headaches. Then, financial crises in 1819 and 1820 caused banks to call in their loans and when speculators like Lytle could not come up with the cash the banks took their lands.[23]

The surveys done by Lytle's grandfather followed the "Virginia custom," meaning the surveyors relied on natural markings such as rivers or piles of stones to set boundaries. This system was not very accurate and led to problems, as William Haines Lytle's grandfather (and many of his unfortunate clients) discovered. When the first settlers arrived, these inaccurate measures were not as critical, but as more and more people moved west, the errors became problematic.[24] For their services, deputy surveyors often received 20 to 50 percent of the lands they surveyed as compensation. They could also be paid in cash, although hard currency was scarce at the time. An 1803 newspaper article gives an idea of how transactions were conducted in the beginning. It stated that people wishing to buy land could apply to Mr. William Lytle and that "two thirds of the payment will be taken in Horses, the balance in Cash, for which a considerable credit will be given." Mr. Lytle did not even expect payment until the following spring.[25]

In September 1820, the Bank of the United States got a judgment against William Lytle for $111,000. Lytle won a time reprieve from the Common Pleas Court of Ohio, but they did not set aside the judgement. He claimed he deposited more than $150,000 (more than four million dollars today) to settle the claims. The Lytle family had proof that at least $120,000 of that amount was claimed by the Bank. In that case, the Bank took $9,000 more than the $111,000 Lytle owed but the family also claimed the Bank owed them for a total of $39,000 ($150,000 minus $111,000) for the overpayment. The government, of course, did not return the money and the family would never forget or forgive this injustice.[26]

Amid all this financial heartache, William Lytle's wife, Eliza, died on May 15, 1821.[27] A little more than a year after the death of Eliza, he married Margaret Smith Haines.[28] Margaret's children from her previous marriage were Ezekiel Smith Haines (a successful lawyer who went by "Smith"), Elias Henry, and two daughters, Joanna and Elizabeth.[29] Because of his legal losses and to keep the house out of the hands of the Bank of the United States, in April 1824, William Lytle transferred the deed of the Lytle mansion to his stepson Smith Haines.[30]

William Lytle, fighter, writer, collector, surveyor, philanthropist, leader. He was truly a Renaissance man, as his grandson would be (from the collection of Virginius Cornick Hall, Jr.).

William's son, Robert Todd Lytle, graduated from Cincinnati College.[31] He also fell in love with his stepsister, Elizabeth, and their relationship developed quickly. They decided to marry in 1822. However, they were deemed too young at that time, so Robert went to Louisville to study law and Elizabeth traveled East to stay with family for a year.[32]

Mr. William Henry Venable, an early biographer of William Haines Lytle, described Elizabeth as "a lady of rare culture and beauty."[33] Robert Todd Lytle would have agreed with that assessment. In an undated letter, Robert gushed about his love to Elizabeth. Though not as gifted as his son would be, Robert tried his hand at poetry. Robert wrote, "The secret contained within, is the name of a young lady whose beauty and accomplishments would distance the most unbounded panegyric...." Robert's love poem included these lines:

"In majesty bright, embracing the sight,
Jealous of matching her galaxy light....
Every spark outshining the diamond true
Will serve but in Egyptian darkness to render
Heaven's rubies, eclipsed by the Beauty of you."

He closed with this instruction: "read, destroy it, and oblige me, Robert."[34]

Robert's law instructor was his uncle, a distinguished Kentucky lawyer and politician named John Rowan. (Rowan, a native of Pennsylvania, had married William Lytle's sister Agnes "Ann" Lytle. As a wedding gift, William Lytle gave them 325 acres near Bardstown, Kentucky. There, Rowan built a house he called "Federal Hill.")[35] Robert Lytle successfully completed his studies and in 1824 was admitted to the Ohio Bar at age 20.[36] Elizabeth and Robert resumed their relationship and on November 30, 1825, were married by the Presbyterian minister Joshua Lacy (J.L.) Wilson.[37] The newlyweds lived with their parents at the Lytle mansion and a little less than a year after their wedding, on November 2, 1826, their first child, William Haines Lytle, was born.[38]

Chapter 2

OUR DEAR BOY

The baby brought new life, changes, and challenges to the household. There are many "firsts" in the life of a newborn. These were not recorded by the Lytles but other everyday events were. One thing that is evident from the letters is that even the grizzled old "Indian fighter" William Lytle loved the baby, and the little boy reciprocated that love. When Lytle traveled for business, he would often ask about Will in letters home.[1] Grandma Margaret kept her husband informed on the family and their little grandson. She noted, for example, how when William was out of town on business, 18-month-old Will would trot to his grandfather's office and look all over for him. She also said Will was a chatty child and "one of the smartest little fellows you ever saw." Robert Todd kept his father up to date on the activities of little Will also. The boy apparently had quite an appetite and Robert wrote about the difficulty of keeping him fed.[2] Robert also said his young son "is a prodigy for his age in every respect." Elizabeth agreed, writing, "a smarter boy never was seen."[3]

With a new mouth to feed and having successfully obtained his law license, Robert Todd Lytle unexpectedly pivoted to politics, a pursuit which often kept him away from the family. He was handsome, an excellent speaker (he was known as "Orator Bob" for his oratorical excellence) and the son of William Lytle. These were all important attributes that would contribute to his early successes. Another important asset was the Lytle family friend, Andrew Jackson, whose hardline views against the Bank of the United States no doubt pleased William Lytle. When Andrew Jackson and his wife, Rachel, stopped in Cincinnati, they were entertained by the Lytles.[4]

For all his strengths, Robert Todd Lytle also had weaknesses, one of which apparently was gambling. Perhaps worse than the habit itself was the fact he was not always good at it. A September 29, 1828, *National Gazette* (Philadelphia) article reported Robert had lost nearly $1,400 (nearly $40,000 in today's dollars) by gambling at a card game called Faro

Chapter 2. Our Dear Boy

Robert and Elizabeth Lytle, silhouette from life, shows the couple at home. Both would die young from tuberculosis, known then as "consumption" (from the collection of Virginius Cornick Hall, Jr.).

and that he intended to sue the winners. Despite the gambling losses he ran for and won a seat in the Ohio House of Representatives in October 1828.[5] But he soon demonstrated a frustrating lack of focus that his son would inherit. Not satisfied with his newly-won seat, Robert wrote that he found political life "somewhat monotonous."[6] Even so, and despite his father's objections, "Orator Bob" continued to pursue a career in politics.[7]

Just over two years after the birth of Will, on November 6, 1828, Margaritta "Mag" Lytle was born.[8] Adding to this good news, in May 1829 William Lytle was appointed surveyor general for the states of Ohio, Indiana, and the Michigan Territory by his friend, President Andrew Jackson.[9] These were good times for the Lytles.

They doted on their children and lavished them with love and attention. Now an older brother, Will, embraced that role. His parents and grandparents noted his maturity for his age. Grandma Margaret recalled with pride the night the Lytles hosted a party for about 50 little boys and girls and Will acted as host "quite like a man." He also developed a love for horses in his childhood and enjoyed going riding with his uncle nearly every day. Even as a small child he was able to ride by himself, in part because of special straps installed on the saddle to keep the boy safe. Even though he acted older than his age, he was still a child. While he could be fun, smart, happy, and intelligent, Will could also be mischievous and a troublemaker. One time he forgot his role as protective older brother and applied a hot poker to sister Mag's backside causing her to be laid up in bed for a week.[10] And a lifelong addiction likely began in Will's childhood.

Because the city of Cincinnati struggled to produce a healthy water supply, citizens often turned to alcohol as an alternative. Robert and Elizabeth gave little Will brandy-laden drinks and convinced him to consume them by saying they were "Grandpa's grog." Unfortunately, Will learned to enjoy these beverages and carried his love of strong drink into adulthood.[11]

Robert Todd Lytle decided not to run for a second term in the Ohio State House of Representatives.[12] He was concerned about the health of Elizabeth who was pregnant and gave birth to Josephine "Josie" Roberta Lytle on October 2, 1830.[13] He was also worried about the health of his father. Elizabeth wrote to Robert on March 10, 1831, that their father, William Lytle, was "lying on a sick couch" and there seemed to be no hope for his recovery. He was dying. Shortly before he passed away, the old man called for his grandson, took him in his arms, and said, "Thank God I have now a boy who will keep up the name of Lytle when the rest of us are laid in the dust."

Around seven o'clock in the evening of March 17, 1831, William Lytle died.[14] Reflecting on her loss, Margaret wrote, "_death_ has made a breach which no length of time or years can ever make up."[15] Robert advised family friend Andrew Jackson of their loss. He wrote that it was his "melancholy duty" to advise the president of William Lytle's death. Robert concluded the letter by saying that his father's soul had "abandoned its wretched tabernacle of suffering, for a home where care comes not & where sorrow never enters."[16] Sorrow would soon enter the Lytles' lives again, though.

Less than a year later, on February 18, 1832, a major flood hit the Queen City. From April through June 1832, measles was the top cause of death in Cincinnati and one of those victims was Margaritta Lytle who died on April 7, 1832.[17] A despondent Elizabeth dealt with her grief by leaving for the East for six months to visit relatives. She left Will and Josie in the care of her mother and her siblings.[18] Five-year-old Will was sent to stay with Uncle Smith Haines and his wife, Charlotte. They soon tired of caring for the boy and sent him to Elias Haines.[19] Robert Todd Lytle dealt with his grief by deciding to run as the Democratic candidate for a seat in the United States House of Representatives.

Chapter 2. Our Dear Boy

Will attended a political parade in June 1832 which featured his father. He enjoyed the pomp and excitement of the festivities. Elizabeth never liked politics, but she worked to support her husband's efforts and Robert Todd Lytle won election to the Twenty-Third Congress, representing Ohio's First Congressional District. His term began in March 1833.[20] Robert would make some good friends while in Washington, D.C., including fellow first-term Democrats Franklin Pierce of New Hampshire and Thomas Hamer of Ohio.[21]

Elizabeth visited her husband in Washington, D.C., and loved socializing. Whereas Robert found the city and the politicians nearly intolerable, Elizabeth attended parties as often as possible and enjoyed her time there. During one memorable week she and Robert attended parties every night. While in the capital she also collected autographs. Andrew Jackson wrote in her book, "Seek Wisdom. This is more precious than rubies, for all her paths are peace, and lead to a happy immortality beyond the grave." Despite making Whig and Democrat friends, Elizabeth concluded that politics is "a game of chance at best" and "success always makes enemies."[22]

Elizabeth enjoyed attending sessions of Congress and listening to the men deliver their speeches, although she felt the press "garbled in a ridiculous manner" one of Robert's speeches. She also noted how well Will was progressing. Referring to him as "Our dear Boy" she said he was exceeding her high expectations of him. The proud mother said Will's memory was excellent and that he had a "fondness for books."[23]

As a political figure, Robert Todd Lytle found himself squarely in the sights of political opponents, including a local Whig newspaper editor and Lytle-hater named Charles Hammond. Hammond used his paper, the *Cincinnati Gazette*, to accuse Robert of "wild and dissipated habits" and being a "spendthrift and a gambler" who was "unworthy of the trust of the people." Robert responded that those were "unqualified falsehoods."[24] Lytle's friend, Moses Dawson (who ran the rival *Cincinnati Advertiser*, which later became the *Enquirer*), said of Hammond, "since he has been a political character, has been infamous for slandering the best and bravest men his country has produced."[25]

The Whig Party had been formed in opposition to "King" Andrew Jackson.[26] The Ohio Anti-Jacksonian Whigs nominated Bellamy Storer, a native of present-day Maine, to run against Lytle for his seat in the House of Representatives. Lytle made a grievous error by trusting in and confiding to a constituent that his stance on the Bank of the United States could be changed. The constituent handed over the incriminating letter to Storer who ambushed Lytle on the campaign trail with it. Storer won by 96 votes. After the loss Elizabeth remarked that "working for the public" resulted in "neither profit, thanks, nor honor...."[27]

Despite the defeat there was still good news. While staying with family in Princeton, New Jersey, Elizabeth gave birth on January 10, 1835, to Elizabeth "Lily" Lytle.[28] The following month Elizabeth took Will and the newborn baby to visit Robert, who was still in Washington. Robert took Will to visit President Jackson in the White House.[29] Robert and Elizabeth made friends in the capital, including Tennessean James Knox Polk and his wife Sarah, with whom they shared a boarding house for a time.[30]

Jackson appointed Robert Todd Lytle to be surveyor general of public lands in Ohio, Indiana, and the Territory of Michigan. This was the same position his father had held. Ohio Governor Robert Lucas appointed him major general of the First Division of the Ohio militia. Despite these honors, "Orator Bob" was never nominated for public office again.[31] Back home, perhaps attempting to revive Robert's irreparably damaged political career, the Lytles hosted a party in Cincinnati which was attended by the Whig Congressman from Massachusetts, Daniel Webster, and his wife. Elizabeth was thrilled that Webster escorted her to the table that evening and felt this would "make the Whiggles mad." Elizabeth was also pleasantly surprised that Mrs. Webster was so friendly to her.[32]

After his term in office, Robert traveled with Elizabeth to the East for leisure. Margaret took Will and Josie to visit relatives who lived near Washington, Kentucky. There, Will and his second cousin, William Lytle Blanchard, hunted before breakfast then swam and fished the rest of the

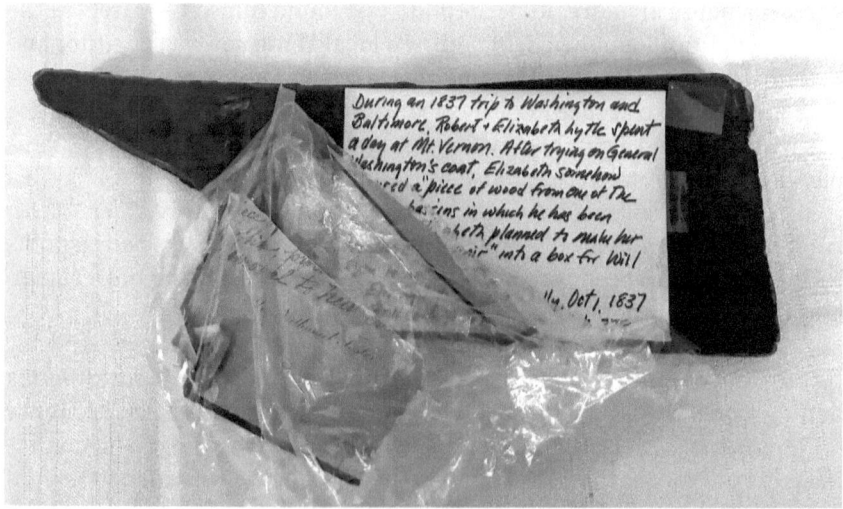

This is the piece of wood taken by the Lytles from the outside of George Washington's coffin. Elizabeth intended to make a box for Willie (photograph by the author).

day. Margaret and the children loved their time with the Blanchards.[33] Coming from the filth and stench of the growing city of Cincinnati to the open fields and fresh air of the country, they enjoyed dining on chicken, hams, buttermilk and, as Margaret noted, "plenty of ice and Corn." They also enjoyed local fresh fruit such as apples, cherries, and plums.[34] One eventful day during that idyllic summer, Will was riding a horse that got away from him. Despite his best efforts, the out-of-control horse bolted down the road and threw the future Civil War hero into a stone wall. When the men from the farm reached Will they helped him up and praised him for his coolness and attempts to manage the runaway horse.[35]

On their trip through the East, Robert and Elizabeth took a side trip to Mount Vernon. Elizabeth wrote to her sister, Joanna Reilly, "…tell Willie I had on Genl Washington's coat." Elizabeth also had managed to procure a piece of wood from "one of the outside bassins" of President Washington's casket. She planned to use the wood to make a box for Willie.[36]

Despite his loss in the election, Robert Todd Lytle had many friends and he and Elizabeth enjoyed their travels together. Their time, however, was growing short.

Chapter 3

THE MANTLE FALLS

The 1830s saw a rise in abolitionist efforts to end slavery and the city of Cincinnati was caught in the middle of the growing divide over that issue. New Englanders who moved to Cincinnati brought their political views, including abolition. Cincinnatians had close ties to slaveholding Kentucky and the rest of the South and therefore were not quick to embrace the growing abolitionist movement. In fact, Robert Todd Lytle was a leader in the abhorrence movement, so named because its members abhorred abolition.[1] Social tensions over a number of issues led to frequent riots in the Queen City leading one abolitionist writer to claim that Cincinnati was not the Queen City. "It is the Mob City—the Queen of Mobs."[2]

Adding to this chaos, Robert Lytle ended up involved in three controversies. The first involved a runaway slave. Lytle's law firm represented the slaveowner. The case contributed to the political rise of one of the runaway's attorneys, Salmon Portland Chase.[3]

Cincinnati's riverfront was lined with coffee shops, produce stores, and other merchants and when steamboats stopped there, passengers would often leave their boat and visit these shops.[4] On a Sunday evening in June 1836, a steamboat angled toward the Ohio shore and berthed along the Cincinnati waterfront. The passengers were told that, due to the amount of freight that needed to be loaded and unloaded, they would be detained until Monday evening. The passengers departed the boat and made their way along the waterfront, seeking refreshments and lodging in the Queen City.

One of the passengers was a veteran of the War of 1812 named Larkin Lawrence. He and his daughter, Matilda, and other members of his family were traveling from Maryland to their new home in Pike County, Missouri. Sometime between Sunday evening and Monday night, Matilda and her younger sister slipped away into the crowds. When it came time to leave, Mr. Lawrence and his nephew searched for the missing girls. They found the younger sister, but the 20-year-old Matilda was gone. Lawrence left for Missouri without Matilda and once in Missouri, he contacted a man named John Riley to find the missing woman. Mr. Riley specialized in finding missing persons of this sort because he was a slave catcher and Matilda, besides being Mr. Lawrence's daughter, was also his slave.[5]

In Cincinnati, Matilda had ended up at the home of noted abolitionist James Gillespie Birney. She was found, arrested, and held while next steps were determined. The team representing the slave owner consisted of Robert Todd Lytle, Nathaniel C. Read and Mr. M.N. McLean. Birney hired Samuel Eells and his law partner, Salmon Portland Chase, to represent Matilda.[6] Chase had represented James Birney earlier in 1836 after Birney had been attacked by mobs in Cincinnati.[7]

In 1817 an Ohio judge had declared that slaves brought into the state of Ohio by their masters were free. But in Matilda's case, her owner (father) did not bring her into Ohio, they were there because the boat required more time to load and unload. Samuel Eells, attorney for Matilda, said she should be free because when a master brings a slave into the free state that makes the slave free. Robert Todd Lytle's partner, Mr. McLean, argued that the master and slave had not resided in the state and that Lawrence had been simply going down a "public highway" (the Ohio River) and was detained for unforeseen reasons (loading/unloading freight). Chase did not address the issue of slaves in transit or raise the issue of whether she should be considered someone freed in transit or a fugitive. Instead, he attacked the federal fugitive slave law. Salmon Chase would earn the nickname "Attorney General for Fugitive Slaves." This case helped launch Chase's career as his courtroom speech was published throughout the country.[8] Judge D.K. Este, however, ruled for Lawrence saying Matilda should be returned to her master.[9]

The next controversy was the so-called "Toledo War" which traced its history back to the Northwest Ordinance of 1787. At that time, the boundary line between the Michigan and Ohio Territories was based on the southern tip of Lake Michigan. Subsequent surveys showed the tip of Lake Michigan was farther south than originally thought. Ohio commissioned a survey by William Harris in 1817 which produced results favorable to Ohio. Michigan ordered its own survey, the Fulton Survey, which followed the original Northwest Ordinance information. The gap between these two surveys came to be known as "the Toledo Strip." The issue came to a head when Michigan applied for statehood in the mid–1830s. When Michigan and Ohio called out their militias to protect their interests, the standoff was known as the "Toledo War." Lytle acted as an intermediary between the representatives of the two areas. One of his jobs was to keep them from killing each other. Ohio's political clout prevailed, and President Jackson signed a congressional act on June 15, 1836, awarding the

This photograph of the Lytle mansion was taken after the front of the house was moved from the south side to the Lawrence Street side in 1867 after additions to the Sisters of the Poor convent on Third Street obstructed the Lytle mansion entrance (from the collection of Virginius Cornick Hall, Jr.).

disputed area to Ohio. Michigan did achieve its most important goal and became a state in 1837. As compensation for giving up the Toledo Strip, Michigan was awarded 9,000 square miles in what is today known as the Upper Peninsula. The final say in the matter did not actually occur until 1973 when federal courts ruled that the disputed areas near Lake Erie belonged to Ohio.[10]

The third crisis arose in 1838 when Robert Todd Lytle resigned as surveyor general due to questions regarding financial mismanagement. Surveyors claimed they were not receiving money owed to them. The total amount owed was at least $30,000. (A Whig newspaper claimed Lytle owed $40,000.[11] The *National Gazette* of July 13, 1838, said the amount was actually more than $52,000. The amounts were suspiciously similar to the amount the Lytles felt the government owed them for William Lytle's court-ordered payments years earlier.) The government did not want Robert to resign, they just wanted the complaints to stop. The complaints continued and Robert offered no feasible explanation.[12] Lytle wrote to a Louisville newspaper and said the matter would soon be closed and that he planned to run for the United States Senate. With help from Smith Haines, he settled the account and resigned. Lytle did not run for the Senate and Haines was appointed to take his place as surveyor general.[13]

Robert Todd Lytle was also a member of the Texian Central Committee and favored the annexation of Texas. In October 1836 Lytle received a letter from an old friend. The writer requested, "I pray you to start the fever in Ohio in favor of the annexation of Texas to the states." It was signed by Sam Houston.[14]

As the world changed around the Lytles, their influence waned. When the Queen City held a dinner to celebrate its anniversary the Lytles were not consulted during the preparations. This insulted the Lytle men who felt this was a slight to their father's memory. Robert's brother, John, wrote that the legacy of their father was being "slighted" despite the important roles he had played in the development of the city. John Lytle said their father had made more of a contribution to Cincinnati "than all the damned skinflints—soulless sons of bitches—who guzzled bear meat & swallowed Nick Longworth's sour wine."[15]

Amid all these crises, Robert Todd Lytle contracted consumption, now referred to as tuberculosis. The strain of the conflicts no doubt contributed to his inability to fight the dreaded disease and as the decade closed, an ill Robert Lytle decided to go south to try to recover his health. He wrote to Elias Haines that he recognized that the letter "may be my farewell scrawl to you in time & Eternity." Lytle boarded the *Queen of the West* in late November. In Louisville he developed a bad cough. His condition worsened in New Orleans.[16] On December 22, 1839, at the Verandah Hotel in New Orleans, Robert Lytle struggled to breathe and made a dying request that his remains be sent back to Cincinnati. "Let me sleep in the Land of my fathers." He then said, "my wife, my children," and died.[17]

Elizabeth Lytle learned of her husband's death from a notice in the *Nashville Whig*.[18] She wrote to a relative "I need not say to you how bereaved and afflicted the loss of my dear Robt has made me." However, she took some comfort from firsthand accounts that indicated, "He met his death with the firmness of a man and the resignation of a Christian." She said Robert was "the only person I have ever known who truly seemed to love his neighbors as himself...."[19]

As the Lytles came to grips with their grief, tributes began to pour in. The *Nashville Whig* said, "while we differ widely from him in politics, we never for a moment doubted his honesty or sincerity. As a friend he was brave, generous, and warm hearted, as a husband and father he was kind and affectionate."[20] *The Madisonian* of Washington, D.C., declared, "General [Robert] Lytle possessed a heart that had no faults, save its unlimited generosity."[21]

An article from the *State Journal* suggested his epitaph should be, "Here repose the ashes of a man, who had the courage to be a friend when friendship was dangerous! We never would have paid him this compliment, in his lifetime—we trust it will be viewed as the offering of sincerity now."[22] Robert Todd Lytle's funeral, on February 5, 1840, was attended by thousands in Cincinnati. The second great Lytle male had fallen, and the Queen City paid homage.[23]

The Lytle legacy now fell squarely upon the not-so-broad shoulders of a 13-year-old boy who liked hunting, fishing, playing marbles, and riding horses. Young William Haines Lytle had always been called upon to act older than his age. Now he would have to do more than act like a man, he would have to be one but first he needed to continue his education.

That summer, before beginning school at Cincinnati College, Will spent time with his Uncle Elias in Sandusky, Ohio, and went sailing on Lake Erie. The summer flew by and soon it was time to start school. Once college started in the fall, Will became close friends with another student named James Findlay Harrison. "Fin" was a grandson of William Henry Harrison.[24] Lytle always enjoyed making new friends and getting together with them. He did well in his studies and developed an ability to deliver effective speeches. A newspaper account from 1840 predicted, "when the ardor of youth shall have been tempered by a judicious course of study, much may be expected of him."[25]

He also began writing poetry. Lytle wrote "The Soldier's Death" in 1840 and some later attributed a prophetic tone to this poem, especially the death scene which read,

> Upon the waste so stained with blood,
> Beside a great and rushing stream,
> A worn and weary soldier stood.
> Like a phantom raised in a feverish dream....
>
> The night has passed—the morn has come,
> With rosy hue the east is flushed,
> And on that spot seemed nature dumb,
> So tranquil was the scene and hushed.
>
> When mortals by the wayside passed,
> The soldier's last deep breath had flown,
> With naught to cheer save the midnight blast,
> On the battlefield had he died—alone.[26]

Elizabeth encouraged her son to read. Specifically, she instructed him to read biographies as she believed this would help him with his speech writing in the years to come.[27] With Robert gone, Elizabeth took comfort in the fact that Will was developing into a fine young man.[28]

Chapter 3. The Mantle Falls

After the loss of her beloved husband, Elizabeth called on John Rowan to settle pending legal matters. Rowan refused to acknowledge one of her property claims. She took Will with her to Louisville to settle the matter. John Rowan was friendly and flattering as he told her he would contest her right to the 15 acres. At the conclusion of their meeting, Elizabeth rose, kissed Mrs. Rowan and their girls, and said good evening. The next morning, she found the best lawyer in Louisville who said she was entitled to that land. With this determination, she got her property.[29]

Despite her legal victory, Elizabeth struggled with the lingering sadness from the loss of her husband. She wrote about longing for that home "where there shall be no more separation or sorrow." She lamented that in this world a widow is left alone without even so much as an "approving smile" or "expression of interest...." One way she chose to deal with her grief was by collecting items related to her late husband to help ensure he would be remembered. That summer of 1841, however, Elizabeth began complaining of ongoing pains in her side and night sweats.[30] She, too, was dying of consumption.

She had been young once, and pretty and active and fun. She had tried on George Washington's coat, reveled with important politicians, and enjoyed picking (and eating) blackberries and peaches from the grounds of the mansion.[31] Now her short life had run its course. On December 29, 1841, at age 35, Elizabeth died.[32] Margaret became the primary caregiver and Elizabeth's sister, Joanna Haines Reilly, moved into the Lytle mansion to help take care of the children.[33]

Will and his sisters were now orphans. There is something final about the loss of the second parent and the three Lytle children, Will, Josie, and Lily, would grow closer over the years. Margaret and Joanna would love the children and do their best to help and care for them, but their parents were gone. He had been the only male in the house since the death of his father, and now Will would continue to be surrounded by loving female relatives.

Life goes on, whether we want it to or not, and Will was still a student in pursuit of a degree. Despite his mother's death, Will determined to focus on his schoolwork. He confided to his friend, Fin Harrison, that it was important to him to be considered the best.[34] Lytle continued to write poems, but instead of focusing his efforts on developing that talent, he seemed to write poetry the way other people doodle.

There is a piece of paper in the Lytle collection on which he began two or three poems and signed variations of his name in large, flourished letters around the perimeter of the page, "Wm. H. Lytle," "Bill Lytle," and "Wm. Lytle." He wrote the letters "L" and "B" in his own name larger and in a flourished script and wrote "Lord Byron" in large letters and then just

Silhouette from life. Grandma Margaret Haines seated. Standing are her grandchildren, Will, Josie and Lily (photograph by the author).

"Byron." It is possible that Byron was an influence on Lytle's poetry. William Haines Lytle's father had acknowledged that in his youth he had read almost all the works of Scott and Byron, perhaps from the Lytle family library. It is possible his son read the same books.[35] On that same page, in the middle, Will started a poem. At the top of the page were the words, "A voice within." There were lines scratched out and added in, words modified. What is left on the page is this:

> She loves me no longer,
> the vision is past,
> and the chain that has bound us is broken at last.
> To its nest the dove cometh,
> expelled by the rain but peace to my bosom comes never again.[36]

On February 3, 1843, the 16-year-old William H. Lytle delivered an oration at school titled "Law and the Legal Profession." A Cincinnati newspaper called it "the gem of the evening" and described the young man as "an uncommonly good speaker; the mantle of his parent seems to have fallen upon him...."[37] The writer described Will's voice as "musical" and appreciated his "wit and humor."[38] More than fifty years after hearing Lytle speak, a Cincinnatian recalled that the young man spoke with "an ease, elegance and impressiveness that was astonishing in a mere boy" and that he had a "chivalrous bearing about him that was fascinating."[39]

Not everyone was so complimentary of his speech. Will received a letter from a neighbor, Ida Drake. The writer had heard and liked Lytle's recent speech but felt he needed to point out to young Will some opportunities for improvement. "First, your gestures have too much ... angular motion to be graceful.... Second, it is not in good taste to translate Latin quotations, for where they are made before an audience ignorant of the Latin language they have a character of pedantry." The writer ended by saying he wanted William to do well and grasp "the richest rewards of society."[40]

William Haines Lytle graduated first in his class from Cincinnati College in 1843.[41] He considered going east to continue his studies there, but ultimately decided to stay near his grandmother and study law with his uncle Smith Haines in Cincinnati.[42] He would follow in the footsteps of his father.

Chapter 4

VOLUNTEERS

Studying law required effort and Will set a schedule that demonstrated his commitment. He began each morning at five o'clock and did not finish his daily studies until around six in the evening. From six to nine he focused on politics and recreation. Will loved socializing and looked forward to getting together with his friends. He confided to Uncle Elias, though, that there was not much to do in town and there had hardly been any parties among the "elite" for quite a while.[1] To pass the time Will read. He recorded, "I am a lover of books and I have a decided mania for them...."[2]

Since the death of their parents, Will and his sisters carved time out of their schedules to be together. For instance, during the summer months the Lytles took tea at home between 5:30 and 6:00 each evening. The downside of spending so much time together is that the sisters soon learned that Will could be critical of their habits. In one letter from 1846 he commented on Josephine's daily routine. He noted that his sister would sleep until mid-morning, rise, eat breakfast then snack on biscuits until lunchtime. After lunch "Miss Housekeeper" would have the carriage brought around for a ride after which she would return to the house, drink a cup of tea, and go back to the couch.[3]

Another outlet for Will continued to be his writing. It is not known how many poems he composed because, according to his friends, he threw away many of them. One that survived is titled "The Farewell." Written in the 1840s, the poem begins:

> My bark is clearing a path of light
> Over the waters fair,
> In whose crystal depths the Queen of Night
> Is bathing her golding hair,
> Silence and beauty are throned above,
> In the vaults of the summer sky,
> And the river murmurs a tale of love
> To the stars as it ripples by...[4]

Chapter 4. Volunteers 31

He would return to the image of a bark in a later poem, written on his 36th, and last birthday. What was on his mind in April 1846 was the Lytle mansion, which was still under the control of Smith Haines. Will wanted Smith to return the house to the Lytle family. What he feared more than anything was that "the old place may be sacrificed and pass from the family." When Smith and Charlotte Haines built their own house across the street, they returned the mansion to the Lytles.[5] Another topic on the minds of many was talk of war with Mexico.

After Mexico gained its independence from Spain in 1821, the new government in Mexico City encouraged immigration into the northern section of their country. Americans, including Southern planters and their slaves, moved in but in 1830 Mexico passed laws to limit immigration and slavery which led to rebellion and the eventual creation of the Republic of Texas.[6]

President Andrew Jackson did not annex the Republic because he believed that would lead to war with Mexico. American Northerners did not want to annex Texas because they knew it would come in as a slave state or, worse, perhaps more than one if the large territory were divided into different states.[7]

William Henry Harrison of Cincinnati (Fin's grandfather) was elected president in 1840. The first Whig president, he died not long after taking office and his vice president, John Tyler, assumed the presidency. Known to foes as "His Accidency" (because of the way he became president) Tyler planned to annex Texas.[8] In 1844 the Whigs did not nominate Tyler to be their candidate for president. Instead, they nominated Henry Clay (an acquaintance of Lytle's grandfather). The Democrats chose Robert and Elizabeth Lytle's old friend, James Knox Polk.[9] Polk narrowly defeated Clay in the election of 1844 and on March 1, 1845, not long before leaving office, President John Tyler admitted Texas to the union.[10]

The annexation caused turmoil in Mexico and Mexican General Mariano Paredes overthrew his country's president, José Herrera, with a promise to take all of Texas back from the United States.[11] Polk sent General Zachary Taylor with 4,000 men to the Rio Grande River. Mexico reacted to this move by sending troops across the river. Taylor sent out patrols to investigate the river crossings and Mexican forces ambushed one of those groups, killing several American soldiers.[12]

As the country prepared for war, William Haines Lytle completed his education and Margaret Haines Lytle tried to keep Will from going off to Mexico. She wrote to Ann Lytle Rowan (her sister-in-law) and Alice (Rowan) Shaw Wakefield on September 30, 1847. Margaret poured on the guilt. Her beloved grandson "Whom at his Birth—his dear Grandfather like Simeon of old took in his arms and blest" had grown up with many advantages. She felt that by going to Mexico he was "throwing himself away...." Margaret closed her anguished letter with these thoughts, "Williams field of labour should be in his Law Office—and let fools Idlers and loafers do the fighting the army I have Ever thought—a school of vice Immorality and depravity."[13]

Alice Rowan Wakefield tried to calm down Margaret, reminding her that Margaret's late husband, William Lytle, had been a soldier "when the savage was the horror of the whole West...." Will's grandfather had shown courage and answered the call to fight for his homeland. Ms. Wakefield closed her letter stating that she believed if William Lytle were "now alive ... he would say go my son and defend the flag and honor of your glorious country."[14] Margaret then appealed directly to her grandson's sense of guilt, writing to Will that her time might be growing short and he should keep this letter as a "little memento" to remember her.[15]

A lifelong Democrat, William Haines Lytle supported Polk's policies to expand the United States and in September he volunteered with the Second Regiment of Ohio volunteers. Elected first lieutenant, Lytle and the regiment mustered in on October 5, 1847.[16] Before leaving for Mexico, Lytle wrote to Elias Haines. He wanted his uncle to know that in the desk by his bedside were papers he valued highly. In case of his untimely death, he hoped that at least a few of the items he wrote might be published. Lytle also hoped the papers "will aid in grappling my name to the memories of my friends."[17] He wanted to be remembered.

As a believer in the "Young America" movement, which supported the expansion of the United States into territories to the south and southwest, Lytle was an enthusiastic proponent of the war. He wrote a poem titled "The Volunteers," the first stanza of which clearly lays out his beliefs.

> What time the yet unconquered North
> Pours to the wars her legions forth,
> For many a wrong to strike a blow
> With mailed hand at Mexico.[18]

The Ohio volunteers went to war via the Ohio and Mississippi Rivers. The first stop was Louisville, a town Lytle would visit many times over the years. They then continued to New Orleans, the city where his father died. In letters home, Lytle does not mention the connection to his father's death, nor does he make any reference to visiting the Verandah Hotel where his father passed away. He did try, unsuccessfully, to meet with the expedition's commander, Major General William Orlando Butler, a Kentuckian who would have known the Lytle family through the Rowans. Lytle wanted to obtain a staff position, but Butler did not grant him an interview, which offended Lytle.[19]

Chapter 4. Volunteers

On November 22, Mexico announced a commission to negotiate peace, meaning Lytle arrived in Mexico just as the war was about to end.[20] Even so, there was still work to be done. Mexican guerrilla fighters were a constant threat as Lytle and his men escorted wagon trains and performed garrison duty.[21] The Ohioans traveled over the great national road of Mexico and near San Juan they passed one of General Santa Anna's haciendas which had been burned by American Rangers. One morning Lytle was on his way to visit the house when his group spotted a herd of wild horses. The Americans forgot all about the hacienda and chased the horses, capturing several mustangs as a result. The next day they visited a large natural bridge. Climbing a hill Lytle spotted a ship in the distant harbor of Vera Cruz.[22]

On December 24, 1847, at Rio Frio, Lieutenant Lytle was elected captain of Company L, Second Ohio Volunteers, to fill the vacancy left after the death of Captain William Kennedy.[23] His men not only elected him captain, but they also built a fine log cabin, complete with windows, for him. Lytle confessed to Elias Haines, though, that soldiering was new to him, and he had much to learn.[24]

Margaret informed her grandson that Franklin Pierce, a friend of Will's father, had stopped by the Lytle mansion. Pierce told Margaret he wanted to meet Robert's children. Upon hearing (perhaps with a bit of theatrics from Grandma Margaret) that Will had gone to fight in Mexico, Pierce said that if Will had the skills of his father that he should use those skills as a statesman instead of a soldier.[25]

On February 2, 1848, the United States ambassador to Mexico signed the Treaty of Guadalupe Hidalgo and American troops were able to go home. Lytle and Company L, Second Ohio, returned to Cincinnati July 15, 1848. Back in town, though, the soldiers of the Second were not all happy. The *Lancaster Gazette* ran an article on August 4, 1848, which included a letter to Major General William Orlando Butler from the officers of the Second Ohio volunteer infantry. The officers protested orders they received to muster out where they were formed. They thought they were out of the service as soon as they were back on United States soil. Because they did not have proper uniforms or money to get back to Cincinnati the men felt the order was "unjust and illegal, an arbitrary exercise of power which the necessities of the soldier alone compel him to obey." Lytle was one of the officers who signed his name to the letter. No records exist if Butler replied. Upon their return there was a grand celebration that included a march from Fourth Street through the city's center to the Merchants Amphitheater on Ninth Street where there was a dinner.[26]

Lytle's sister Josie returned to Cincinnati after attending school in the East in mid–July. When Will, Josephine, and Lily reunited in Cincinnati

Lily noted it was a "grand scene" and she was happy that "Bubby & Sissy" were all back together with her again.[27] His sisters had missed him and his sense of humor as well as his "merry laugh." They also missed his singing. Sometimes Josie would play the piano and Will would sing to his sisters.[28] They likely did not miss, however, his teasing. On one occasion he advised Lily not to cry so much otherwise her tears would raise the level of Lake Erie. He teased Josephine about her baby talk.[29]

Back home, Lytle attended to business matters and in December 1848, he was admitted to practice law in the state of Ohio.[30] Having gained admission to the Ohio Bar, the young man went to work at the law firm of Haines, Todd, and Lytle (Alan Todd was a friend of Lytle). Their law office was located at Number 15 Third Street, between Main and Walnut, an easy walk from the Lytle mansion.[31]

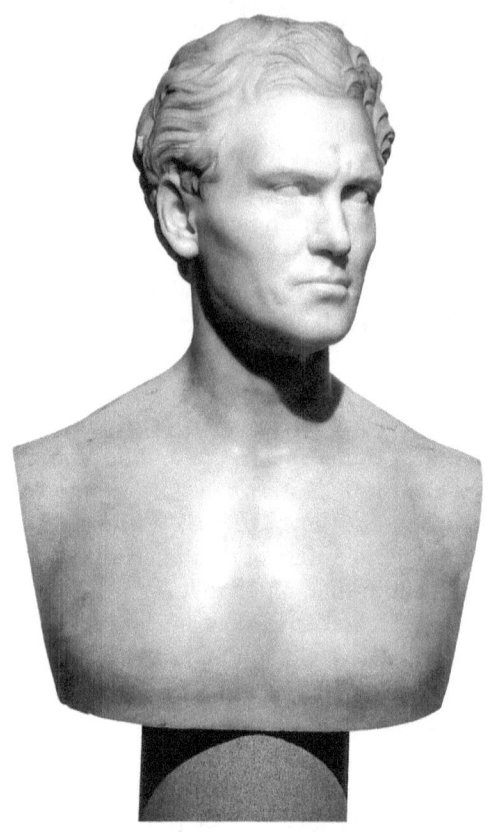

Hiram Powers' bust in marble of Robert Todd Lytle. Will placed the bust in the Arts Union Gallery for a short time to allow friends of his father to view it (from the collection of Virginius Cornick Hall, Jr.).

Settling back into civilian life, Lytle wrote to the famed sculptor Hiram Powers and asked him to create a bust of Robert Todd Lytle in marble. Will's mother had begun the task of collecting items that would remind her and their friends of Robert. On January 26, 1849, Powers replied that he would gladly do this project. The bust is still in the Lytle family.[32]

As the 1840s closed, William Haines Lytle stood on the precipice of a decade that would bring him fame, love, and a brush with death.

Chapter 5

THE FOLLY AND THE BEAUTY

Unhealthy conditions in Cincinnati contributed to cholera outbreaks. Known as the Queen City, Cincinnati also had another nickname: the city of pigs or "Porkopolis." One new Cincinnatian, Mrs. Frances "Fanny" Trollope, noted that pigs roamed the streets of Cincinnati to eat the city's garbage. In her book, *Domestic Manners of the Americans*, she noted that upon arriving in Cincinnati, her landlord told her how to dispose of trash. He told Fanny, "I expect you don't know as we have got a law what forbids throwing such things at the sides of the streets; they must all be cast right into the middle, and the pigs soon takes them off."[1] In addition to pigs roaming the streets eating garbage, an article in an 1845 *Cincinnati Commercial* noted "the deplorable conditions of the City reservoir—dead animal carcasses floated on the surface, dirty water ran in, surrounded by dead and dying vegetation, and twenty feet from the reservoir a chemical establishment chimney poured out 'poison gas.'"[2]

An 1849 cholera outbreak led to the deaths of four percent of the city's population.[3] Harriet Beecher Stowe, who was living in Cincinnati in June 1849, wrote, "This week has been unusually fatal…. Hearse drivers have scarce been allowed to unharness their horses…."[4] Lily Lytle and Aunt Joanna Reilly developed severe cases but recovered fully. Agnes (Ann) Lytle Rowan, the wife of John Rowan, died from the dreaded disease while visiting her daughter in Cincinnati.[5]

William Haines Lytle was stricken with cholera in 1850, and the case was so severe that doctors did not expect him to survive. Thanks to the loving care of his Aunt Joanna and his otherwise good health, he recovered from his illness. To celebrate, he, Josephine, and Smith and Charlotte Haines traveled to Sandusky, Ohio, to see Elias Haines. From there they went on to Niagara Falls.[6] Returning home, they attended the grand opening of the Burnet Hotel, at Third and Vine. Tickets to the "Grand Ball" cost $10 each and 600 people were invited to the spectacle.[7]

That same year, 1850, might have produced a chance encounter. A young Irishman, new to the country, lived in Cincinnati for a few months. While there he boarded at Mrs. Hanson's and worked at a drug store owned by a Mr. Salter. That drug store was right around the corner from the law offices of Haines, Todd, and Lytle. The Irishman's name was Patrick Cleburne and in the next war, he would rise to great fame and face Lytle across the field at Perryville.[8]

The Lytle siblings were concerned about their beloved grandmother. Margaret Haines Lytle had loved and cared for them for many years. Never one to hold back her thoughts, she had guided the children through the difficult years after the deaths of their parents and now she, too, was dying. On June 14, 1851, after a long and painful illness, Margaret Lytle passed away. No doubt her death left a "breach" as she once described it. Aunt Joanna Reilly, Margaret's daughter, assumed the role of maternal leader and caretaker of the Lytle household.[9]

William Haines Lytle was young, handsome, articulate, and now, a military veteran, making him a perfect candidate to run for public office. When approached by local Democrats he agreed to run for a seat in the Ohio state legislature and won by a wide margin. A torchlight parade celebrated his victory. Hundreds of fellow Democrats cheered the results in the streets of the Queen City. Even Whig opponents said Lytle's speeches were better than those delivered by their own candidates. The newly elected representative advised Uncle Edward Lytle that he would use his energies to do his best on behalf of the people who elected him. After her brother's victory, Lily predicted that her brother would one day be elected president of the United States.[10] Lytle served during the winters of 1851–52 and 1852–53 as a member of the Ohio House of Representatives.[11]

While in the legislature, Lytle introduced bills about money matters, securing property, and enabling creditor parties to enforce their securities.[12] On February 26, 1852, the *Cincinnati Enquirer* reported that Lytle offered an amendment to a bill requiring foreign insurance companies to deposit $25,000 to secure policies insured by them. There followed a lengthy discussion, but no vote was taken. In 1853 Lytle offered a proposal to pay Hiram Powers to create a marble bust of George Washington. Lytle said, "Above all, it will be a fitting mark of homage to the character, and the memory of 'the father of our country.'" The *Summit County Beacon* (Akron, Ohio) March 16, 1853, recorded the result. "An amendment making an appropriation of $10,000 for a statue by Hiram Powers was lost, yeas 20, nays 44. An amendment of $10,000 for the purpose of warming the Lunatic Asylum with steam was agreed to."[13]

Lytle also served on the judiciary and enrollment committees but his time in office was less than spectacular.[14] It should be noted, though, that

Chapter 5. The Folly and the Beauty

he was the youngest elected member in the House of Representatives in Ohio at that time.[15] Lytle decided that a return to the practice of law would allow him to do more good and attain greater accolades. In other big family news, his sister Josephine became engaged to marry Cincinnati physician Dr. Nathaniel Foster.[16]

William Haines Lytle, the poet who would often write of love, did become romantically interested in a local beauty named Therese Chalfant. She was a beautiful, cultured young lady and would have been a good match for Will. However, another Cincinnatian, George H. Pendleton, who would gain success in politics, beat Lytle to the punch and won her hand. When Will learned of her engagement, he wrote that if he were in Cincinnati he "might contest the prize." He did not pursue her.[17] There would be other loves in the future.

Despite the setback in his love life, other political opportunities came his way. Lytle family friend Franklin Pierce won the presidential election of 1852. President-elect Pierce offered Lytle appointments in the government, but he declined the offers.[18] In Ohio, state delegates had been instructed to vote for him for secretary of state of Ohio.[19] The young Lytle decided not to accept this offer either.[20]

Instead, he turned his attention to his cousin Eliza Macalester. Known as "Lily Mac," she was the daughter of Robert Todd Lytle's sister, Eliza Ann, who died of consumption in 1835 at the age of 29. Lily Mac's father objected to the union, at least in part because of the family history with that dreaded disease.[21] However, Will must have done something right because Josie wrote to her brother in an undated letter (likely around February 1853), that Lily Mac was about to leave for Washington, D.C., for the inauguration of Franklin Pierce and hoped to meet Will there.[22]

There are no letters in the Lytle collection between Will and Lily Mac. Other correspondence, though, indicates word reached Mr. Macalester that Lytle had "bad habits" which were "unacceptable," and the relationship collapsed in June 1853. Stunned, Will turned to his Aunt Charlotte and Uncle Edward for advice. Edward advised William to "drop the matter forever."[23] As it turned out, Edward had spoken to Lily's father about Lytle's bad behavior and therefore played a role in the rejection. Lytle and Lily Mac never rekindled the flame.[24] (Lytle's mother Elizabeth never liked Edward, describing him as a "disgrace" to the family.)[25]

After the disappointments in his love life, Lytle stayed home more in the evenings. He enjoyed receiving guests at the house and having get-togethers with family and friends.[26] Lytle told his sister, "I know something of the folly & something of the beauty of Life. I have had my troubles...." Continuing, he added, "All I mean to say is that a firm & resolute heart can not be subdued...."[27]

As a public figure, Lytle's actions were often witnessed and sometimes reported. They were not all flattering. Uncle Edward Lytle fired off a stinging letter to his nephew from Pittsburgh dated June 28, 1853. "… your habits have been bad during the winter time!"[28] Edward might have been referring to a news story that was reported a couple of months earlier regarding Lytle.

The *Pomeroy Weekly Telegraph* (Pomeroy, Ohio) of March 1, 1853, reported a physical assault in Columbus. Lytle's friend, a Mr. Gest, was upset about something written by Sullivan (S.D.) Harris, editor of the *Ohio Cultivator*. Harris and Mr. S. Plumb, a member of the House from Ashtabula County, were leaving the capitol building when Gest and Lytle attacked them. Lytle "seized" and "violently" threw Plumb to the pavement while Gest attacked Harris. As Gest was pummeling Harris, Gest's friends from the House stood around and shouted, "Gest, give him hell! Give him hell!"

Despite the reports of rowdy conduct, on July 26, 1853, the state of Ohio appointed Lytle inspector general with rank of lieutenant colonel, First Division, Ohio Volunteer Militia.[29] He also went back to work for his law firm.[30]

The Lytles lived in an area rich with the influence of many cultures. Near their property were the homes and luxurious gardens of well-to-do families. Just a few blocks to the south was the Ohio River. From their front door the Lytles could see The Beautiful River and hear the steamboat whistles. They might also have heard the chanting and singing (and likely swearing) of the stevedores who loaded and unloaded the boats that brought and carried away valuable cargoes. The Lytles and their servants could walk over to Broadway, which was just west of their mansion, and make the easy walk down towards the river to the Pearl Street Market to buy food and other items.[31]

Nearby shops offered jewelry and clothing from far-off London, Paris, and New York.[32] If, instead of walking south they turned and headed north up Broadway they might end up at the homes of other wealthy friends. Just behind the Lytle property ran Fourth Street. Walking up Lawrence to Fourth, they would turn left, or west, cross Broadway, continue down Fourth and find themselves among shops, government buildings and churches, including the beautiful Episcopal Christ Church Cathedral. To the north of the Lytles' home was also the western edge of Bucktown, home to African Americans (including former slaves) and Irish immigrants. To the east was the newly completed Miami Canal that connected the Ohio River to Lake Erie.

Dunning Foster lived across the street from the Lytles. He liked Cincinnati and reached out to convince his younger brother to come to the

Chapter 5. The Folly and the Beauty 39

city and work with him.[33] The younger brother accepted and worked as a bookkeeper for the Irwin steamboat commission firm.[34] (The Irwins also lived right across the street from the Lytles and their daughter, Mary Jane, was good friends with Josie and Lily Lytle.) At some point during his stay in the Queen City, Dunning's younger brother visited Federal Hill, the home of Lytle's great-aunt and uncle. Legend has it that after the visit Dunning's brother, Stephen Collins Foster, wrote a song about the house. That song, published in January 1853, was "My Old Kentucky Home."[35]

William Haines Lytle liked Kentucky where he had family and many friends. At the wedding of his cousin, Mary Blanchard, near Maysville, Kentucky, Lytle enjoyed the after party immensely. People danced upstairs and downstairs and everyone had a great time, including Lytle. After the wedding, he and several other guests took a steamboat back to his home in Cincinnati to continue partying.[36]

Travel to and from Louisville was made easier by the steamboat. When Lytle's grandfather's family traveled down The Beautiful River, they had relied on the current to carry them downstream. The arrival of the first steamboat in 1811 meant travel up and down the river would be possible. Steamboats left the wharf in Cincinnati at the foot of Vine Street at 5:00 p.m. and arrived in Louisville at 6 the next morning. A meal was included for no extra charge. The speed of these magnificent boats could reach about 18 miles per hour going downriver and 10 miles per hour going upriver.[37]

The eventful year of 1853 ended on a sad note. In November Lytle's uncle, Elias Henry Haines, who had spent most of his Ohio years in the Sandusky area, died in Cincinnati. Before his death, Mr. Haines purchased a vault in Spring Grove Cemetery, section 57, lot 63. It was cut into a hillside, on high ground, because at that time the lower section of Spring Grove Cemetery suffered from flooding.[38] Mr. Haines was buried in the vault. In the years to come, other family members would join him on that hillside.

Chapter 6

Tensions Mount

To connect its farms and markets with the Ohio River and Southern customers, Ohio built canals. The work on the canals began in the 1820s and required hundreds of laborers. Immigrants from Ireland and Germany moved to Ohio for the opportunity. Irish and Germans (and other Europeans) also moved to Cincinnati to escape political persecution after the Revolutions of 1848 that swept across Europe. By 1850, 27 percent of Cincinnati's population had been born in Germany.[1] Many, but not all, of the newcomers were Catholics and the native-born Protestants clashed with them over their religious and cultural differences. People who had lived in Cincinnati for years began to feel threatened and crowded by people who looked, spoke, and worshipped differently than they did.

Religion and nativism were two causes of tension in Cincinnati and the country, but the issue that emerged as the main conflict was slavery. On March 4, 1850, United States Senator John Caldwell Calhoun, the pro-slavery firebrand from South Carolina who had challenged President Andrew Jackson with the nullification crisis (Calhoun believed protective tariffs meant to help Northern manufacturers and which also hurt the southern states were unconstitutional and therefore could be declared null and void at the state level), delivered his last speech. He declared, "I have, Senators, believed from the first that agitation of the subject of slavery would, if not prevented by some timely and effective measure, end in disunion." Calhoun said the problem was that there was no longer "equilibrium" between the two sections of the country.[2] In 1854 an attempt at an effective measure, the Kansas-Nebraska Act, was put forth by Stephen Arnold Douglas, United States Democratic senator from Illinois.

When the country planned to build a transcontinental railroad that would link East and West, one of the main concerns was whether the newly created states would come in free or slave. Senator Douglas proposed the Kansas-Nebraska Act which would allow for slavery above the line established in the Missouri Compromise of 1820. This meant that any new state

Chapter 6. Tensions Mount

created in the Great Plains, which before had been off limits to slavery, might now allow it. Douglas's legislation would rely on "popular sovereignty," meaning the settlers of the various territories would determine whether their state allowed slavery or not.[3] One of the outcomes was "Bleeding Kansas," which resulted in guerrilla warfare between pro and anti-slavery forces.

Despite the ongoing turmoil in the country, Lytle was often bored and sought ways to entertain himself. On one occasion he rode his horse up the Courthouse steps into the Recorder's office.[4] He participated in civic activities and on February 16, 1855, at a charity benefit at the National Theater, played the role of "The Ghost" as part of

A self-portrait by Lytle, drawn sometime in the 1850s, perhaps after one of his local charity performances. In the upper right-hand corner, he playfully wrote, "How do you think I look?" (W.H.L. self-portrait, Lytle Papers, Mss qL996p, box 32, item 474; Cincinnati Museum Center).

a performance of the third act of Hamlet.[5] During that summer of 1855 Lytle advised his sisters that he was quite busy not only in his private life, but also in his law practice and political activities. In his free time, Lytle attended the opera, played billiards, and socialized with friends and family.[6] During the summer he also spent time in Louisville and sent several letters to his sisters. Referring to himself as "Bub" he wrote, "Bub has been very busy lately...." In another, "I know you would like to hear from Bub if it was only a line...."[7] Busy as he was, more appointments came his way.

On July 18, 1855, Lytle was promoted to division inspector and assistant adjutant general of the First Division Ohio Volunteer Militia.[8] It was also in 1855 that he was involved in another romantic relationship. Sarah Du Bois "Sed" Doremus was a relative on his mother's side. Born in New York, she was eight years younger than Lytle, but the age difference did not bother them. There are no letters between Sed and Will in the Lytle collection but there is a letter from Lytle's sister Lily suggesting that he had asked Sed to marry him. Lytle family lore claims that Sed refused because she thought it proper to reject the first proposal and expected he would ask again, and that Lytle did not ask a second time because he wasn't really that interested in her anyway.[9] Lily's letter and Lytle's subsequent communications seem to indicate otherwise.

The first four pages of her letter are lost or were removed. Lily said her brother had written two letters that "wounded" Sed. Regardless of the letters, Sed's father, Thomas Doremus, would not consent to the marriage due to "information" he received from Charlotte Haines (Lytle's relatives liked to meddle). Something happened between Sed and Will on a Sunday which led to his harmful letters to her. The specifics of the incident are not mentioned. Sed had told Lily that before she received those letters she had not given up on her relationship with Will and would have approached her father for his blessing, which she believed he would have given. The two letters, however, seemed to bring their relationship to an end. Even with the letters, however, Sed "solemnly declared & made up her mind never to marry till you do." Lily feared Sed might never recover or be happy again. Lily ended her letter, "I had never seen anyone whom I would so love to have as a sister."[10] Lytle responded to his sister that after Therese Chalfant, Lily Mac and now Sed, regarding "love, that star with me has set—forever, most probably."[11]

There are no love letters to or from any of the women mentioned above. However, there is a love letter written to a lady identified as "Miss Camp." His tone and playfulness are evident in that letter and one can only imagine what he must have written to Sed and Lily Mac and other later lovers. One of the lines in his letter is a plea. "Perhaps too [sic] thee, beautiful Miss Camp the admired—the belle—the courted has forgotten her young lover. Write—do write my dearest girl."[12]

Lytle also continued to write poetry. One of his efforts is buried in the Lytle papers in Cincinnati and likely has not seen the light of day since it was filed away years ago. It will probably never be included in any anthologies of his poems. It begins innocently enough and then takes an unexpected turn.

> Fair lady, when in other lands
> Beyond the broad Atlantic

Chapter 6. Tensions Mount 43

> You feel disposed to dream awhile
> In humor quite romantic
> Of moonlight hours long time flower
> Birds, lovers, flowers, lutes
> Bestow an idle thought on me
> And don't forget—the boots!
>
> Let others praise the garter trim,
> with neat coquettish air,
> High heeled! or slippers bright with gold,
> Dark eyed Sultanas wear.
> Or Ienners [?] shoes or moccasins
> Or "chaussure" [shoes] such as suits
> Of calf, morocco, silk or kid
> But <u>we</u> say, "go it boots!"
>
> Yes <u>boots</u>! The regular stagy kind—
> It boots not how to tell
> All Paris why in western lands
> We love such boots so well.
> So "honi soit qui mal y pense" ["shame upon him who thinks evil
>   upon it"—the motto of the Royal Order of the Garter]
> And waiving all disputes
> But leave us men the pantaloons,
> And you may take our boots!![13]

The same person who wrote about the boots he loved so well could also write:

> Night garlanded with stars, the universe
> Teeming with rich benevolence, shall teach
> Our hearts to mingle in a sweet communion,
> So warm and glowing that the hoary Earth
> In love's sweet light shall wear another youth
> And bloom as in the old primeval garden.
> The sands of life shall all be turned to gold,
> Our lives, unchilled by frost, or storm, or hail,
> Shall slowly wear away, till like ripe fruit
> We yield our spirit to the gleaner—Death.[14]

The February 20, 1856, *Cincinnati Enquirer* reported Lytle was on the Invitation Committee for the National Celebration of George Washington's birthday. The 1856 Democratic National Convention was held in Cincinnati. It was eventful. The Democrats chose not to nominate the incumbent president, Franklin Pierce. Instead, they chose "Old Buck," James Buchanan.[15]

Lytle gave a speech in favor of the candidacy of James Buchanan, and said England was responsible for slavery in the United States. He blamed abolitionists for the failure of the Missouri Compromise and praised Southern courage and patriotism. Lytle predicted the Southern states would leave the Union if the new Republican Party were successful in winning elections.[16]

In family news, on November 12, 1856, Lytle's youngest sister, Elizabeth (Lily), married Cincinnati attorney Samuel Broadwell. Sam and Lily took up residence near the Lytle mansion.[17] The following month, William Haines Lytle spoke to a group of fellow Democrats. The *Fremont Weekly Journal* December 5, 1856, reported that the idea of annexation of Cuba was discussed at the meeting which was attended by Ohio Democratic party leaders.[18] The *Cincinnati Enquirer* printed an article suggesting Southerners stop wasting their time on Kansas and look to expand into other areas, like Cuba.[19]

The Ohio Democratic platform of 1855 favored the annexation of Cuba and the Sandwich Islands (Hawaii).[20] Lytle's speech to the Democrats was lauded as "the gem of the evening." Referring to Cuba as "the lovely damsel," Lytle said, "If the old bachelor of Wheatland [James Buchanan] should be so hardhearted as to decline receiving her through the front door of the Union, 'Young America' [which became a faction of the Democratic Party that attempted to unite the party with an emphasis on nationalism] would slide her in through the back window." (Wheatland was James Buchanan's home.)

James Buchanan won the presidential election with less than half the popular vote and the country edged ever closer to civil war.

Chapter 7

ANTONY AND CLEOPATRA

William Haines Lytle was promoted to major general and command of the First Division of Ohio Militia. A newspaper account declared he combined "all the qualities to give grace in time of peace, and efficiency in time of war...."[1] Republican Governor Salmon P. Chase signed off on the promotion September 19, 1857.[2] However, there was apparently some type of dispute over the results.[3] Governor Chase conferred with Sullivan D. (S.D.) Harris about the "disputed election of major general of militia in Hamilton County." A second election followed a court challenge and Lytle emerged as the winner again. Chase noted in his journal, "Gen Harris declined to interfere as to Maj Gen Ham [Hamilton] Co."[4]

The September 23, 1857, *Cincinnati Enquirer* detailed the events. "Governor Chase has a notion that peace men and those who, it is believed, will run away upon instinct if they should ever see a shot fired in anger, make the best officers." The article stated that Lytle won the election to major general in the Ohio militia "by a great majority.... The election was contested, and the court decided that there was no ground to set it aside." The article said that once Lytle was nominated "Chase refused to issue the commission." A second election was held, and Lytle won again. "We suppose Chase will be compelled to issue the commission now."

Ohio Democrats selected Lytle as their candidate for lieutenant governor. On the campaign trail, Lytle told crowds that the South should be free to resolve the slavery issue for themselves.[5] The *Ohio Statesman* reported on Tuesday, September 1, 1857, that Lytle "was greeted with nine tremendous cheers. His speech ... was received with the most unbounded applause...."[6] The *Cadiz Sentinel* described Lytle as "one of the glorious young Democrats of that Gibraltar of Ohio Democracy, Hamilton County." The reporter said Lytle was "making an excellent impression everywhere."[7]

While campaigning in Port Clinton, Ohio, a city his grandfather had helped found, Lytle took time off from the campaign trail to visit the lake shore where he observed fishermen at work. He also visited a nearby Native American burial mound. His grandfather had been interested in archaeology and visited Native American sites. The elder Lytle wrote articles about his findings. The mound William Haines Lytle visited overlooked the lake and while exploring there Will found some Native American artifacts which he sent home for safe keeping.[8]

Despite Lytle's best efforts and excellent speeches, in the state general election Republican Governor Salmon P. Chase defeated the Democratic candidate Henry B. Payne 160,568 to 159,065, a total difference of 1,503 votes. In the lieutenant governor race, Martin Welker defeated Lytle 159,827 to 158,826, an even smaller 1,001 vote difference, a margin of less than one-half percent of all votes cast in the race.[9]

Even though he had failed to win the election, Lytle was still very much in demand as a speaker and as a friend. There are examples of invitations from friends in the Lytle papers. One states, "you must come up Friday evening or Saturday morning—I claim you as my guest for a few days."[10] In July 1858 he accepted an invitation to speak at a July 4 celebration in Clermont County but admitted to his sisters, "what a bore!" He also confided to Lily he was bored by the requirements of his position as major general in the state militia.[11]

Throughout the years, Lytle's darker side sometimes manifested itself. In 1858 Lytle did something that physically injured his sister, Lily. The injury is not recorded. Whatever happened to her, it took some time for her to recover. She said she would bear the pain and that her brother had it in his power to make those who loved him "either perfectly happy or entirely wretched."[12]

Lytle did not confine his bad behavior to his family members. A Mr. A.D. Bullock of Cincinnati wrote to his wife that Lytle was seen "most gloriously drunk" with his friends at the St. Charles Exchange.[13] Uncle Edward Lytle read an article that prompted him to write to his nephew, "If there is a shadow of truth in the foul publication—leave Cincinnati forever! In Gods name let me know if there is any truth in the filthy story! If true, I would ten thousand times sooner have heard of your death—My scorn of rowdyism, and vulgar debauchery is and always has been inexpressible." The article Edward saw was likely the one that had been printed in the October 1, 1857, *Wyandott Pioneer* (Upper Sandusky, Ohio). The paper reported that Lytle had attended a Christmas supper at the Neill House in Cincinnati and "shocked the company by one of the most outrageous and blasphemous sentiments ever uttered." As the gentlemen were enjoying "a good Christmas supper," Lytle proposed a toast. As the revelers stood with raised glasses, Lytle said, "Here's to the hero of the day—Jesus Christ!" Will assured his uncle the report was the work of political enemies.[14]

Chapter 7. Antony and Cleopatra   47

From the profane to the profound ... Uncle Edward's letter about Will's behavior is dated July 25, 1858. On Thursday, July 29, 1858, the *Cincinnati Commercial* printed a poem. The newspaper editor, William Whiteman Fosdick, predicted, "The following lines from our gifted and gallant townsman, Gen. Wm. H. Lytle, we think constitute one of the most masterly lyrics which has ever adorned American poetry; and we predict a popularity and perpetuity for it unsurpassed by any Western production."[15]

Over the years there would be many different versions of how or when Lytle wrote his most famous poem. The *Semi-Weekly Times Democrat* (New Orleans) July 7, 1911, reported that a copy of the poem was found on Lytle's body after he was killed at Chickamauga, leading to the story that he had written it on the field as he died or had written it the night before the battle. A man named H. Martin Williams claimed Lytle wrote the poem "while very drunk."[16] The *Cincinnati Enquirer* July 11, 1886, ran an article written by Rowan Buchanan, a relative, who recalled that Lytle and his friends had met at the Debolt Exchange restaurant. Members of what Buchanan described as "the gang" had gathered to talk about literature. The gang included W.W. Fosdick, Buchanan Read, George Pendleton, George Pugh, Robert McCook (who, along with his father and brothers, would fight in the Civil War), and others "the like of which I shall never look on again."

Lytle sat and listened until he said, "I've scribbled off a little thing which I want to read to you; tell me what you think of it." Lytle removed a few sheets of paper from his coat pocket and began to read "in a low tone, so as not to disturb the other gentlemen engaged in conversation." Lytle began, "I am dying, Egypt, dying." Near the end of the first verse Ohio Senator George Pugh interrupted him. "Who wrote that, Billy?" His friends insisted the poem be published and Lytle responded that "it is not worth publishing."

The *Altoona Tribune* March 8, 1871, printed an article by William S. Irwin who said Lytle's friends had gathered at the Lytle mansion to congratulate him on recovering from an illness. They talked for a while until Lytle went over to his table and began to write. Having finished his work, Lytle "pushed the paper on which he had been writing carelessly over among loose scraps...." In this version, W.W. Fosdick went over, read the poem, put it in his pocket and determined to publish it. Irwin said Lytle "was a man whom no one could help loving..." with "delicately winning manners and affectionate disposition...." Irwin predicted Lytle's poem "will live while the English language is spoken."

Lytle's Civil War aide and friend, Alfred Pirtle, said Lytle wrote it in his room at the Lytle mansion and that the poem "was the fruit of weeks of

Stairs at the Lytle mansion leading to the upper level where Will's room was. From childhood to manhood, Will went up and down these stairs many times (from the collection of Virginius Cornick Hall, Jr.).

preparation and research, though put upon paper in a few hours after he had in his mind arranged each line."[17] The Buchanan, Irwin and Pirtle stories cannot all be true in their entirety, but it is possible that there are elements of truth in each of them.

Lytle's poem was published throughout the country. One of Lytle's friends, Thomas Means, wrote a letter to Lytle praising the work and encouraging him to write more. Means wrote, "A gloomy disagreeable Sunday that keeps us all in the house has led me to rummaging among the contents of my table basket and finding a certain exceedingly profane poem called Antony and Cleopatra amongst them.... I am delighted with it and wish you would let the world learn more of your powers in that and other directions...."[18] Another person who read it was a Kentuckian named Josiah (J.) Stoddard Johnston.

While traveling to Arkansas where he had a cotton plantation, Johnston was standing on the deck of a steamboat, waiting to depart. A stranger, mistaking Johnston for Lytle, walked up and began speaking to him. Johnston knew who Lytle was because he was also a Democrat. Later, when Lytle's poem "Antony and Cleopatra" was published, Johnston read it, liked it, and continued to follow Lytle's career and determined that someday he would like to meet the famous Cincinnatian.[19]

William T. Coggeshall included "Antony and Cleopatra" in his book, *The Poets and Poetry of the West*, published in 1860. A noted actor of the day, James Murdock, read the poem to an overflow crowd at a theater in Boston during the Civil War. When Murdock finished reading Lytle's poem to the Boston crowd, "the audience broke out in loud and prolonged applause, many rising to their feet and waving their handkerchiefs to emphasize their appreciation of it."[20]

The famous first line of Lytle's poem is borrowed from William Shakespeare's *The Tragedy of Antony and Cleopatra*. In Act 4, scene 15, Mark Antony tells Cleopatra, "I am dying, Egypt, dying." When the Cincinnati *Commercial* first published the poem, just under the byline for the poem it says, "'I am dying, Egypt, dying' (SHAKE.)"

In poetry we often find the most beautiful thoughts and feelings of the human race. William Haines Lytle was a poet. His words moved people, still move people. This is his most famous poem.

Antony and Cleopatra

I am dying, Egypt, dying,
Ebbs the crimson life-tide fast,
And the dark, Plutonian shadows
Gather on the evening blast,
Let thine arm, oh! Queen, support me,

Hush thy sobs, and bow thine ear,
Hearken to the great heart secrets,
Thou, and thou alone, must hear.

Though my scarred and veteran legions
Bear their eagles high no more,
And my wrecked and scattered galleys
Strew dark Actium's fatal shore,
Though no glittering guards surround me,
Prompt to do their master's will,
I must perish like a Roman,
Die the great triumvir still.

Let not Caesar's servile minions
Mock the lion thus laid low;
'Twas no foeman's hand that slew him,
'Twas his own that struck the blow.
Hear then, pillowed on thy bosom,
Ere his star fades quite away,
Him who, drunk with thy caresses,
Madly flung a world away!

Should the base plebian rabble
Dare assail my fame at Rome,
Where the noble spouse, Octavia,
Weeps within her widowed home,
Seek her, say the Gods have told me,
Altars, augurs, circling wings,
That her blood with mine commingled,
Yet shall mount the throne of kings!

And for thee, star-eyed Egyptian!
Glorious Sorceress of the Nile,
Light the path to Stygian horrors
With the splendors of thy smile.
Give the Caesar crowns and arches,
Let his brow the laurel twine,
I can scorn the Senate's triumphs,
Triumphing in love like thine.

I am dying, Egypt, dying:
Hark! the insulting foeman's cry.
They are coming—quick my falchion!
Let me front them 'ere I die!
Ah! no more amid the battle
Shall my heart exulting swell,
Isis and Osiris guard thee,
Cleopatra! Rome!—farewell! [21]

Chapter 8

ON THE EVE OF WAR

William Haines Lytle had friends and family throughout the country. As a result, he traveled extensively. He had been to Mexico to serve his country during the war. He had close ties to the South with family and friends in Kentucky. He also had relatives in the Northeast. For example, his mother's first cousin, Daniel Haines, was the governor of New Jersey in the 1840s and into the early part of the 1850s.[1] Will spent time in New Jersey, Washington, D.C., New York, and Pennsylvania, where his uncle, Edward Lytle, lived. He liked New York City. ("It is fast and noisy and head over heels....") He did not care for Philadelphia. ("I think this town a humbug and always did.")[2] Throughout his life, as he traveled around the country for business or leisure, he took note of his surroundings and often commented on the things he saw and did.

A popular mode of travel for Lytle was the steamboat but by the 1850s the railroad connected Cincinnati with other parts of the country. Three trains left Cincinnati every day, except Sunday, at 6 a.m., 10 a.m. and 10:15 p.m. The Little Miami Railroad connected in Columbus, Ohio, with other railroad lines.[3] In April 1860 Lytle boarded a train to Pittsburgh. The journey was cursed with delays and bad weather. At one point during the trip the passengers were forced to board a boat for part of the journey. There was a rainstorm and Lytle was afraid his trunk of clothes would get wet. With the aid of the barkeeper, he protected his trunk from the rain by placing the luggage of the other passengers on top. He felt justified in this action because he believed their clothes "would probably be benefited by a little washing." After a similar frustrating travel experience, he wrote a short poem not to be found in any anthology of his work.

Impromptu

What a terrible bore
To be waked up at four
By a thump at your door
Interrupting a snore!

No growling I beg!
Boot on the wrong leg!
Pants all inside out
But now here about
As bad as the wars
Thus to wait for the cars
At 4 o'clock in the morning.[4]

That trip to Pittsburgh was also notable because Lytle ran into some old political acquaintances who were on their way to Charleston, South Carolina, for the Democratic National Convention.[5] At that convention Northern Democrats nominated Stephen Arnold Douglas as their presidential nominee. Southern Democrats nominated Vice President John Cabell Breckinridge, splitting the party.[6]

Republican Abraham Lincoln won the presidential election of 1860. One month later, on December 20, 1860, the Charleston, South Carolina, *Mercury* declared, "The Union is Dissolved" and the Palmetto State became the first state to secede. As Lytle predicted, other Southern states followed.

There are books written and arguments made about the causes of the Civil War. People have offered states' rights, economic sectionalism, and conflict of cultures as causes. But these issues were made more important because of slavery. It was an old wound that had never healed and by 1860 many Northerners and Southerners had gotten to the point where they simply did not like each other and were ready to fight.

The Milwaukee *Sentinel* said Southerners were lapsing into "barbarism" and that in the South "there are but few schools, and the masses are growing up in ignorance and vice." The Muscogee (Georgia) *Herald* claimed that the North was merely "a conglomerate of greasy mechanics, filthy operatives, small-fisted farmers and moon-struck theorists…" who were "devoid of society fitted for well-bred gentlemen." In 1856 South Carolina Congressman Preston Brooks famously pummeled the United States senator from Massachusetts Charles Sumner in the old Senate chamber. Brooks took offense to Sumner's "The Crime Against Kansas" speech that singled out Brooks' relative, then took his cane and beat the Massachusetts politician senseless. That act contributed to the Northern belief that the Southerners were a violent people.

Abolitionist John Brown, after his murderous work along Pottawatomie Creek in Kansas, hoped to start a slave uprising by leading a raid against the Federal arsenal at Harper's Ferry in 1859. His revolution failed and he was hanged. In December 1860, United States Senator Alfred Iverson of Georgia delivered a speech that stated, "Sir, disguise the fact as you will, there is an enmity between the northern and southern people that is deep and enduring, and you never can eradicate it—never!"[7]

Chapter 8. On the Eve of War

Lytle, though, would fight for the Union without hating Southerners. And Southern officers would see in Lytle someone they considered to be like themselves, a gentleman. He believed in the rights of the Southern people to determine their own fate, and he believed in the preservation of the Union. He believed abolition would cause huge problems for the country, socially and economically. His father and grandfather had both been strong supporters of Andrew Jackson, who believed in the preservation of the Union and had stood against Senator John C. Calhoun's claims that states could nullify federal law. With the nation spinning out of control, Lytle decided to run for office and sought the Democratic nomination for the United States House of Representatives. George H. Pendleton, the incumbent (and Therese Chalfant's husband), was nominated instead.[8]

On the eve of war, William Haines Lytle stood 5'6" tall. His long, soft hair, moustache and beard were brown with an auburn tint and his eyes were hazel. (He had been clean-shaven for three years in the 1850s because he felt like the beard interfered with his ability to eat soup.)[9] A Cincinnatian recalled seeing Lytle on the streets as the young poet passed by one day just before the war. "He was rather short in stature, thin in the flanks, but broad, full-chested.... He walked erect and, as was his wont, very leisurely, and with a side-to-side swing.... His reputation at the time was that of being highly social and possessed of winning politeness, a modest bearing and chivalrous spirit."[10]

His work up to this point had been uneven. He had shown flashes of brilliance, and he had shown indifference. Lytle could be charming and loveable, and he could also be destructive and careless. Boredom and "bad habits" had appeared from time and time. "Antony and Cleopatra" clearly showed his talent as a poet. His speeches indicated he could be a great statesman. His intellect promised he could be a powerful lawyer. But before the Civil War, he had yet to harness his considerable talents and focus his efforts.

Chapter 9

CLEAR THE WAY

As Southern states left the Union, Southerners seized Federal properties. One Federal property sought by South Carolinians was Fort Sumter in Charleston Harbor. Refusing to abandon this site to the nascent Confederacy, President Abraham Lincoln ordered supplies sent to the fort. Confederate harbor batteries fired on the supply ship and drove it away, and no further action occurred. Then, on the morning of April 12, 1861, a Rebel cannon fired a shell that arced through the darkness and exploded over the parapets of Fort Sumter. On that signal, Confederate guns from the batteries in Charleston opened fire and the American Civil War began. The fort's commander, Kentucky native Major Robert Anderson, surrendered to the Rebels. Kentucky, birth state of Anderson as well as Confederate President Jefferson Davis and United States President Abraham Lincoln, announced its official policy of neutrality. Lytle's Kentucky relatives, William Lytle Rowan and William Lytle Blanchard joined the Confederate army.[1]

Three days later Lytle, a major general in the Ohio militia, was in Columbus when President Lincoln called on the loyal states for 75,000 volunteers to put down the rebellion. The following day, Lytle received a telegram from Ohio's recently elected Republican governor, Cincinnati native William Dennison, ordering him to establish a camp near Cincinnati to train the expected volunteers. Lytle rushed back to Cincinnati on the next train, met his staff at the Burnet House, and began recruiting. Captain William Starke Rosecrans chose the site for the training camp which would be named Camp Dennison. Sixteen miles northeast of Cincinnati, the camp was near enough to the Queen City to draw supplies but far enough to prevent too many distractions to the new recruits. The Little Miami Railroad connected the camp to Cincinnati and Columbus.[2]

Thousands of men rushed to fill the ranks. Militia units at least had some notion of discipline and drill, but volunteers who had never served would have a lot to learn. They signed up, showed up at camp, and began

Chapter 9. Clear the Way

Camp Dennison was established to train new recruits before sending them off to war. "Middleton, Strobridge & Co., Lithographer. *View of Camp Dennison: 16 miles northeast of Cincinnati, Ohio / lithographed by Middleton, Strobridge & Co., Cincinnati, Ohio.* **Camp Dennison Ohio United States, ca. 1865." Camp Dennison, Ohio: Published by Swan & Litchfield (Library of Congress).**

the transformation process from civilian to soldier. They learned to respond to bugle calls and drumbeats. They learned to march and handle weapons. They dealt with health issues, bad weather, and insufficient quality and quantity of food. They elected their officers (which meant that, in the beginning, many inexperienced men led other inexperienced men with predictably bad results). Lytle, although not a West Point graduate, did have the benefit of Mexican War experience as well as being an officer of the state militia.

The army would be organized in this manner. A *company* was commanded by a captain, who oversaw a first lieutenant, a second lieutenant, and 97 men for a total of 100 soldiers. Within a year of the beginning of the war this number typically dropped to an average of 30 to 50 soldiers. For the artillery, this sized unit was called a battery. Companies were designated by letters, such as, Company H.

Regiments were commanded by a colonel, assisted by a lieutenant colonel, a major, an adjutant, a quartermaster, a surgeon, and an assistant surgeon. They were raised by state governments which usually meant that men from the same area served in a regiment. Regiments were designated by number and state. The Tenth Ohio, for instance, was drawn from Cincinnati. Ideally, ten companies of 100 men each, or 1,000 men total, would be in a regiment. By the spring of 1863 an average Union regiment would field between four and five hundred men due to deaths, illnesses, and other losses. For example, the Tenth Ohio Volunteer Infantry regiment, which Lytle would soon command, began the war with 958 men and ended the war with 310. During the Civil War, a regiment that failed to muster ten companies was often called a battalion.

A *brigade* was commanded by a brigadier general (or a colonel). Brigade commanders were assisted by aides, adjutants, and various staff such as a quartermaster, a topographical engineer and so forth. Brigades included from four to six regiments, though the number varied as the war went on. In the Southern armies, the brigade was usually known by the name of the commander of that brigade such as Adams's Brigade or the famous Stonewall Brigade whereas in the north they were more commonly referred to by a number designation such the Seventeenth Brigade or the First Brigade.

A *division* was commanded by a brigadier general or a major general. Divisions could include 12,000 men with as few as two and as many as six brigades in the division.

A *corps* was commanded by a brigadier general or a major general. Before November 1862, Confederate divisions would be grouped into wings or "grand divisions." Composed of two or more divisions, in the north each corps was given a number such as XX Corps.

An *army* was commanded by a major general and comprised multiple corps. Union armies were usually named after rivers such as the Army of the Potomac or Army of the Cumberland, whereas Confederate armies were normally named for a geographical area like the Army of Northern Virginia or the Army of Tennessee.[3]

Governor Dennison offered George Brinton McClellan, who was living in Cincinnati at the outbreak of the war, command of Ohio's troops. McClellan accepted. (Mrs. McClellan had discovered she was quite taken with Cincinnati people during their time there. She remarked, "They are really quite Eastern—and quite *civilized*....")[4] One thing her husband discovered was how unprepared Ohio was to outfit an army for war. The Ohio state arsenal had only old smooth-bore muskets, most of which were rusted and damaged. There were also no accoutrements such as belts and cartridge boxes.[5]

One of the regiments formed was the Tenth Ohio Volunteer Infantry regiment. Drawn from the Irish and German communities in Cincinnati, it would be known as an Irish regiment, but there were two companies of Germans or "Dutch" as they were called. Six companies were indeed Irish and the other two were a mixture.[6] These men were not all gleaned from among the elites of Cincinnati. These were rough men, unaccustomed to the order and structure of military life. "The Irish," one prejudiced contemporary opined, "can do nothing but dig, and seldom rise in the social scale."[7] At its formation, the Tenth was described as "a mob."[8]

On May 6 Lytle resigned his position as major general of Ohio militia to accept his new command as colonel of the Tenth Ohio.[9] Fellow Ohioan and military officer, Jacob Dolson Cox, noted "the brilliant Lytle" gained control over his regiment right away and said the Tenth "had fallen into competent hands."[10] Lytle said of his new regiment, "The sons of Erin, enthusiastic and daring, and the undaunted, untiring Germans have joined hands with the native citizens, and sworn to vindicate the laws and maintain the Constitution."[11]

On May 16, Lytle's lawyer friends from the Cincinnati Bar presented their former colleague with a sword. Thomas Gallagher made the presentation speech and said his fellow lawyers "appreciate and understand your character as a gentleman and as a soldier." Other friends presented Colonel Lytle with a handsome black charger named *"Faugh-a-Ballaugh,"* an ancient Irish battle cry meaning, "clear the way."[12] A group of Cincinnati ladies presented the new regiment with flags.

Upon receipt of the flags, Colonel Lytle responded: "On behalf of the Tenth Regiment, I tender to the ladies of Cincinnati, through you, our heartfelt thanks for these beautiful flags. When these wars are over we will bring them back again to the Queen City of the West, without spot or blemish. You see around you a thousand men who to-day say good-by to their sweethearts and their friends. God bless the city, the state, the Union, and the ladies. We make no promises, but when it comes to the clash of steel, remember the Tenth ... tell the ladies that there is not a man in these ranks who will not shed his heart's blood like water beneath these colors. We bid you good-by, and God bless you all. *Faugh-a-Ballaugh!*"[13]

As Lytle led his regiment the men grew to respect and later form a very strong bond with him. A newspaper correspondent reported his observations during one of the Tenth's first marches. "During the brief halts by the wayside he was amongst the first to procure water for his thirsty command, and in every case was amongst the last to wet his own lips. His appearance at any place along the line was the signal for cheers."[14]

Many of the Irish Catholics, for example, knew that the Lytle family had been friendly to them. Those who did not know were advised of this fact when Father Richard Gilmour, of St. Patrick's in Cincinnati, spoke to the Tenth Ohio. He told them that "the first territorial donation to the Catholic Church in Ohio, was a gift ... in Brown County, from the grandfather of their Colonel."[15]

During their training at Camp Dennison there was nearly a riot between the Tenth and Thirteenth Ohio regiments. A member of the

Tenth was reportedly shot by a sentry of the Thirteenth. "The tenth being hot-blooded, flew to arms," reported a correspondent. Other troops were called in to separate the two Ohio regiments. To avert their fury, Lytle ordered the Tenth into line of battle. By the time the Tenth had formed, the Thirteenth had been dispersed and all had time to cool off without any further violence. The correspondent noted, "The entire affair may be charged to the credit of Captain Barleycorn." ("Captain Barleycorn" was a slang term for alcohol.)[16]

Fortunately, the Tenth Ohio received orders to march to western Virginia on June 24. Under the overall command of Major General George B. McClellan, of the Department of the Ohio, their goal was to secure the Baltimore and Ohio Railroad near Grafton, (West) Virginia.[17] (The state of West Virginia had not yet been formed. This Union offensive would help secure its creation.) Lytle was allowed a personal servant to accompany him, so he brought along Mr. John Wilson, an African American, from Cincinnati.[18] Upon his arrival in camp, Mr. Wilson showed the colonel a letter from Mrs. Wilson saying she was starving. Will asked Lily to help Mrs. Wilson. Lily responded by renting out Will's room at the mansion and giving some of that rent money to Mr. Wilson's wife.[19]

As the Tenth marched to the train station to depart the Queen City, well-wishers crowded the streets, waving handkerchiefs and cheering. Flags hung from the windows of the city's buildings. Workmen stopped their tasks and cheered as the soldiers filed past. A newspaper correspondent noted that the ladies in the crowd, besides crying, shouted encouragements like "God bless you!" and "Fight for the Union!" Once aboard the train the men heard "one long and loud shout" as they departed.[20] Unfortunately, the Tenth suffered their first fatality soon after, when Private William Houlihan, Company H, was accidentally killed while changing trains in Columbus.[21]

On the march, soldiers toted their full backpacks and heavy rifles through drenching rains and the mountainous terrain of western Virginia. Soldiers might carry forty to fifty pounds of equipment and, including unplanned halts, be able to cover two miles in an hour of marching. Officers needed to keep the troops moving. A war correspondent observed that Lytle "has been unceasing in attention to the soldiering progress of the men, while his courtesy and affability has everywhere won him the regard of the Virginians." On the march, loyalists or "Union men" would smile and supply water readily to the advancing Federal soldiers. In contrast, "Secesh" supporters "sat quietly at their doors and at the requests for simply a glass of water, pointed with dogged silence to the well."[22]

Lytle wrote proudly to his sisters in late June that his men had performed their duties well and their behavior had won "great praise" from the citizens along the way.[23] He was not pleased, however, with the fact that at the time he wrote the letter his regiment was still waiting for the rest of their equipment to arrive. On July 8, 1861, he recorded that his regiment marched 32 miles while conducting a 124-wagon train safely. As he did before departing Cincinnati to go to war in Mexico, he considered what should be done with his papers should there be an "accident." He wanted his law partner Alan Todd, and his friend William Fosdick to review his writings he had left in his room at the Lytle mansion and burn any that were not worth keeping. He closed his letter with this request. "Your letter Lil enclosing Sed's … is just rec'd to my great delight…. Remember me affly to Sed Doremus." So, it is obvious that Sed and Will stayed in contact with one another, family lore to the contrary.[24]

Lytle had a close call one night when his black charger tripped over a large tree beside the road and landed on Lytle's leg. He and his horse were fine, but they had come very close to rolling down a steep hillside. Lytle took time to praise *Faugh-a-Ballaugh*. The black charger was a magnificent animal and had but one fault, the horse was "a little tender in the feet…."[25] Lytle said that his horse was well known amongst the men and seemed to know them as well. He said his horse was "the pet of all the boys…."[26]

Between May and July McClellan's Federal forces took control of the Trans-Allegheny counties of western Virginia as far south as the Kanawha River. However, farther east, on July 21, Confederate forces routed the Federal army at the Battle of First Manassas or Bull Run, which was only thirty miles from Washington, D.C. The resulting chaos threw the Capitol into a panic and the Federals brought in McClellan to reorganize the shattered Federal army around Washington. Rosecrans replaced McClellan as commander in the Trans-Allegheny theater.[27]

In the ranks of the Federal forces in western Virginia was John Beatty, a native of Sandusky, Ohio, and a banker before the war. He had enlisted with the Third Ohio as a private, and by the time of the Battle of Perryville would be their colonel. He kept a journal throughout the war. When the Third marched into Virginia with the Tenth Ohio, Beatty noted in his journal that the people in the area had been "grossly deceived by their political leaders." They believed that the Federal troops had come to free the slaves, lay waste the Southerners' property, and kill their families. The Southerners believed it was the Federal troops that were trampling on the constitution, and they were "simply defending their homes and fighting for their constitutional rights."[28]

Rosecrans established his headquarters in Clarksburg, Virginia, and ordered Colonel E.B. Tyler to move the Seventh Ohio Infantry to patrol the areas around an important river crossing known as Carnifex Ferry. The Confederates pinned their hopes for the defense of this region on

An artist's rendition of Lytle on his horse, *Faugh-a-Ballaugh* (from the collection of Virginius Cornick Hall, Jr.).

Brigadier General John Buchanan Floyd. A former secretary of war in President Buchanan's cabinet, Floyd was placed in command of the "Army of the Kanawha." Unfortunately for the Confederates he did not get along with the other area commander, Brigadier General Henry A. Wise. Both were ex-governors of Virginia and political foes.

Chapter 9. Clear the Way

Wise had no military background whatsoever, yet he won a victory over Federal forces at the Battle of Scary Creek in July. (The Confederate forces were led by Wise and Lieutenant Colonel George S. Patton, grandfather of George S. Patton of World War II fame.) After the Battle of Scary Creek both sides withdrew. Despite their stated intentions to work together, Wise and Floyd did not cooperate well. There was added pressure on Floyd because the pro–Union populace in the western part of Virginia wanted to create a new state and had scheduled a vote for October 24 in Wheeling to determine their path forward on that matter.[29]

Floyd and Wise managed to work together long enough to devise a plan to strike at Carnifex Ferry. Floyd was reinforced by the Twenty-Second and Thirty-Sixth Virginia regiments on August 24.[30] At dawn on August 26 Floyd launched a surprise attack on Colonel Tyler's Federals at Cross Lanes. The battle resulted in another victory for the Confederates. Tyler managed to escape as did a contingent under Major John Steven Casement but the Federal army under Cox was in danger. Floyd established Camp Gauley on the bluffs overlooking Carnifex Ferry and waited for more reinforcements.[31]

As secretary of war under President Buchanan, Floyd had sent half a million muskets to the South. He also ordered the transfer of 121 heavy guns from Pittsburgh to the Gulf Coast for forts that were not scheduled to be built for several years. And he was accused of taking $870,000 in bonds from the Department of the Interior. He was cleared of the charges but many in the North still thought of him as a thief. Even fellow Southerners had their doubts about him. After meeting Floyd, Confederate Colonel Henry Heth said, "I had conceived an idea that a man who had been Secretary of War knew everything pertaining to military matters. I soon discovered that my chief was as incapacitated for the work he had undertaken as I would have been to lead an Italian opera."[32]

McClellan ordered Rosecrans on August 29 to join Cox and trap Floyd. Colonel Lytle accompanied Rosecrans to Sutton, Virginia, on September 4. Cox was at Gauley Bridge and skirmished with Rebel forces under Wise. Robert E. Lee warned Floyd that Rosecrans's army was approaching but Floyd thought he could whip any army sent against him.[33]

Rosecrans's First Brigade, commanded by Brigadier General Henry Washington Benham, consisted of regiments he considered to be his best, including Lytle's Tenth Ohio. The Tenth had performed well in their scouting duties and a small portion had been involved in a skirmish on the Bulltown Road, but for most of the men the upcoming battle would be their baptism of fire.[34]

Born in Connecticut, Benham attended West Point and graduated in 1837 at the head of his class. He joined the Corps of Engineers and worked on coastal defenses. He was promoted to captain. A veteran of the Mexican War, Benham was appointed chief engineer of the Department of the Ohio at the outbreak of the Civil War and served under McClellan during Mac's campaign in northern (West) Virginia. Jacob Cox described Benham as a "stout red-faced man, with a blustering air, dictatorial and assuming...." Rosecrans described Benham as "a selfish, conceited man." Nonetheless, Benham led the First Brigade, which included the Tenth Ohio.[35]

At 9 a.m., Saturday, September 7, the Federals began to advance south from Sutton. Two companies from the Tenth Ohio and two from their Camp Dennison nemesis, the Thirteenth Ohio, were sent out ahead as scouts. The Tenth led the First Brigade followed by the Second and Third Brigades. The Twenty-Third Ohio, of the Third Brigade, had in its ranks Major Rutherford Birchard Hayes and Private William McKinley, both future presidents of the United States.[36]

The Confederate fortifications at Camp Gauley were set up in a horseshoe-shaped bend in the river. Mr. Henry Patterson's farm was about one hundred and fifty yards in front of the Rebel works. Besides Patterson's two-story house, the property included a cornfield, a log barn, and other outbuildings. A road ran in front of the house. The Rebel camp, just up the hill, sat more than four hundred feet above the river. Behind the Confederate camp was the road leading down to the ferry. Since the Federals would approach through Mr. Patterson's property that narrow, dangerous, steep path was Floyd's only escape route.[37]

(There is some confusion as to the correct spelling of the last name of the Civil War owner of the house, Henry Patterson. According to Rick Proctor of Carnifex Ferry Battlefield Park, in the cemetery at nearby Zoar Baptist Church, Henry Patterson's name is spelled Patterson on his side of the tombstone while his wife is buried under the name Mary A. Patteson. And the "Great Persuader," former West Virginia Governor Okey Leonidas Patteson, was a grandson of Henry Patterson.)

The Twenty-Second, Thirty-Sixth, Forty-Fifth, Fiftieth, and Fifty-First Virginia regiments manned the Rebel defenses. Floyd had two artillery companies, four or more cavalry companies and sixty local militia men. Henry Guy's Goochland Artillery comprised four six-pounders and Lieutenant Thomas E. Jackson's Horse Artillery had three guns. All told, Floyd had around 2,000 men for the coming battle.[38]

In front of their position, Rebels cut down trees and formed an *abatis*. This earthen redoubt in front of the camp ran for around one hundred yards and included a parapet battery positioned with the artillery guns on a platform to fire over the fortification rather than through an opening. On each side of the redoubt were irregularly constructed palisades. The left flank had open ground about 4,500 feet long and a double line

Chapter 9. Clear the Way

The "rushing Gauley" River. The Rebels only way out was down a steep, narrow path to the river more than 400 feet below (photograph by the author).

of log breastworks. The right flank was equal in length but had a slope in front. Dense woods protected each flank. In the middle of the line Floyd placed the Goochland Artillery's four six-pounders. The Forty-Fifth Virginia defended the right flank. The Fiftieth Virginia was stationed on the right and left of the artillery. The Fifty-First Virginia was on the left with the Thirty-Sixth Virginia on the left flank. The Twenty-Second Virginia was in reserve behind the Thirty-Sixth on the left and three artillery pieces threatened any advance, situated between the Thirty-Sixth and Twenty-Second.[39]

Floyd liked his defenses. Wise thought the position was indefensible and should have been established on the south side of the river and referred to Floyd's defenses as "a ditch in a meadow."[40] Very soon Floyd's position would be tested.

Chapter 10

THE FIRST FALL: CARNIFEX FERRY

Tuesday, September 10, 1861.
Carnifex Ferry is located eight miles south of Summersville, (West) Virginia, near the confluence of the Gauley River and a southern tributary, the Meadow. The wild, narrow Gauley, with steep banks on either side and rough, rocky stretches throughout, widened at Carnifex Ferry into a long smooth body of water. Here, a large force could cross the river.[1]

There are at least three possible spellings of Carnifex. In some records it appears as "Carnifix." The version most often used (and the one that will be used in this chapter) is "Carnifex." Most likely the correct spelling is "Carnefix," based on the tombstone of the man, Mr. William Carnefix, who owned and operated the ferry.[2]

Federal troops rose at 3 a.m. on Tuesday, September 10. They ate a hasty breakfast and began their march in a heavy mist around 4:15. When they reached McKee's Creek, Confederates opened fire on the lead detachment. An order went out to send up ten Federal infantrymen to assist. The orders were misinterpreted and instead of sending ten men, the entire Tenth Ohio advanced. Colonel Lytle heard the shots and shouted, "That is John Hudson!" (Hudson was captain of Company C of the Tenth Ohio and one of Lytle's scouts.) The Tenth rushed forward and drove off the Rebels.[3]

The Federals continued to Carnifex Ferry and at 2 p.m. chased Confederates from a hilltop camp. Because the Rebels departed suddenly, they left behind tents, uniforms, clothing, provisions, weapons, burning campfires and fifty head of beef cattle. Moving forth from the abandoned camp, First Lieutenant James T. Hickey, Company C, Tenth Ohio, noted that the path they would now take was "a muddy, slushy road between two hills." Rosecrans instructed Benham to move forward "slowly and cautiously" and not to engage the enemy unless there was "an evident opening." Company C, Tenth Ohio, was left to guard the abandoned camp. The Tenth and

Chapter 10. The First Fall: Carnifex Ferry

The "muddy slushy road" taken by the Tenth Ohio to get to the battlefield (photograph by the author).

the Thirteenth Ohio advanced as Rosecrans rode to the top of a nearby hill to observe.[4]

Around 3 o'clock the Tenth Ohio moved forward. Lytle sent out flanking parties to the right and left and skirmishers in advance of the column.

As the first Federals appeared from the dark woods a Confederate officer heard one of his men say, "There they are." The Rebel officer, on horseback, could see over the breastworks and noticed the blue-coated enemy coming out of the woods.[5]

Confederates opened fire on the Yankee skirmishers around 3:30 p.m. Lytle pushed his regiment forward along the narrow road, through the dense woods until at last they saw light breaking through the trees ahead, to their right. Emerging from the forest, they saw a cleared field which rose to the left of the road. On the far side of the field, to their front, was the Patterson House. What they did not see was that just beyond the top of the rise the entire Rebel force was waiting.[6]

Coming into the clearing, Lytle saw Rebels posted in force behind what he described as an "extensive earthwork." When the front of the Tenth Ohio's column reached the right center of the Confederate works, the Butternuts opened fire. A war correspondent accompanying the Ohioans noted, "Words were never framed to give expression to the terrific effect of that awful sound. But we knew what it was and prepared for the shock of battle. I watched the men closely. There was quivering of lips and blanching cheeks; but I saw no man falter, thank God."[7] Lytle ordered his colors to the front with the intent of assaulting the Confederate battery.[8]

While deciding his next move, Lytle's men fell around him "in great numbers."[9] As hundreds of muskets cracked and rattled and the Rebel cannon roared, a war correspondent described the Rebel volleys as "sharp as peals of thunder."[10] Caught in this storm of lead, the Tenth recoiled and broke ranks but reformed. Hickey recalled, "There was not an inch of ground, or tree, nor a blade of grass that did not receive its share of fire."[11]

Fortunately for the Ohioans, the Rebel fire was not very accurate, or it could have been a massacre. As the Butternuts fired downhill many of their bullets and shells flew high of their targets. Benham ordered his artillery to return fire and the Twelfth and Thirteenth Ohio were ordered forward but the Tenth was about one mile ahead of the rest of the First Brigade when the battle started so they would fight for some time without support.[12]

Around 4 p.m., seeing his men still pinned down and with no sign of relief, Lytle decided to attack without Benham's consent. Not everyone in his regiment heard the commands so only companies A, B, C (which had come up from the Rebel camp) and E advanced. Riding *Faugh-a-Ballaugh*, Lytle waved his sword and shouted, "Forward, follow. Men of the Tenth. Advance the colors!" The Federals emitted "wild unearthly screams" as they advanced. The American flag and the Tenth's regimental flag became targets for the Confederates. Private Michael Fitzgibbon, Sergeant Daniel

Chapter 10. The First Fall: Carnifex Ferry   67

O'Connor, and Captain McGroarty were all shot down while carrying the flags.[13]

Faugh-a-Ballaugh, the beautiful charger with the tender feet did not flinch amid the noise and smoke. He faithfully carried his master toward the Rebel lines. When Lytle reached the top of the hill, he wheeled *Faugh-a-Ballaugh* to the right and encouraged his men as they advanced up the slope. Captain John Preston Sheffey of the Eighth Virginia cavalry said Lytle rode up to within 75 yards of their entrenchments. The Virginian claimed one of his men from Company A fired at Lytle with a "double-barreled gun, loaded with musket cartridges...." One of those lead projectiles struck Lytle in the left calf, cut through his boot, passed near an artery, scraped the bone, and exited the other side of his leg before tearing into *Faugh-a-Ballaugh*.[14]

After being hit, *Faugh-a-Ballaugh* reared up, threw Lytle to the ground, and ran toward the Rebel lines.[15] The Rebels captured Lytle's horse and it died of its wound later that evening. Sheffey said, "Lytle was a very brave man and it seemed almost a pity to shoot him."[16]

The wounded Lytle ordered his men to take cover. Some rallied behind

This photograph is taken from the road that cut across to the Patterson House. The row of stones in the middle of the photograph is approximately where Lytle fell. The Confederate works were up the hill (photograph by the author).

two log houses in front of the Confederate battery and kept firing for about an hour. The rest of the regiment, on the right, under Lieutenant Colonel Herman J. Korff took cover in a cornfield. Part of the left wing of the Tenth under Irish-born Major Joseph Walter Burke moved through the woods on the left of the road and fired at the Confederates across a deep ravine.[17]

Lytle continued to issue orders until he became faint from loss of blood. He finally ordered his men to fall back. Part of the Tenth retreated to the edge of the woods, while others sought refuge behind the Patterson house. Because of their fighting spirit and the losses they suffered at this battle, the Tenth Ohio earned the sobriquet, the "Bloody Tenth."[18] A Northern correspondent noted, "I tell you, the Irish of the Tenth stood up … like heroes."[19]

Once removed to relative safety behind the Patterson House, Lytle noticed one of the wounded soldiers was his private secretary, John H. Green, who had been hit in the chest. Lytle asked, "Mr. Green, why in heaven's name did you expose yourself to this casualty?" Green replied, "I came because I thought it would encourage the men."[20] When offered water, Lytle took the cup and immediately passed it to Green. Green replied, "No, no Colonel, after you, thank you, sir, after you, sir."[21]

The Thirteenth Ohio was the next regiment to reach the battlefield, followed by the Twelfth. When Colonel John W. Lowe of the Twelfth Ohio reached the field, he said he wanted to go where Lytle and the Tenth were because that was where the fighting would be the hottest. Lowe had been accused of cowardice after the fight at Scary Creek and he longed for redemption. Colonel Lowe raised his sword and shouted, "Follow me my men! Charge!" As he turned to face the Confederate lines, a bullet smashed into his forehead, and he fell dead. Federal reinforcements continued to arrive, but they were unable to take the Confederate position.[22] As the last light of the September day began to fade, Rosecrans ordered his men back to the camp they had captured earlier. He planned to resume the attack in the morning. William McKinley noted in his diary, "while on our way back we met the Tenth Ohio Regiment with their dead and wounded. The sighs and groans were pitiable."[23]

At midnight Floyd ordered the retreat of his exhausted Rebel soldiers. Early on the morning of September 11 Floyd got his entire army down the steep, slippery path behind their camp to Carnifex Ferry and across the Gauley River. Shortly after daylight a man walked into the Federal camp and reported that the Rebels had escaped during the night. The Rebels destroyed the footbridge and flatboats as they left. Since Rosecrans did not have any way to repair the bridge quickly and get across the river and his men were "much fatigued" they did not pursue. Colonel Hugh B. Ewing proceeded into the abandoned enemy camp around 7 a.m., where

Chapter 10. The First Fall: Carnifex Ferry

his men took prisoners and two stands of colors. The Federals fired off a few rounds of canister at the fleeing Confederates and then took control of Camp Gauley.[24]

The South saw Floyd's defense and withdrawal as a victory. Confederate Secretary of War Judah Benjamin wrote to Floyd, "I take great pleasure in communicating to you the congratulations of the President, as well as my own, on this brilliant affair...."[25] The goodwill did not last long. Floyd and Wise continued to argue to the point that Robert E. Lee had to split them up. Floyd attacked Federal forces under Jacob D. Cox at Gauley Bridge and lost. As a result, the Army of the Kanawha left (West) Virginia forever. Floyd was then transferred to command the Confederate forces at Fort Donelson in Tennessee.[26]

A Northern war correspondent who witnessed the battle and had accompanied the troops on the campaign offered his view on the outcome. "I am constrained to regard it as a victory without triumph." Acknowledging the Rebels abandoned the field, the correspondent noted, "they escaped without serious damage, and they were enabled to prevent us from pursuing until it was too late to overtake them." The Confederates were able to carry off their weapons but left their flag and other items. He concluded, "Floyd's evacuation of the place is a mystery to all of us."[27]

As a result of the battle, the loyal government of western Virginia met in Wheeling in October, paving the way for West Virginia statehood. Of the Federal officers on the field at Carnifex Ferry, 12 would go on to become generals and two became presidents of the United States. The Federals suffered 27 killed. Of those, 15 were from the Tenth Ohio. Of the 103 wounded, 40 were from the Tenth Ohio. Floyd's Confederates suffered 32 casualties: nine wounded and 23 captured.[28]

The Cincinnati newspapers published the names of the fallen heroes of Carnifex Ferry. A newspaper clipping in the Lytle scrapbook titled "The Battle in Western Virginia" listed the killed as: "Calvin Darr, M. Folly, Sgt. John Kennedy, George S. Murphy of Co. E, German and Marhouse of Co. A, Hammerschan Wilhelm Markiworth of Co. B, Louis Schneck Co. D, Thomas C Madin Co. I, John Keigl Co. G."[29] Per the official roster of the Tenth Ohio, the actual names of the killed were: Sergeant John Kennedy, Company E, aged 22; Thomas German, Company A, aged 23; William Moorehouse, Company A, aged 38; Herman Schramm, Company B, aged 28; William Marquardt, Company B, aged 20; Louis Shuck, Company D, aged 18; John Kirsel, Company G, aged 33; Harry Rooney, Company A, aged 24; James Peters, Company C, aged 35; Sergeant Patrick Kavanaugh, Company A, aged 27; George S. Murphy, Company E, aged 38; Charles Medary, Company I, aged 27; John Anderson, Company E, aged 28. Calvin

Darr and Michael Fitzgibbon are not on the roster but were reported as killed in action.[30]

In his official report of the battle, General Benham wrote, "The personal gallantry and chivalrous daring of Colonel Lytle are attested by his wound and the exposed position in which he received it." Privately, he referred to Lytle's attack as "the ridiculous assault of the hare-brained colonel."[31] William S. Rosecrans recorded, "I beg leave to signalize Col. W.H. Lytle for the gallantry with which he led his troops into action...." John Green, the polite, wounded soldier, wrote, "Lytle realized every idea of chivalry I had formed from romance or history."[32]

In his baptism of fire, Lytle had performed bravely. He should not have attacked without Benham's permission, but once committed he did not falter or flinch. The Tenth Ohio performed bravely as well. The bond between Lytle and the Tenth Ohio grew stronger on the bloody fields of western Virginia.

Chapter 11

RECOVERY AND REUNION

Lytle traveled back to Cincinnati on the steamer *Silver Lake*. The correspondent onboard wrote, "A trip down the Ohio River is very pleasant. The scenery is very beautiful; no other words can express it."[1] The boat arrived in a heavy downpour, but there was still a large crowd to welcome Lytle and receive the body of Colonel Lowe, who had been killed at Carnifex Ferry.[2] Lytle would recover at the home of Sam and Lily Broadwell.

A local reporter interviewed Lytle in the parlor of the Broadwell house. Lytle, needing a crutch to move around, rose and welcomed the reporter and then explained that the bullet that had torn through his leg had also pushed leather from his boot into his calf. As a result, the wound was not healing properly, causing much pain and discomfort. Doctors were finally able to remove the leather piece and the healing began, though his leg continued to cause him problems.[3]

The Tenth Ohio arrived back in Cincinnati in November and marched over to see their commander. As Lytle watched from the doorway of the Broadwell house, the Tenth stood at attention and their regimental band played "Rory O'More."[4] The soldiers cheered wildly for their wounded leader and waved their stained caps. The Tenth's tattered flag was then displayed in the window of Shillito's department store.[5]

Later that month Lytle was invited to attend the First Anniversary of the Dedication of the Catholic Institute. The *Cincinnati Daily Commercial* reported that the Union Hall was "crowded" for the event. The colonel sat on stage for the program. The first speaker, Father Edward Purcell, after praising the courage of the Irish soldiers noted, "I could not help thinking to myself there is not a man living bold enough to stand up and challenge the allegiance of the foreign-born citizen." The next speaker was an officer who also spoke of the bravery of the Irish. At the conclusion of his talk, the crowd repeatedly and loudly called for Lytle. Not expecting to speak, he sat for a few minutes before rising from his seat, supported by his crutch.

The cheering increased as Lytle moved forward. Lytle always rose to the occasion when called on to make a speech. The reporter observed how "the glow of enthusiasm mantled his face and brow, and gleamed from his eye, as he paused until the cheering subsided." Looking out at the excited crowd, Lytle told them, "When I go back and tell my men, for their sakes, you have received their Colonel here tonight, *I know they will feel very proud.* They often think of you my fellow citizens—and the brother, mother, wife or sister among you, in spirit, visit the soldier as he rests in his chill tent beside the rushing Gauley!"

Lytle praised his soldiers and said he would return to his command and tell them that "they have your prayers. And though we may never return, many here will yet hear the voice of the bird of the morning—and it will be for them to tell the story ... how ... freemen sprang to arms and restored the American Union!" The correspondent noted, "The effect of Col. Wm. Lytle's well chosen, deep, earnest words ... seemed to strike a chord in the innermost recesses of every bosom in the assembly.... Lytle sat down amid great cheering and murmurs of applause."[6]

The men of the Tenth, after their brief respite, were ordered to report for duty and go back to the war. However, only about one third of the men reported on time for their departure to Louisville. The rest, according to one historian, were found "in bars, brothels, and jails."[7] The Cincinnati *Daily Press* of December 3, 1861, recorded, "Files of soldiers were busy this morning hunting up the Carnifex heroes, wherever they could be found...." The writer opined that the men of the Tenth Ohio had "a tendency to stimulants" and that they now needed to report for duty and continue in the fight to preserve the Union. "The Tenth has had a glorious season with their friends, and they are now needed in Kentucky. Do not lose the good opinions you have gained. Let the cry be, 'to Nashville and beyond.'"

Before leaving Cincinnati, Colonel Lytle took time to write a thank you note to Mrs. Isabel Carlisle for the donations of the Ladies Aid Society to the Tenth Ohio. The ladies had supplied mittens, shirts, towels, socks, drawers, gowns, and handkerchiefs. Lytle graciously accepted these donations on behalf of his regiment.[8] He also purchased a horse to replace his lost steed. A newspaper reported that the horse was "a fine large dark gray."[9]

On the second day of January 1862, Lytle boarded the mail boat for Louisville to rejoin his regiment in the Army of the Ohio. The *Cincinnati Daily Press* reported that the colonel would take command of the Seventeenth Brigade in Kentucky. On his way to the new camp, Lytle made an unexpected stop to see an old family friend. Alfred Pirtle noted in his journal, "At noon today were agreeably surprised to receive a call from Mr. Broadwell and Col. Lytle, from Cincinnati!"[10]

Chapter 11. Recovery and Reunion

Alfred Pirtle was born March 25, 1837, in Louisville, Kentucky. His father, Henry, was a well-known and respected judge. "Alf" received his education at the finest schools in Louisville and prepared for a career in civil engineering but went to work instead for the Louisville and Nashville Railroad. Before the war he was a member of an elite military unit called the "Citizen's Guards" led by Simon Bolivar Buckner. When the Civil War began, Pirtle was neutral but sided with the Union and joined the Louisville Home Guards in September 1861. Lytle offered him a commission as first lieutenant in the Tenth Ohio and Pirtle accepted. He would be mustered in at Bacon Creek, Kentucky, on February 7, 1862.[11]

Lytle's friend, aide, and chronicler, Louisville native, Alfred Pirtle ([PC16.0074] Alfred Pirtle carte-de-visite. The Filson Historical Society, Louisville, KY).

The commission Pirtle received was as second lieutenant, Company H, Tenth Ohio Volunteer Infantry. Pirtle's mother wrote Lytle and asked for an explanation for the discrepancy. Lytle replied that he did not know why Alfred had not received the commission Lytle had applied for. "However, his promotion will be certain after a while." The colonel also assured Mrs. Pirtle that her son's "sterling qualities will soon be appreciated by officers and men."[12]

When Lytle reported to Bacon Creek he received orders from General Don Carlos Buell, commander of the Army of the Ohio, to go back to Louisville and take command of the barracks there. Pirtle reassured Lytle that Buell probably assumed he was still recovering in Louisville and did not intend to separate him from his command. Lytle wrote home that the duty itself would not be difficult because, "the Barracks are *not built*—though you need not mention this out of the family."[13]

Less than a week later Lytle decided the Louisville duty wasn't so bad after all, writing home from the Louisville Hotel that he was tending to his

Despite promises to his sisters, Lytle kept this traveling liquor cabinet throughout the war (General Lytle liquor cabinet and glassware [CHS.1977.31.1]; Cincinnati Museum Center).

wounds. The popular Cincinnatian also kept a busy social schedule, calling on local ladies. He also responded to his sister, Lily who begged him to stop drinking alcohol. He replied, "My dear Lil, if it *will contribute any way to your happiness I most cheerfully give you the promise you ask. So put your mind at rest.*"[14] It should be noted Lytle had a traveling liquor cabinet that went with him throughout the war, so his promise notwithstanding, physical evidence indicates perhaps otherwise.

Lytle met with General Ormsby MacKnight Mitchel at the Galt Hotel. Mitchel, a noted Cincinnati astronomer (his men called him "Old Stars"), had attended parties at the Lytle mansion before the war. (Mitchel's name would soon become associated with Andrew's Raiders and The Great Locomotive Chase.) He assured the young colonel that Lytle had been ordered to Louisville not as a slight, but to "make all things right" and that Lytle would be reunited with the Tenth Ohio in the event there was an advance made by the Federal troops.[15]

On January 16, 1862, Buell issued Special Orders Number 12 and ordered Colonel Lytle to Bardstown, Kentucky, to relieve Brigadier General Thomas Wood in command of Camp Morton.[16] Lytle knew this was an important opportunity and planned to carry out his duties successfully. Lytle took time to write home to reassure his sisters that he intended to keep his promise regarding the drinking.[17]

Settling into his new command, Lytle continued to win friends and influence enemies. A Bardstown newspaper voiced its approval of Lytle taking over at Camp Morton, noting his "stern justice and sterling integrity." The author of the article stated his belief that Lytle was "one of the best officers" in Kentucky.[18]

There were six regiments at Camp Morton and four hundred men in the hospital. Lytle described his duties as "onerous" and confessed he wanted to get back with his old regiment. In the meantime, he visited his Rowan relatives at nearby Federal Hill ("My Old Kentucky Home"). He noted sadly that the old Rowan place had not aged well. The house reminded Lytle of his home in Cincinnati, but Federal Hill's condition was not as good. "The glories of Bardstown have pretty much departed...." The wallpaper was torn, the doors creaked when opened and closed and the entire house presented "an air of decayed splendor...."[19] Perhaps the visit put Lytle in a reflective mood because he wrote another poem.

In Camp 1862

> I gazed forth from my wintry tent
> Upon the star-gemmed firmament;
> I heard the far-off sentry's tramp
> Around our mountain-girdled camp
> And saw the ghostly tents uprise
> Like specters 'neath the jeweled skies.
> And thus upon the snow-clad scene,
> So pure and spotless and serene,
> Where locked in sleep ten thousand lay
> Awaiting morn's returning ray,—
> I gazed, till to the sun the drums
> Rolled at the dawn, "He comes, he comes." [20]

In Bardstown the Federal post band often played four or five songs at sunset in front of the courthouse, near Lytle's headquarters. Lytle loved music and made sure that his band provided entertainment for himself and the locals who began showing up to listen to the performances. These acts by the Yankee commander won over many of the people who had had strong pro-secession leanings before his arrival. As he had done before and would continue to do, Lytle won over people with his charm and grace.[21]

Lytle managed to break away from his duties long enough to meet and dine with his friend Lieutenant Colonel Joseph W. Burke of the Tenth Ohio. He also met with the Rowans again. His cousin, Josephine Rowan, daughter of Rebecca Rowan and the late John Rowan, Jr., informed the Cincinnatian that the Rebel General Pierre Gustave Toutant-Beauregard had recently put his troops to work building a railroad that stretched forty miles. Lytle replied, "Yes, we always thought he would be good at '*making tracks*.'" The busy colonel also had tea with Mr. William Beckham, son-in-law of former Kentucky Governor Charles Anderson Wickliffe. Lytle, always observant of beauty in its many forms, remarked that Mrs. Julia Wickliffe Beckham was quite attractive and that he had fallen "quite in love with her."[22]

In February Lytle reported to his sisters that he had become romantically involved with a young lady named Miss Brown. There is no further mention of Miss Brown, so the romance did not last long. Lytle was a handsome, charming, dashing officer and he drew the attention of ladies wherever he went. He playfully returned their affections. But Lytle's flirtations sometimes went further than intended.

Miss Jennie Springer was a member of an elite Cincinnati family. She asked Lytle for a photograph and a military button, which he sent to her with a note asking if she would like an army correspondent. Not intending to begin a courtship, Lytle was surprised to learn a month later that Miss Springer took his offer more seriously than he intended. To nip that in the bud he sent a polite letter stating he had merely wanted to exchange letters from time to time as he had done and was doing with several other lady friends. She did not reply to this note and Lytle considered her lack of response "ill bred." He felt he deserved "a respectful declination." The situation proved comical to his buddies. "Burke and Alf Pirtle are much amused at the whole performance."[23]

Chapter 12

Lytle Moves South

As the month of March began, Lytle prepared to rejoin his regiment, but his leg was still bothering him, and he was concerned that it was taking so long to heal.[1] Pirtle noted in his journal that March "came in like a lion." The Tenth moved south without Lytle and endured snow, rain, and hail and by 1 p.m. on March 1 had reached the Tennessee state line. The officers quartered at the Magnolia House, which was owned by a man who had two sons in the Confederate army. The owner's daughter, whom Pirtle thought "rather good looking," was a staunch secessionist who stated her hope that the Federals would "soon go back double quick to the Ohio River and she hoped but few of us would be left to tell the tale."[2]

On March 6 Lytle still had not rejoined his command and was in Louisville. His leg was better, but he noticed with displeasure that two more brigadier generals had been appointed from Ohio while he remained a colonel. He wrote to his sisters that it seemed to him that politics drove the promotion process more so than actual performance in the field. Lily replied that she believed that he had been passed over for promotion because of his drinking and pleaded with him to stop. She believed that promotions, respect, and achievement of his ambitions required him to forego alcohol. Lily questioned his "moral courage" and wondered if he were strong enough to quit the booze to obtain the rewards he deserved.[3] Lily's harsh words were still in his mind when he also learned of the death of his old friend, William W. Fosdick, who had died in Cincinnati at the age of 37. The news shocked and saddened the Cincinnatian.[4]

Although not promoted to brigadier general, he was about to take command of the Seventeenth Brigade, of the Third Division, in the Army of the Ohio.[5] The Seventeenth Brigade comprised the Forty-Second Indiana, Fifteenth Kentucky, Third Ohio, and the Tenth Ohio. Having received his orders, Lytle left Louisville to join his command and traveled first to Nashville, Tennessee.[6] John Beatty noted in his March 22 journal entry, "Colonel Lytle, of the Tenth Ohio, will assume command of our brigade."[7]

On March 26 Colonel Lytle left Nashville for Murfreesboro to join the brigade. With his new orderly, Joe Guthrie, driving, he rode most of the way in an ambulance to save his leg from the stress of riding a horse. A few miles from the Federal camp Lytle mounted his horse and rode the rest of the way. As he approached, the Tenth Ohio advanced to meet him. Pirtle recorded, "The boys were all excitement...." They gave him three cheers. Pirtle observed that Lytle "looked pale and excited and gracefully acknowledged the salutes as he rode slowly down the line." The horse was "much alarmed by the sound and the waving caps." The soldiers of the Tenth called Lytle "Old Bill."[8]

Pirtle also recorded part of the address Lytle made to the troops. The colonel spoke "with a quivering voice" and told the men, "Comrades of the 10th Ohio I am happy once more to meet you." He continued, "Yes! In the language of the Sage [Andrew Jackson] whose ashes are now mingled with the dust of the state you are in, 'By the eternal! The Union shall be preserved!' (Prolonged cheers)." Lytle ended his short speech with this promise, "Above the smoke of the battlefield I shall see those cherished flags borne so proudly at Carnifex ... and louder than the rattle and the crash of rifles and the roar of artillery, will be heard the battle cry of the 10th *Faugh a Ballaugh!*"[9]

A correspondent of the *Cincinnati Enquirer* gave his version of what happened when Lytle arrived at Camp Van Buren, Murfreesboro. "While I write, I hear a tremendous cheering, and go out to learn what it means." Expecting to see a dignitary the reporter was surprised to see a "very modest-looking trooper, who, on closer inspection, turned out to be Colonel William H. Lytle." When the "boys recognized him, a cheer went up that called out the whole camp; hats, caps, and guns went up in wild confusion, and the scene presented by the enthusiastic Tenth beggars description."[10]

Once he had moved into his new headquarters, Lytle accompanied General Mitchel and other officers to a dinner given at the home of a local man named William Franklin Pitt Lytle. The Tennessee Lytle was a wealthy slaveowner who owned more than three thousand acres.[11] After that first evening, Colonel Lytle often visited the Lytle house in Murfreesboro where he would dine with W.F.P. Lytle and his wife, Sophie Dashiell Ridgely Lytle.[12]

For some reason, in letters home Lytle referred to Mr. Lytle as "David." The colonel said that "David" had met Robert Todd Lytle in Nashville several years before. The two "compared notes" and determined they were related. In fact, both sets of Lytles had originated in Ireland, then moved to Pennsylvania but the Tennessee Lytles first settled in North Carolina whereas the Ohio Lytles had first gone to Kentucky. He described the Tennessee Lytles as being wealthy and well-connected.[13]

Chapter 12. Lytle Moves South

The Tennessee Lytle family did not call W.F.P. Lytle "David." Their nickname for him was "Billy Creek" and he outlived his first two wives. His third wife was the beautiful Sophie Dashiell Ridgely. Mr. Lytle liked to walk his property, especially through a grove of cedar trees, north of the turnpike, where he would go to clear his head. When the Yankees arrived, they cleared the land and cut down the trees for their fortifications.[14]

His elegant two-story brick house was built in 1810, a year after the Lytle mansion in Cincinnati. The spacious hallway entry was wall-papered with scenes from Sir Walter Scott's "Lady of the Lake." There was a wing on each side of the entry. One contained the office-library the other contained a bedroom. A large dining room was attached to the rear of the office-library. This Murfreesboro home was a comfortable and friendly respite during these troublesome times.[15]

Will told Josie that Mr. Lytle even knew about Josie and Lily and their marriages. His source for that information was none other than Captain William Lytle Blanchard of General George Bibb Crittenden's staff, who had also been a guest of the Tennessee Lytles a few weeks before. (Note: The "List of Staff Officers of the Confederate States Army" does not include a William Lytle Blanchard. Perhaps he was serving in another capacity under Crittenden.) Will was given a letter from a Lieutenant Frank Henderson Lytle, Company C, Eighteenth Tennessee, who had been captured at Fort Donelson and was imprisoned at Johnson's Island, near Sandusky, Ohio. Frank Lytle claimed kinship and asked his Northern kinsman to help him "secure a liberation on parole." Lytle wrote home and asked his sisters to help the Rebel. Whether they intervened is not known but Frank Lytle would be exchanged in September 1862 and serve under General Joseph Wheeler.[16]

Colonel Lytle named Alfred Pirtle as an aide-de-camp. This allowed the Kentuckian to notice his commander's habits and tendencies, one of which was punctuality. For instance, on March 31 Lytle held a review which began "precisely" at 8 a.m.[17] On April 3 Pirtle wrote in his journal that the command left camp in Murfreesboro at "precisely" 1:00 p.m. to march to Shelbyville and Lytle galloped his horse up to the head of the column, "with colors flying, bands playing, and everyone putting on his parade bearing and step...."[18]

Pirtle also made note of Lytle's staff. Lieutenant Colonel Joseph Burke was about twenty-seven and a native of Ireland. He was short, "tolerably well shaped," had a florid complexion, with hair and beard approaching red. Burke's hair was short, and his beard was neatly shaved except for his moustache which Pirtle said was a "Zouave-like goatee." Major R.M. Moore was about fifty and well-liked by the men "for he lets them have their own way too much." Dr. Muscroft was from Cincinnati and had a "ferocious moustache" and wore glasses. Pirtle described Father William O'Higgins as a "highly educated, travelled gentleman but guileless as a child about a great many things ... tells a tale remarkably well...." Pirtle noted in his journal that the town of Shelbyville, Tennessee, was "so decidedly Union in sentiment that the Rebels called it 'Little Boston.'"[19]

While in Shelbyville Lytle's band serenaded residents who came to watch the dress parades. He found the people to be quite friendly and received many invitations to dinner, but declined them all because of his demanding schedule. Some of the Shelbyville residents had read of the Carnifex Ferry battle and heard he had been killed. He told them, "'not *permanently* and that I had brought down my own remains.'"[20]

Alfred Pirtle was a sensitive, intelligent man who wrote detailed and interesting letters to his family and kept a journal during the war. His insights allow us now to see Lytle from an outsider's perspective. Granted, he liked Lytle very much, but his contemporaneous records are not cleaned up and refined the way later writings often were. He simply recorded what he saw. For example, during the march through southern middle Tennessee, Lytle decided he wanted to smoke a cigar but could not find a match anywhere. As they passed a house along the road, they saw a woman leaning on a fence watching the Yankees. Lytle noticed smoke coming from the chimney and asked if he could have a light. The woman took the cigar, went inside, and came back puffing on it. He took the cigar from the woman and, "With all the style he would have used in addressing a duchess, he returned his thanks and rode off puffing a cloud in our faces." His staff officers struggled to keep from laughing. When they were well away from the house, Lytle finally broke into laughter, and his staff followed suit.[21]

To Pirtle, the colonel was "as kind and affectionate as ... a warm hearted affectionate brother...."[22] A war correspondent who had known Lytle since Cincinnati wrote, "Almost as long back as I can remember, the elegant form of Gen. Lytle, upon prancing steed, at the head of marching columns, in the streets of Cincinnati, has been familiar to me. There is not, perhaps, in all the army, a more thorough soldier...."[23]

At least one company of soldiers under his command decided to test Lytle. For their march to Alabama, Lytle ordered the men to carry their knapsacks to reduce the weight of the loads in the wagons. Company E of the Tenth Ohio refused. He told the soldiers that his orders were issued to be obeyed and that the first man who refused to carry his knapsack when ordered would be shot. Lytle gave the men five minutes to comply. For the first two minutes he sat motionless on his horse. When he began to unstrap his holster, Pirtle noted, "The boys knew exactly what to expect and all of them obeyed the order." The march resumed and the Seventeenth

Brigade crossed the Alabama state line on their way to Huntsville on April 15.[24]

Lytle described Huntsville as "one of the most beautiful towns in America." From there he led a raid that advanced 12 miles into Tennessee and captured two carloads of Confederate mail.[25] In addition to the mail, the Federals captured two pieces of artillery, a Confederate flag (which Lytle kept), military supplies, and forty or fifty prisoners. General O.M. Mitchel reported that Lytle's expedition "has proved a success."[26]

In early May, the "Thunderbolt of the Confederacy," Rebel raider John Hunt Morgan, attacked a Federal force in Pulaski, Tennessee, capturing 268 men and officers, one of whom was a son of General Mitchel.[27] Lytle later spoke with a Federal officer who had been captured and managed to escape. Lytle was impressed that the Thunderbolt had been courteous to the officer and concluded, "Morgan is certainly a gallant gentleman—A man quite after my own heart."[28]

Morgan, though, was not viewed as kindly by other Federals. He was a constant threat to the Union supply lines. However, John Beatty noted in his journal his thoughts on Morgan. "Our boys find Alabama hams better than Uncle Sam's sidemeat, and fresh bread better than hard crackers. So that every time this dashing cavalryman destroys a provision train, their hearts are gladdened, and they shout 'Bully for Morgan!'"[29]

Seizing private property, though, was officially discouraged. Mitchel sent an order to Lytle, "See that your men do not pillage and plunder.... I would prefer to hear that you had fought a battle and been defeated in a fair fight than to learn that your soldiers have degenerated into robbers and plunderers." The same day he sent a dispatch to Colonel John Basil Turchin ordering Turchin to remove his troops from Athens "as early as possible."[30] Mitchel was sensitive to the conduct of the troops in north Alabama because of an incident that took place in Athens on May 2, 1862.

Ivan Vasilovich Turchinoff was a native of Russia and a former soldier in the service of Czar Alexander II. Turchinoff and his wife emigrated to the United States, settled in Chicago, and Americanized their names. Ivan became John Basil Turchin. In June 1861 Turchin joined the Nineteenth Illinois and was commissioned a colonel. In February 1862 Colonel Turchin was placed in command of a brigade which two months later captured Huntsville, Alabama. It was what happened next, though, that earned Turchin a court-martial.[31]

Turchin's troops entered Athens, Alabama, without any resistance. The citizens seemed to be mostly pro–Union. On May 1 Confederate cavalry swept in, surprised the Federal garrison, and drove them from the town. As many as a hundred of the townsmen joined the Confederate cavalry to pursue the Federals. The following day Turchin led a counterattack and retook the town. Believing the townspeople had acted treacherously toward his men, the Russian-born Turchin rode to the middle of the square and shouted to his officers, "I shut my eyes for two hours." What followed was the sacking of Athens. At least one woman allegedly was raped, and homes and businesses were ransacked and pillaged. Residents of the sacked city later made claims against the United States for damages of nearly $55,000. (The claims were denied.)[32]

Don Carlos Buell ordered a court-martial for Turchin and his officers. Unrepentant, Turchin declared he believed he was waging war the way it should be waged. Turchin said, "I have tried to teach rebels that treachery to the Union was a terrible crime." The court-martial, led by Ohio native Brigadier General James Abram Garfield, found him guilty. He was relieved of command and recommended for dismissal from the service. Many Federal officers, including Lytle, were disgusted by what the Russian had done to Southern civilians. However, others in the North saw his actions as justified and Turchin's wife appealed directly to President Lincoln who set the verdict aside and reinstated the "Russian Thunderbolt."[33]

Dr. Malone of Athens was an acquaintance of Lytle's and made sure the Cincinnatian knew that Malone's two sisters had been robbed by some of Turchin's soldiers. This type of behavior from the Yankees hardened the hearts of the Southerners. Unlike Shelbyville, Lytle experienced open hostility from the people in this area. The citizens would not speak to the Federal troops and Lytle said "the women are *venomous*...."[34] Colonel Beatty agreed with Lytle about the local inhabitants. He noted, the men of the town "settled down to a patient endurance of military rule. The women, however, are outspoken in their hostility, and marvelously bitter."[35]

Even during this hectic, dangerous time of his military career, the Cincinnati poet found time to take pen in hand and compose a patriotic piece.

'Tis Not the Time
1862

'Tis not the time for dalliance soft
In gentle ladies' bowers,
When treason flaunts her flag aloft
And dares to tread on ours.
Again the swords our fathers wore
Must in the scabbards rattle,
And we will sing the songs of yore,
When marching forth to battle.

From every pine-clad mountain side,
From every dimpled valley,
The bugles ringing far and wide

> Invite the brave to rally.
> And far to East and far to West
> Our iron line advances,
> While freedom's flag, by freemen blessed,
> In glory o'er us dances.
>
> But when the birds of morning sing,
> And all the wars are over,
> Our lances at your feet we'll fling
> And then we'll play the lover.
> And all will say 'tis time to wed,
> As gayly drums shall rattle,
> Before our conquering column's head,
> When marching home from battle.[36]

General O.M. Mitchel recommended Lytle for promotion to brigadier general, but Lytle had not heard anything from the government regarding his possible advancement. Despite his disappointment, Lytle pledged to stay in the fight to the end. Mitchel had no word on the promotion but did advise Lytle that he had invited his daughter to come visit and suggested Lytle's sister, Lily, come down too. Will advised Lily not to make the trip because it was too dangerous. He also asked Lily, "Do the people ever talk of me at home? How are all the pretty girls?"[37]

Lytle's camp headquarters in Huntsville was surrounded by magnificent oak trees. He had a view of the town from his command post. An artillery battery was posted to one side and just below were the soldiers of the Tenth Ohio. His other regiments were located nearby.[38]

The workload took its toll on Lytle. Pirtle noted on June 14 the colonel was "very sick."[39] Lytle decided to take the camp doctor's recommendation and get some rest, which helped him but he still felt weak.[40] On June 30 Lytle wrote a letter to his sisters labeled "PRIVATE." He admitted that his health was not good, and he was also concerned about his lack of promotion and threatened to resign if he were replaced as commander of the Seventeenth Brigade. Lytle was furious that he had been passed over again. Turchin's appointment to brigadier general was particularly vexing for the poet-soldier. Lytle was not alone in his concerns about the Russian's rise to higher rank, because of what had happened at Athens. "The promotion of Turchin causes much talk." The sisters had evidently informed Will that his friends had not forgotten him. "You do not know how glad I am to hear that my friends remember me." He closed the letter by referring to a letter he had received from "Seddy."[41]

Lytle and several other officers took time from their schedules to go up Monte Sano (Spanish for "Mountain of Health") outside of Huntsville. There they enjoyed lunch beside a spring near the top of the mountain.

View from the picnic area on top of Monte Sano. The mountains of north Alabama fade into the distance. Originally a health colony promoting the benefits of spring water and clean mountain air, Monte Sano has drawn visitors for more than 200 years. True to its name, the mountaintop helped restore Lytle's health (photograph by the author).

Pirtle recalled, "Col. Lytle did the honors with his usual grace and dignity, looking better than I ever saw him, while he made himself agreeable to a lady on each hand…." The afternoon hours passed quickly. Pirtle recalled there was a gentle breeze and as the participants enjoyed a "merry conversation" the band played softly creating "a scene that shall long live in my memory...."[42] The group sang the "Star Spangled Banner," "Bold Soldier Boy," "Benny Haven's Oh!" They ended their outing by singing "Old Lang Syne." As the men and women made their way back down the mountain at sunset, the fading light on the mountainside presented a beautiful scene. True to its name, the mountain seemed to restore Lytle. He wrote of the excursion, "It has been indeed a day long to be held in remembrance...."[43]

One afternoon a thunderstorm pounded the Federal camp. The lightning and thunder were "terrible" recalled Pirtle and the wind was so strong that it blew down trees and leveled tents. Lytle's tent was hit, and his papers were scattered "in every direction...." The colonel was soaked from the storm but joked about the situation as he gathered his papers, "concluding that was better than to grumble...." Lytle's positive spirit was infectious, and his staff soon found themselves enjoying picking up debris from the muddy fields. Lytle "was particularly funny—his wit as brilliant as I ever heard it under the most favorable circumstances."[44]

There were trying days ahead, but the terrible war was honing Lytle.

Chapter 13

Hope

On July 26, 1862, representatives from Cincinnati were in Huntsville, Alabama, to present a new flag to the Tenth Ohio. There had been fears in the camp of the Tenth Ohio that the flag had been carried off by Rebel cavalry who attacked the wagon train bringing it down from Cincinnati. Although the raiders carried off many goods, they did not take the flag, much to the relief of Lytle and his men. Many citizens from Huntsville gathered to watch the Yankee ceremony. A reporter remarked, "The scene was one of the most beautiful I have ever witnessed. The hour, the grey of the evening, the morning in the distance, the neat and orderly appearance of the men in waiting to receive so beautiful a testimonial from their fellow-citizens at so great a distance...."[1]

Lieutenant Colonel Joseph Burke of the Tenth Ohio made the arrangements for the ceremony and at his signal the troops moved in step to form a three-sided hollow square. The band was to the right and the colors to be presented were sheathed. Mr. E.M. Spencer, whom Lytle noted was the editor of the Cincinnati *Daily Times*, presented the flag and told the men, "Half a century ago France emblazoned the name 'Borodino' upon the flag of a regiment which had won glory and immortality upon that bloody field. Cincinnati writes the single word 'Carnifex' upon her banner for the Tenth...." Mr. Spencer concluded by telling the men "you are not forgotten at home" and the people of Cincinnati felt "fully confident" that the flag "will never be dishonored...." The regiment responded with three cheers.[2]

Colonel Lytle stepped forward and addressed Mr. Spencer: "It is many a long month since yonder regiment, one of the oldest in the Ohio Line, amid the prayers and benedictions of patriotic men and women, left Camp Dennison." The regiment had suffered losses since that time, but the men were determined to win the war. Lytle said, "when you go home, tell the bighearted, whole-souled, patriotic, generous people of Cincinnati, that the Tenth Ohio ... will again march through the crowded and appealing

Chapter 13. Hope 87

streets of the old town to the stirring music of 'Garry Owen' and 'St. Patrick's Day in the Morning.'"

Then he turned and spoke to his men. He urged them to "let this testimonial from a great and loyal city of the Republic be a still stronger stimulus to exertion." To Lytle, the soldier in the ranks "is as worthy of the applause and gratitude of the nation as the General who conducts the campaign." They performed their duties, whether as a picket or in a battle, "aiming not so much at promotion as to be worthy of it...." The "soldiers of the Republic" marching forth to defend the Union "will be invincible." Lytle exhorted his men to keep fighting to the end. He thanked Mr. Spencer for bringing the flag and making the presentation.[3] Pirtle believed that Lytle's speech was "the most felicitous and beautiful accepting speech that I ever heard" and the soldiers responded with "tremendous cheering...." At the conclusion of the speech the band played "Hail to the Chief."[4] After the ceremony, many of the guests made their way to Colonel Lytle's quarters to, as a reporter noted, "partake of the hospitalities attendant on such an occasion."[5]

Despite his patriotic speech, Lytle still harbored resentment over the promotion issue. Writing to his brother-in-law Sam Broadwell the day after the flag presentation, Lytle expressed dismay that Joshua Sill, five years younger but a West Point graduate, had been promoted to brigadier general July 16. If he did not receive the long-sought promotion soon, he would resign from the army and return to Cincinnati.[6]

Lily assured her brother that the family and their contacts were doing everything they could to help him gain his promotion. She closed by advising Will that President Lincoln had said he was aware of Lytle's performance and intended to promote him.[7] Lytle's sisters were not the only source of love and inspiration from Cincinnati. Aunt Joanna Reilly sent her nephew some cigars and shirts and included a note that read, "May the prayers of your sainted Grandmother be your guide and shield from all danger."[8]

On August 20, 1862, Buell sent Lytle instructions to prepare to leave Huntsville. Communications had become uncertain due to the distance Lytle was from other Federal troops. He was to reach Shelbyville, Tennessee, within four days of receiving final instructions to evacuate. Buell ordered the colonel to "Make your preparations quietly and secretly. Your intention must not be made known even to your own officers."[9]

He did make his intentions known. A Huntsville resident, Mary Chadick, recorded in her diary, August 24, that Mayor Robert W. Coltart advised her that the Federals were going to evacuate later that afternoon. The townspeople were not to celebrate because Lytle said he "could not be answerable for the conduct of the troops when leaving." He did not want another Athens. Before the Federal troops had arrived in Huntsville, residents had been warned of the Tenth Ohio. A Huntsville citizen recorded he had assumed the Tenth would be "wild, lawless men...." The citizens were "surprised that their horses and property were left unharmed." The man praised the Tenth's "discipline and fine bearing...."[10] Then orders arrived delaying the planned evacuation.

Lytle's commander, Brigadier General Lovell Harrison Rousseau, and his staff, departed for Nashville on August 26 and left Lytle with the Tenth Ohio, Fifteenth Kentucky, Kennett's Fourth Ohio cavalry, Loomis's battery, a company of engineers and mechanics and two companies of loyal Alabama volunteers. Pirtle noted, "We are the southern most forces of the Army of the Ohio..." and all the men were keenly aware of their situation.[11]

Lytle liked Rousseau, whom he described as a "thorough Kentuckian." Born in Lincoln County, Kentucky, Rousseau attended local schools until his father died of cholera when Lovell was 15. After the death of his father, he worked construction and helped build the turnpike from Lexington to Lancaster. Rousseau then studied law in Louisville and moved across the river to Indiana where he was admitted to the bar. He served in the Mexican War, was elected to the Kentucky House of Representatives and at the outbreak of the Civil War helped raise troops for the Union.[12]

Approximately one hundred miles away, in Chattanooga, Tennessee, Confederate commander General Braxton Bragg joined up with Major General Edmund Kirby Smith's Army of East Tennessee to invade (or liberate) Kentucky. This would become known as the "Heartland Offensive." Bragg hoped that he could bring the people of the Commonwealth into the Confederacy once they saw the Rebel army there. Kirby Smith moved his forces north and on August 27, 1862, Bragg began his march to Kentucky. In one of the Confederacy's great victories of the war, Smith defeated Union forces at Richmond, Kentucky, at the end of August. One of the Confederate heroes of that battle was Patrick Cleburne, who was wounded in the fighting.[13] The Rebel victory led to the capture of Frankfort, Kentucky, the only Northern capital to fall during the war. No one on the Northern side knew exactly where Bragg was headed but Nashville or Louisville seemed to be likely targets and Lytle was ordered to move north to join the hunt for Bragg.

On August 29 Lytle received orders to forward his wagon trains to Nashville. In his order, Buell told Lytle, "Your communications are rendered so uncertain by the necessity of concentrating the army at a point beyond supporting distance from you that I deem it proper to withdraw your force from Huntsville." He was ordered to take the medical supplies, leave the sick and destroy everything else they could not carry away. The following day he received another message requiring him to get to Shelbyville, Tennessee, in three days.[14] On August 31 Mary Chadick recorded in her diary, "Awoke a little after midnight by the sound of heavy tramping of feet, the sound of voices, uttering the most dreadful curses, the rattling of wagons...." (No doubt the Tenth Ohio contributed to the cursing.) She feared the Yankees "had set fire to some parts of the town." The retreating Federals were destroying food and any other items they felt could contribute to the Confederate war effort but did not burn the town.[15]

Pirtle witnessed slaves, emboldened by hope, swarming the Federals, "loading some of the wagons with their women and children." The African Americans did not know where they were going and what they would do once they got there but Pirtle said they had but one thought and that was "that they were going to be free!"[16] A war correspondent also witnessed the retreat from Huntsville. He described the scene as "ludicrous." The formerly enslaved workers followed the Federal military columns on foot, on horseback and in wagons. Children, furniture, pots, and kettles crowded the overloaded conveyances. Unfortunately for the enslaved people, Lytle eventually turned them all away, stating that he believed it was in their best interests to return to their "homes."[17]

Lytle's command reached Shelbyville, found that the rest of the army had not passed through, and moved on toward Murfreesboro. The officers joked with one another about the possibility of going to Louisville.[18] Lytle was in Murfreesboro by September 3.[19] He reported to headquarters that his troops moved north with a long train of wagons, driving four hundred head of horses and cattle.[20]

Continuing north, as Lytle and his escort galloped along the column of marching troops, the men cheered. Pirtle observed, "'Old Bill'... is a favorite outside of the 'Bloody Tenth.'"[21] A week later Lytle reported from Bowling Green, Kentucky, to his sisters that his march "elicited high compliments" from Buell's headquarters. The column, four to five miles long, had made the march without the loss of a single man, wagon, or animal. During Lytle's march north, a Federal garrison at Munfordville, Kentucky, defended by John Thornton Wilder, put up a stiff fight but finally fell to Bragg's Rebels. The poet-soldier was not involved in the fighting there. On September 26 Lytle and his troops arrived in Louisville and were reequipped and outfitted. He longed for a visit from his family members, but they were unable to travel to the River City.[22]

Rebel forces under Bragg had reached Bardstown, Kentucky, on September 22. Kirby Smith was then near Frankfort, the capital of Kentucky, which had fallen to the Rebels. On September 25 Bragg sent his cavalry commander, Nathan Bedford Forrest, back to Tennessee to recruit more cavalrymen and threaten Nashville which meant that Bragg was virtually blind in terms of intelligence regarding Federal troop movements. Bragg himself departed on September 28 to travel to Frankfort and left Leonidas Polk in command of the troops at Bardstown.[23] (Polk was known as "The Fighting Bishop" because he was a bishop in the Episcopal church. The Rev. Charles Petit McIlvaine consecrated Polk "Bishop of the Southwest" at Christ Church Cathedral in Cincinnati in 1838.)[24]

Before embarking on the crusade to save Kentucky from the Confederates, Buell issued orders to reorganize the Army of the Ohio. He planned to create three corps, each with three divisions. This new structure would be consistent with changes being made in other Union armies. I Corps would be commanded by Major General Alexander McDowell McCook. II Corps would be under the command of Major General Thomas Leonidas Crittenden. Buell intended for III Corps to be commanded by Brigadier General William "Bull" Nelson but Nelson, an aggressive fighter in battle, offended Union Brigadier General Jefferson Columbus Davis, who shot him dead at the Galt Hotel in Louisville the same day Buell's changes were to take place. (Davis was not prosecuted and went on to distinguish himself in future battles, including Chickamauga.) To fill the vacancy in leadership for III Corps left by Nelson's death, Buell selected a man he knew, trusted and liked, Ohioan Charles Champion Gilbert.[25]

On October 1 Buell's 60,000-man army began leaving Louisville. Buell's three army corps left via three separate roads while Joshua Sill led two divisions toward Frankfort to fool the Rebels into thinking that was their target.[26] McCook's I Corps was to

One of the "Fighting McCooks," Ohioan Alexander McDowell McCook would be Lytle's corps commander at Perryville and Chickamauga. Questionable decisions at Chickamauga led to McCook shouldering part of the blame for that military disaster. "Alexander McDowell McCook, Union general, three-quarter length portrait, seated, facing front" (Library of Congress).

Chapter 13. Hope   91

march on Harrodsburg. Crittenden's II Corps was to pass four miles south of Perryville and Gilbert's III Corps was to move directly through Perryville.[27] The Third Division of I Corps was commanded by Brigadier General Lovell Harrison Rousseau. The Seventeenth Brigade, Third Division, I Corps was commanded by Colonel William Haines Lytle.

On October 2, when Bragg discovered Sill's movement toward Frankfort, he believed Buell was moving his entire force there, so he tried to set a trap. Kirby Smith would hold the Federals in front and Polk would lead the Army of Mississippi to hit Buell's force in the flank. "I see no hope for Buell," Bragg wrote in an uncharacteristically hopeful tone. Because Forrest was not there to scout, the Confederate commander was unaware that the bulk of Buell's army was making its way toward Bardstown. Arriving in Frankfort on the third, Bragg received dispatches from Polk indicating that they had detected a large Federal force moving toward them and Polk moved the Army of Mississippi out of Bardstown and toward Danville.[28]

On October 3 Lytle wrote to Lily that they were in Taylorsville, Kentucky.[29] Two days later he wrote Aunt Joanna that a battle seemed imminent. There had been skirmishing for two days and he was fatigued but was still hopeful regarding the future of the Union.[30]

Saturday October 4 Bragg was in Frankfort, Kentucky, where Richard Hawes was to be installed as the Confederate governor.[31] The Rebel party was interrupted by the ominous booming of distant artillery. Bragg received word the Federals were only twelve miles away and sent orders for Polk to go to Harrodsburg to guard their supplies. Without any further ado, Bragg, Hawes, and the Confederate cavalrymen rode out of town. The citizens thought their commander was riding out to attack the approaching Northerners. But this was not an attack. It was a hasty retreat, and soon Federal troops rode into Frankfort and ended the short Confederate occupation.[32]

Bragg's Army of Mississippi was divided into two wings. The right wing was under the command of Major General Leonidas Polk. The left wing was under the command of Major General William J. Hardee. When Polk's Confederate troops moved toward Harrodsburg, Hardee, looking for water, moved toward Perryville. Because that area had access to good roads, he knew he could shift his troops, if need be, in case the Federals appeared.[33]

On October 7 Bragg ordered Polk to join with Kirby Smith at Versailles, west of Lexington, where he believed the crucial battle would be fought.[34] As the Confederates moved towards Versailles, the Federal army was moving towards Perryville. When the Rebels learned that the Federals were closing in, they stopped at Perryville and prepared to fight.[35]

Confederate Major General William Joseph Hardee dashed off a note from Perryville to Bragg warning him, "Tomorrow morning early we may expect a fight."[36] Bragg sent an order to Polk, commander of the right wing, dated October 7, 5:40 p.m., to "give the enemy battle immediately; rout him and then move to our support at Versailles. ... No time should be lost in these movements."[37]

When Buell learned that the Rebels were now concentrating their forces at Perryville, he issued orders for Alexander McCook to change his line of march to Perryville. Buell intended for McCook to march at three o'clock the next morning, but the orders did not reach McCook until 2:30 the morning of October 8.[38] It would be a long day for everyone. For some, it would be their last.

Chapter 14

THE SECOND FALL: PERRYVILLE

Wednesday, October 8, 1862.
Perryville, Kentucky, was settled by a group of Pennsylvanians in the 1770s and originally named Harbison's (or Harberson's or Harbeson's) Station or Fort. In 1817 it was renamed after Commodore Oliver Hazard Perry and in 1836 the Kentucky state legislature voted to build a turnpike from Springfield to Danville, running through Perryville. With the Mackville Road intersecting there as well, the town became a crossroads and a market for nearby farms.[1] There were approximately four hundred residents in the town in 1862. The Chaplin River runs through Perryville and the Chaplin Hills loom nearby, to the west. The upcoming battle would come to be known as the Battle of Perryville or Chaplin Hills.[2]

The sun would soon rise into a hot, cloudless sky, but before daybreak on October 8 Lytle, at Mackville, eight or nine miles from Perryville, had originally been ordered to begin his march at 6 a.m. but received new orders to move immediately. His brigade was on the road within twenty minutes.[3] Lytle's Seventeenth Brigade comprised the Third Ohio (Colonel John Beatty commanding), the Tenth Ohio (Lieutenant Colonel Joseph W. Burke), the Fifteenth Kentucky (Colonel Curran Pope), the Forty-Second Indiana (Colonel James G. Jones) and the Eighty-Eighth Indiana (Colonel George Humphrey) with the First Battery, Michigan Light Artillery (Captain Cyrus O. Loomis).[4]

The Third Ohio originally organized at Camp Jackson in Columbus for three-months' service. At Camp Dennison in Cincinnati, they reorganized for three-years' service in June 1861. They had campaigned in West Virginia, Kentucky, Tennessee, and Alabama. The Fifteenth Kentucky organized at New Haven in December 1861. They served in campaigns in Kentucky, Tennessee, and Alabama. Both had been with the Seventeenth Brigade since late 1861 and both were involved in the capture of Huntsville, Alabama. The Forty-Second Indiana organized at Evansville in October

1861. The Hoosiers had been transferred from the Fourteenth Brigade to the Seventeenth earlier in 1862 and had campaigned in Tennessee and Alabama. The Eighty-Eighth Indiana was the newest regiment in the brigade, having organized in Fort Wayne in August 1862. They had been attached to the Seventeenth Brigade in September. This would be their first action. The First Michigan Light Artillery, Battery A or "Loomis's Battery" was originally attached to state militia and tendered its services to the government in April 1861. They had campaigned in West Virginia, Kentucky, Tennessee, and Alabama.[5]

Rousseau's three brigades moved with Lytle's Seventeenth leading the way, followed by Colonel Leonard Harris's Ninth Brigade. Colonel John Converse Starkweather's Twenty-Eighth Brigade brought up the rear.[6]

Major General Alexander McCook's younger brother, Colonel Daniel McCook, Jr., commanded the Thirty-Sixth Brigade, III Corps. They had marched directly to Perryville as planned and arrived west of Perryville along the Springfield Pike on the night of the seventh. Colonel McCook received orders to move forward at 2 a.m. on the eighth and seize nearby Peters Hill. He sent three of his regiments into the darkness where they fought for and took the hill.[7]

Despite this firing on his left and Bragg's orders from the previous night, Polk claimed he did not know what "immediately" meant and did not comply with the orders to commence the morning attack. He also did not bother to tell Bragg he was not carrying out the order. Polk would later claim that he and other generals had met and decided to "adopt the defensive-offensive" and "await the movements of the enemy, and to be guided by events as they developed." (Bragg would later write of Polk's "acknowledged disobedience.")[8] As a result, the Rebels missed an opportunity to hit the Federals before more troops arrived on the field.

Confederate Brigadier General St. John Liddell, on the Confederate left, was not confused. Shortly before 7:00 a.m., he sent his Arkansans to retake Peters Hill. They were driven back. Recently promoted Brigadier General Philip Henry Sheridan joined Colonel McCook and ordered more Union troops forward. Dismounted Federal cavalrymen were sent out as skirmishers. Confederate artillery opened fire and the Federals brought up two pieces which silenced the Rebel guns. Approximately three miles from Perryville, the Federal troops of I Corps, including Lytle's Seventeenth Brigade, heard this artillery fire from their right front and the men picked up the pace.[9]

I Corps reached the Dixville Crossroads and turned right onto the Mackville Road. Lytle's troops halted near a two-story white house, owned by John Calvin Russell, on the south side of the road around 10:30. Rousseau formed Lytle's and Harris's brigades into a line of battle anchored on the Russell house and ordered a reconnaissance force to go to the front and left. Lytle sent the Tenth Ohio forward.[10] Rousseau ordered the Forty-Second Indiana ahead to assist the Federal cavalry on the right. By this time, though, the firing had ceased. Rousseau noted, "Everything indicated that the enemy had retired and it was so believed." Lieutenant George Landrum of the Second Ohio recalled, "We all supposed they [Confederates] were leaving, as we could see nothing of them." Men relaxed and ate food from their haversacks. Many of the soldiers were disappointed there had not been a battle.[11]

The Federal soldiers needed water and Doctors Fork or Creek was right up the road. Rousseau sent orders to send out skirmishers, then send out a regiment at a time to find water. Lytle sent the Tenth Ohio forward as skirmishers to clear the way then ordered the Forty-Second Indiana to search for water. Once at the creek they stacked their arms and fanned out along the creek bed, north and south of the road. Due to the recent drought, the creek was mostly dry and all they found were small puddles covered with green scum, but the Hoosiers found if they scraped that away they could still boil the water for coffee. The remainder of the Federal column continued its march down the Mackville Road around noon. Lytle thought he heard gunfire coming from the front and left and thought it might be coming from the skirmishers of the Tenth Ohio.[12]

Rousseau and McCook rode up to the ridge where two Parrott rifles from Cyrus Loomis's First Michigan Light Artillery battery had been moved. A Parrot rifle gave its artillerists the advantage of range. For instance, a 12-pounder Napoleon smoothbore gun had a range of around 1,600 yards. A Parrott could fire a projectile nearly 2,000 yards.[13] A correspondent described the report of the rifled Parrott guns as "sharp, quick."[14] They fired into the distant woods until the Rebels could no longer be seen then the Federals waited for orders.[15]

Unaware of any lurking danger, Rousseau, McCook, their staffs, and several other Northern officers, including Lytle, passed around a bottle of liquor. They could see clouds of dust in the distance, coming from the Harrodsburg Pike, and assumed the Confederates were moving away to join Kirby Smith. Rousseau did not believe other Confederates were anywhere near.[16] Lieutenant Landrum looked through his field glass and saw Rebel skirmishers appearing from the distant woods. Rousseau believed the distant troops were Union soldiers. Landrum replied, "If so, they were dressed in 'Butternut' clothes." Rousseau still didn't believe it until a Rebel shell flew over the heads of the Federal officers and struck nearby. Landrum noted, "such a skedaddling to get out of range I never saw before…. I could not help laughing; at the same time I felt as though I would be safer a little farther off." Federal artillery responded.[17]

Rousseau called up the rest of Loomis's battery and Peter Simonson's Fifth Battery, Indiana Light Artillery. They positioned themselves on the western ridge of a large ravine that separated the two forces. The guns were lined up on the north side of the Mackville Road, across from Henry P. "Squire" Bottom's farm. As the artillerists of both armies dueled, Lytle positioned his men for an expected Confederate attack. Artillery batteries from Alabama, Tennessee, Mississippi, and Louisiana fired at the Yankee lines.

Lytle looked through his field glass and saw "heavy masses of Rebels apparently deploying into line of battle."[18] North and east of the rest of their brigade, well in front of the rest of the line, the Tenth Ohio was stationed along Doctors Creek. To the left of the Tenth Ohio was the Thirty-Third Ohio of Harris's brigade, which had also been thrown forward as skirmishers. Lytle's Third Ohio, Fifteenth Kentucky and Eighty-Eighth Indiana comprised the right flank of the emerging Federal position. The Third Ohio was ordered to the crest of the hill behind or west of the Bottom house and barn and the Fifteenth Kentucky moved to support the Third, behind the ridge. The Eighty-Eighth Indiana was farther back, behind the Russell house in a wooded area. Simonson's battery was still posted to the left of Loomis's battery along the ridge of the ravine through which any Confederate attack must move. Shells exploded all around. Lytle's clerk, James Robb of Company E, Tenth Ohio, was hit in the side by a spherical shot and killed instantly.[19]

Bragg was unaware he was facing an entire Federal corps. The Federal commander, Don Carlos Buell, on the other hand, was unaware a battle was going on at all. He was at the home of a local named Dorsey getting ready to eat lunch. Buell later claimed he did not hear the battle. Some later historians justified Buell's statements and blamed the rolling Chaplin Hills and "acoustic shadow" or "sound refraction" for Buell's inability to hear the major battle being fought nearby. When he did at last hear the booming of big guns, he thought his men were wasting powder or "shelling the woods." He sent orders to "stop that firing." Acting Major General Charles C. Gilbert said he would ride to the front and see what was going but Buell ordered him to stay and eat lunch with him.[20] Much later, when the sound of the distant firing became continuous Buell said, "that is something more than shelling the woods; it sounds like a fight."[21]

Episcopal Rev. Charles Todd Quintard, who traveled with the Confederate army as their chaplain, looked out toward the Yankee positions and remarked, "They are fighting for water now. I am informed they have had none for two days." A Southern bystander chimed in, "I hope they will never get a drop till Father Abraham sends it to them by Lazarus."[22]

Confederate Brigadier General Sterling Alexander Martin (S.A.M.)

Chapter 14. The Second Fall: Perryville

As this sketch shows, the Federals stood in line and held their ground against the Rebel attack before falling back to establish a final defensive line. "The Battle of Perryville, Kentucky, fought October 8, 1862" (Library of Congress).

Wood's brigade moved towards the Tenth Ohio in anticipation of advancing on the Federal lines. (Wood, a native of Alabama, had graduated from St. Joseph's College in nearby Bardstown, Kentucky, in 1841.) Wood's brigade would follow behind Major A.T. Hawkins's Mississippi sharpshooters. The Thirty-Second Mississippi, then the Thirty-Third Alabama, followed by the Thirty-Third Mississippi would move forward one after the other. To Wood's right was the brigade of Colonel Thomas Marshall Jones which would be followed by the brigade of Brigadier General John Calvin Brown.[23]

After firing for nearly two hours, Loomis informed Lytle he was running out of long-range ammunition. Lytle accompanied Loomis to the rear and reported to Rousseau who ordered Lytle to hold the line as long as possible and if necessary, retire in good order. The poet-soldier assured Rousseau he could hold his position "easily." Riding back to the front Lytle saw Loomis's battery limbering up and leaving. Not expecting this, the Cincinnatian sent a message to Rousseau asking if he should change his positions since the artillery had withdrawn. He did not get a response and shortly after 2:00 p.m. the Rebel artillery let up and the Confederate infantry advanced.[24]

Seeing the large mass of enemy troops approaching, and determining they were greatly outnumbered, the Thirty-Third Ohio fell back but the Tenth Ohio held its position. Jones's Mississippians moved toward the "Bloody Tenth." Confederate Brigadier General Daniel Adams's brigade began moving to threaten Lytle's Third Ohio, the far right of McCook's Corps.[25]

At Carnifex Ferry the Tenth had moved along a wooded trail, marched through mountains, and attacked up a hill toward an entrenched enemy. Today they found themselves in a rather bleak landscape of dry wispy grass and cornfields. This allowed the Tenth Ohio to see they were badly outnumbered, so they fell back to join their comrades along the ridge. The Rebels continued to press forward.[26] More Confederates joined the assault as Brigadier General Bushrod Rust Johnson (a native of Ohio) launched his men toward the Bottom House and Doctors Creek where the Forty-Second Indiana still waited for orders. Brigadier General Patrick Ronayne Cleburne's brigade of Tennesseans and Arkansans followed Johnson. Rebel sharpshooters stumbled into the Forty-Second Indiana in the creek bed. One of Lytle's aides finally arrived and told the Forty-Second to get out of the creek bed and reform behind the Union line on the ridge. Major James Shankin of the Forty-Second said he could not hear the orders but figured it was time to leave and started climbing "up the bluff" while "grape-shot" was striking all around. Before extricating themselves, the Forty-Second would suffer 25 percent casualties.[27]

The Tenth Ohio positioned themselves to the right of Harris's Thirty-Eighth Indiana. The Tenth Wisconsin was to the left of the Thirty-Eighth Indiana.[28] Federal artillery fired canister and infantry unleashed volleys into the advancing Confederates, blasting great swaths in the Rebel lines. One Federal soldier recalled, "...we could see awful gaps in their lines & then they would close up...." Confederate riflemen singled out Simonson's artillery battery and their deadly fire killed several of his men and horses, forcing him to fall back three hundred yards to join Loomis southeast of the Russell house.[29]

By 3:00 p.m. Confederates had advanced against the Federal center and left, and the Union center began falling back. In front of Lytle's position, Johnson's brigade crossed Doctors Creek, followed by Cleburne, and began pushing up the hill past the Bottom house toward the Third Ohio's line. The Ohioans stood their ground. A Rebel shell struck the Bottom barn and it caught fire. Wounded men had been crawling to the structure throughout the battle. Now, as the dry barn burned and wind whipped the flames, the sanctuary became a slaughterhouse and the shrieks of the dying men inside added to the awful din of battle. The intense heat singed the faces of the men of the Third Ohio who were near the conflagration. The wind blew the smoke across the Federal lines, from south to north.[30]

Farther to Lytle's left, the Rebel brigades of Jones and Brown moved

Chapter 14. The Second Fall: Perryville

Modern day view of the Perryville battlefield taken from the Union line near where the Tenth Ohio fought. The Rebels were forced to attack across open ground and ascend a steep slope to get to the Federals (photograph by the author).

forward to the left of the Tenth Ohio. Having retreated from the creek bed, the Forty-Second Indiana reformed in the cornfield behind the Tenth, on the north side of the Mackville Road and the Eighty-Eighth Indiana moved across the road and formed behind the Forty-Second Indiana. The Fifteenth Kentucky stayed in position behind the Third Ohio who were fiercely holding their position on the hill.[31]

A Confederate officer in Brown's Brigade summed up the plight of the Rebels who were trying to take the Bottom Farm from Lytle's men. "The only way out of the difficulty was up that hill and over the fence." As the Rebels moved forward a young soldier in Brown's Brigade tried to shout but in his excitement the noise came out as a squeak. "The effect was electric," recalled a fellow soldier and the Rebel yell commenced and turned into a "great roar."[32]

Colonel Daniel McCook went to Sheridan and begged him to hit the attacking Rebels. Sheridan denied the request. McCook asked if he could at least use his artillery because he could plainly see what was about to happen on the Union right (Lytle's position). Sheridan replied, "It might concentrate the fire of the enemy's artillery upon our troops."[33]

Major General McCook sent Captain Horace N. Fisher to find help from the nearest commander. Fisher rode toward the Springfield Pike and first encountered Brigadier General Albin F. Schoepf of III Corps. Schoepf replied that he would first need to talk to General Gilbert. Fisher found Gilbert who told him he would need to go make his request directly to Major General Buell.[34]

Captain Fisher arrived at Buell's headquarters at 3:30 p.m., as the Union left and center were falling back. Lytle was holding his part of the line, but Bushrod Johnson's Rebels had pushed past the Bottom house and Cleburne moved into position to prepare to cross the creek. Adams was closing in on the right of Lytle's line. Brown and Jones were moving forward and applying pressure. The Tenth Ohio held on to the ridgeline and the Third Ohio held on along the fence between the burning barn and the attacking Butternuts.[35]

Confederate infantry advanced to within 150 yards of the Tenth Ohio who kept up a steady fire. Captain C.W. Frazer, Fifth Confederate, recalled, "The shock was terrific—the line swayed as one body, leaving a track of dead and wounded to mark its former position." Lytle said the "rattle of small arms fire" was "deafening." A Northern soldier described the sound of the battle as "like the continuous rattle of ten thousand drums." Despite the Rebel yells and brave attacks, Lytle's line held. A Louisiana soldier of Adams's brigade recalled, it was "the grandest but the most awful sight ever I looked upon ... the enemy stood firm ... pouring heavy fire into our lines with considerable effect."[36]

The Third Ohio derisively referred to the Fifteenth Kentucky as "The Paper Collar regiment" due to their excessively neat appearance. Now the Fifteenth would get their turn in line. Beatty's Ohioans, who had been battling the advancing Rebels, ran low on ammunition and the Kentuckians moved up the hill to take their place. The Third retired behind the hill, leaving behind nearly 40 percent casualties including six color-bearers.[37] The men of the Fifteenth Kentucky made their stand against thousands of screaming, determined Rebels. Nine color-bearers would be shot down and The Paper Collar regiment's Lieutenant Colonel George Payne Jouett and Major William Campbell were both killed. Their commander, Colonel Curran Pope, who moved up and down the line, patting the men on their backs, encouraging them, was also wounded. After the regimental flag, riddled with bullet holes, was shot from its staff, James Brown Forman tied the flag to a fence rail and rallied the troops. For his bravery he would be named the regiment's commander. Known as the "boy colonel" Forman would be killed two months later at Stones River, just two weeks after his twentieth birthday.[38]

When the Kentuckians began to run low on ammunition, the Third

Chapter 14. The Second Fall: Perryville 101

Ohio came back up the ridge to help. With Rebels moving to flank their right, the Federal troops shifted to meet the new threat. The Tenth was holding, and the Thirty-Eighth Indiana was still beside them, but the Tenth Wisconsin bent back as the Rebels pushed forward. Adams's troops closed on Johnson's left to form one long, gray line with Cleburne right behind.[39]

Johnson's men ran low on ammunition, so they fell back and Cleburne's Brigade, brass bands playing, moved forward.[40] Cleburne ordered his Fifteenth Arkansas to the right to prepare to move against Lytle's Tenth Ohio. He saw the Thirty-Eighth Indiana and Tenth Wisconsin fall back away from the crest, so he ordered the Fifteenth Arkansas forward to reconnoiter the ridgeline in preparation for an advance. Captain Dixon of the Fifteenth crept to within thirty steps of the Federal position and returned to advise his commander of the Federal troop dispositions. Cleburne sent out his skirmishers ten paces in front of his main line with the battle flags of his regiments flying.[41]

A war correspondent recorded what he witnessed. His article appeared in the October 14, 1862, *Cincinnati Enquirer*. It was now a few minutes before 4:00 and the correspondent reported on the Rebel assault against the Tenth Ohio. "The bright sun-beams glancing from their bayonets flashed like lightning over the field; and the blue flag with a single star waved all along their lines, as proudly as though it were not the emblem of treason, slavery and death.... Nearer and nearer they come! Great heavens will no one tell the Tenth of their fearful peril? ... The heroes of Carnifex are doomed!"

The Tenth Ohio could not see Cleburne's main battle line because the Ohioans had moved back slightly away from the ridgeline. Once the Rebel skirmishers and flag bearers, including one holding aloft Cleburne's famed blue flag with the white oval, crested the hill, the Tenth Ohio stood and fired. Before the Tenth could reload, the main gray line appeared and poured a murderous fire into their exhausted ranks. The Ohioans turned and retreated down the slight slope into the cornfield behind their position.[42]

Cleburne's men came over the ridge at an angle. Adams's men hit the Federal line at the same time.[43] Lytle moved to the front to rally his troops and intended to make a shock bayonet charge to stop the enemy's attack. He could only manage to gather about 100 men. Lytle then moved forward in the field just north of the road to guide his men to the new defensive line forming near the Russell house. As he was rallying the small rearguard a shell burst nearby and a jagged piece smashed into Lytle's head, just behind his left ear.[44]

Lytle could not see the wound but could tell he was bleeding profusely.

From the last Union defensive line looking toward where Lytle fell. The Confederates were pouring over the ridgeline and moving toward the Union line. The site of Lytle's fall is nearly in the center of this picture, not far from the road (photograph by Chuck Lott).

Determining the wound was mortal, Lytle refused help from soldiers who rushed over to his aid, telling them, "You may do some good yet, I can do no more, let me die here." Had Lytle known that his wound, though painful, was not fatal, he could have walked to the improvised Northern line of defense and safety. Instead, he fell into the hands of the enemy. The wounded Lytle was sent to the Confederate lines and Bushrod Johnson sent him to his surgeon for treatment.[45]

The Forty-Second Indiana joined with the Eighty-Eighth Indiana and formed a line near the Russell house, where the brigade had first formed earlier that morning. Rousseau rallied the men as the Rebels continued to advance. The Confederates moved their artillery right up to the ridgeline vacated by the Fifteenth Kentucky. Adams and Cleburne swept forward with a cheer.[46]

Cleburne's men, yelling "like a thousand savage wolves," attacked and advanced to within a hundred yards of the Russell house and Dixville Crossroads. With their cartridge boxes replenished, the Third Ohio and Fifteenth Kentucky, along with the survivors of the Tenth Ohio and Eighty-Eighth Indiana held the line. Exhausted from attacking up and

Chapter 14. The Second Fall: Perryville

down steep embankments, the Confederates could go no farther. With the Union's III Corps lurking nearby and Federal reinforcements continuing to arrive the Butternuts' chances faded into the twilight. The sun set at 5:32 p.m., ending a long, bloody day.[47]

Colonel Beatty noted in his journal that after the fight his men were hungry and thirsty but, "Few, however, think either of food or water. Their thoughts are on the crest of that little hill...." Beatty wrote that the men had "long sought for a battle, and often been disappointed and sore because they failed to find one; but now, for the first time, they really realize what a battle is...." As they walked among the familiar dead the men now realized the horror of war. "We have looked upon such scenes before; but then the faces were strange to us. Now they are the familiar faces of intimate personal friends, to whom we are indebted for many kindly acts. We hear convulsive sobs, see eyes swollen and streaming with tears...."[48] A Confederate noted that on the hill where the Tenth Ohio had fought, there were two straight lines of dead and dying and the lines reminded the Rebel "more of a wagon road...."[49] After the battle a correspondent for the *New York Herald* wrote, "In a line of six hundred yards, almost as perfect as on dress parade, the dead lay, shot down in their tracks. The position of each regiment could be distinguished by the dead, the figures on their caps revealing their regiments."[50]

That night a bright harvest moon lit up the horrible battlefield. The armies were close enough neither could rest for fear of a night attack. The Confederates had possession of the field, but their enemy held a strong defensive line. This would be the high-water mark of the Confederacy in the western theater. The Rebels in the West would never advance an army farther north than Perryville.[51] Realizing he would face overwhelming odds when the sun rose, Bragg ordered a retreat to begin sometime between 1 and 2 a.m.[52]

Lytle's Seventeenth Brigade suffered heavy casualties. The Forty-Second Indiana went into the battle with 490 men and lost 20 killed, 133 wounded, and 21 missing for a total of 174. That is a 35.5 percent casualty rate. The Eighty-Eighth Indiana fared better, going in with 434 men and losing two killed, 20 wounded, and none missing for a casualty rate of 5 percent. The Fifteenth Kentucky went into the battle with 517 soldiers and suffered 62 killed, 136 wounded, and five missing for a 39.4 percent casualty rate. The Third Ohio went into battle with 500 men and lost 42 killed, 148 wounded, and none missing for a loss rate of 38 percent. The Tenth Ohio started the battle with 528 soldiers and lost 60 killed, 169 wounded, and eight missing for a casualty rate of 44.9 percent. Overall, the brigade lost more than 180 killed and a 32.4 percent casualty rate.[53]

Behind enemy lines, wounded and worried about his future, Colonel Lytle walked through the darkness, fearing his next stop might be the dreaded Libby Prison.

Chapter 15

THE GENERAL AND MRS. LYTLE

After the battle of Perryville, Buell summed up the campaign this way, "An army, prepared for the conquest and occupation of Kentucky, with full knowledge of our means of resistance and with a confident expectation of prevailing over them, has been driven back, baffled and dispirited, from the borders of the state." A disheartened Bragg wrote, "The campaign here was predicated on a belief and the most positive assurances that the people of this country [Kentucky] would rise in mass to assert their independence.... Willing perhaps to accept their independence, they are neither disposed nor willing to risk their lives or their property in its achievement."[1]

The first reports from the battlefield indicated that Lytle was killed in action. One newspaper reported, "Perryville Late Telegraph News the Great Battle in Kentucky Col. Lytle of the 10th Ohio Killed." A *New York Herald* article on October 11 lamented, "We now find that he [Lytle] lost his life while commanding a brigade in the Army of the Ohio." Captain Frank Darr of Buell's staff telegraphed the family with more hopeful news, informing them, "Rebel prisoners say Lytle was wounded and taken prisoner which I think probable." Fortunately, Darr's report was accurate.[2]

When J. Stoddard Johnston, the man who had been mistaken for Lytle years ago in Cairo, Illinois, and who now was a staff officer of Braxton Bragg, learned that Lytle was being held prisoner, he went to the house where the Yankee was being held. He met Lytle in the parlor. Johnston described Lytle as "handsome" with "brown hair inclined to auburn, and beard and mustache of redder hue." Johnston told Lytle the Cairo story of mistaken identity and how much he had enjoyed reading the Yankee's famous poem. The Kentuckian asked if Lytle needed anything and the Ohioan asked if Johnston would send a letter to his family to let them know he was alive. Johnston readily agreed but said he had a better idea and offered to parole the Yankee poet, send him back through the lines, and let him go home. Lytle happily agreed. The offer needed Bragg's consent, which he granted.

The parole was executed before Major Samuel K. Hays of General Buckner's staff on Thursday and on Friday Lytle was on his way back home. He rode back to the Yankee lines in a buggy and reported to General Buell's headquarters immediately after arriving back within the Federal camp.[3] The *Gallipolis Journal* of October 16, 1862, reported that Colonel Lytle was among the 440 Federal soldiers paroled after the battle who had arrived back within the Union lines. Lytle telegraphed his family on October 12 to let them know he was alive. Once paroled, he could not return to active duty until a suitable exchange took place, so he went back to Cincinnati to await further instructions.

(The parole and exchange program allowed prisoners to be "paroled," then "exchanged." The idea was that prisoners could be returned to their own lines [paroled] and after agreeing not to take up arms again until they had been officially exchanged for someone of equal rank from the enemy's side. By early 1863 the system ran into problems, including the introduction of African American soldiers into the United States Army because the Confederacy refused to recognize and treat the Black men as soldiers.)[4]

Anxious to get back to the war and his command, Lytle sent a message directly to Ohio native, Secretary of War Edwin McMasters Stanton. Lytle stated that he would be ready for duty in a few days and asked if his exchange could be effected at once. Stanton replied and instructed the adjutant general to negotiate Lytle's exchange "as speedily as possible" and closed with these words: "Allow me to express my high estimation of your gallantry and hope for your speedy recovery and restoration to your command with appropriate rank." Lytle would recover and await further instructions at the home of his sister Josie and her husband, Dr. Nathaniel Foster.[5]

Stanton's instructions reached Major General Lew Wallace, who after the war would author *Ben Hur* but at this moment was working at the headquarters of paroled prisoners in Columbus, Ohio. Wallace advised the anxious Lytle that he had received his request for speedy action. Wallace congratulated the Cincinnatian on his bravery and "fame." The future author closed by saying, "Courage and a clear head are God's good gifts, and for our country's sake I am glad you have so nobly manifested them as your properties." Wallace advised Lytle to "remain there until you are recovered, exchanged, and receive orders."[6]

Not long after the battle Lytle's sister, Lily, received a letter from Charlotte "Lottie" Doremus, sister of Sed Doremus. Lottie was pleased to know Will was alive for his sisters' sake and because Sed still loved him. Ms. Doremus wrote, "I am sure if Will could only have seen how overwhelmed she [Sed] was by such a shock, he would never have doubted for an instant that her love was not as strong as in days gone by—but I trust God will still spare his life that he may be enabled to judge for himself." She hoped "that they might yet be thoroughly happy in each other's love, and it is this day stronger than ever."[7]

While waiting to rejoin his command, Lytle sat down on his birthday, November 2, and wrote another poem. In the first line he hearkened back to "The Farewell," the sensitive and poignant poem he had written 16 years before, that also referred to journeying in his "bark."

Lines on My Thirty-Sixth Birthday

Swift through the hurricane of life
My shattered bark drives on,
The pilot's hand has left the helm,
Rudder and mast are gone.
I hear the roar of angry seas,
And see the breakers rise,
Revealed amid the sullen gloom
By lightning-lighted skies.

'Tis done! To hope I bid farewell,
Love and her lights may flee,
And youth's entrancing glamor fades
From hope to memory.
Far o'er the Atlantic waves tonight
My true love winds her way,
And many a tear is mingled with
The ocean's briny spray.

Gird on my trusty blade once more.
And saddle my sinewy steed
Dash down the gloomy page to earth,
Whose lore I would not read.
Weave fast your woof, weird sisters three!
Again among the brave,
For freedom and for victory,
Or for a soldier's grave![8]

After the Battle of Perryville, many Northern politicians and officers were furious that Buell had not pursued and destroyed Bragg. Many soldiers were also frustrated they had not destroyed Bragg. A member of the Forty-Second Indiana shared a false rumor that Buell and Bragg were "brothers-in-law, and had supper together the evening before, and that General Buell had promised General Bragg that he would let him go back South without a battle." Major Shankin of the 42nd Indiana simply stated, "Buell is the most stupendous failure on record."[9]

A military commission court of inquiry against Buell was convened. Conducted at the Burnet House in Cincinnati, the commission's first witness was William Haines Lytle. From December 1 to 4, 1862, he appeared before the court. A trained and seasoned lawyer himself, Lytle kept his answers short and, because of his parole agreement, refused to divulge information he had gained while being held prisoner.[10]

When asked for specifics regarding Confederate troops he saw after his capture, Colonel Lytle responded, "I have some delicacy in testifying to these points under the terms of my parole." The government lawyer asked why he could not answer, and Lytle responded, "there is a provision in the terms of the parole 'that I shall not reveal anything that I might have discovered within the line of the enemy.' I therefore decline to testify on these points." Lytle produced a copy of his parole to prove his point.[11]

(After the war J. Stoddard Johnston read Lytle's testimony before the Buell inquiry and saw that Lytle had faithfully upheld his oath not to divulge information regarding what he saw behind the Rebel lines. "It affords me especial gratification to have found how worthily my act of kindness was bestowed, especially as during the sitting of the same commission a number of paroled prisoners disregarded their oaths upon the insistence of the Judge Advocate, whose efforts in the same direction proved unavailing with Colonel Lytle.")[12]

Still waiting to hear about his military status, on January 5, 1863, Lytle wrote directly to the Commissary-General of Prisoners, Colonel William Hoffman, asking for his help. Lytle was agitated because the Tenth Ohio had fought at Stones River without him. He asked for Hoffman's "earliest attention" so that the exchange could occur without further delay.[13]

Rosecrans wired Hoffman on January 19, 1863, that he had seen in the newspapers that all prisoners taken in Kentucky had been exchanged. "Does this include General William H. Lytle of Cincinnati?"[14] Lytle telegraphed Stanton on February 4 advising the secretary that Rosecrans had ordered him to report for duty immediately after he was exchanged. Stanton replied on February 9 that Rosecrans had issued General Orders number 10 which declared all prisoners captured before December 10 in Kentucky officially exchanged. Lytle was now able to report for duty.[15]

General Rosecrans was in Murfreesboro and Lytle would make his way there via Louisville and Nashville. In Louisville he called on the Pirtles and other acquaintances in the River City and in Nashville he called on President James Knox Polk's widow who received him warmly. He noted that she was still very pretty but did not record any specifics of their conversation.[16]

Lytle arrived in Murfreesboro and reported to Rosecrans. Lytle also was happy to be reunited with his friend and aide, Alfred Pirtle, who had

Chapter 15. The General and Mrs. Lytle 109

missed the Battle of Perryville due to illness.[17] While he was away, Lytle's old regiment, the Tenth Ohio, had been detached for guard duty to Rosecrans's Army of the Cumberland headquarters. (When Rosecrans was promoted to replace Buell, the Army of the Ohio was renamed the Army of the Cumberland.)[18]

Having just arrived in Murfreesboro, Lytle went back to Cincinnati on March 2, expecting to testify again in the Buell court of inquiry but was not called. The inquiry did not condemn Buell for his actions, but he never received another command. He was mustered out of the volunteer service in May of 1864.[19]

Although no one knew it then, that brief trip to Cincinnati was the last time Lytle would see his family and his home. Lily sent Will a hasty note that she was home, sick in bed, and would not be able to meet with him. Instead, she sent him the words to her favorite hymn. "I thought you might possibly enjoy reading it—as I remember you too, once liked it on hearing it sung." "*No more a wayward child, I seek no more to roam, I love my heavenly Father's voice, I love, I love His Home!*"[20] Lytle responded that he "had never felt so solemnly on leaving home before." He "could not get over it" and "felt strangely & so deeply."[21]

Lytle had just left Cincinnati when he received the tragic and shocking news that Aunt Joanna Reilly died. The day before her death, Joanna told Josie that it was difficult for her to say good-bye to her beloved nephew because she believed she would never see him again.[22] On her last morning Aunt Joanna told Josie that she had she just seen Will that day and they shook hands before he departed. Josie informed her that was not possible since he was already gone. Joanna said, "I was not asleep—it was no dream." She lingered a while longer, then Joanna Haines Reilly died.[23]

Lytle telegraphed Rosecrans to request a leave to return for the funeral but received no reply. He had to go on because his orders required him to go back to Murfreesboro.[24] Arriving in Murfreesboro Lytle wrote home that he hoped one day the family would be united "in a brighter world." Even in his hour of mourning, Lytle noted happily that Mrs. Lytle of Murfreesboro had invited him to stay at her home. It was now hers because her husband, Mr. William F.P. "Billy Creek" Lytle, had passed away on March 9.[25]

Lytle continued to write poetry. One of the most personal of his works is titled, "When the Long Shadows." There is no date on this poem, which deals with death and remembrance. Unlike many of his other poems, this one is clearly about himself and his feelings. When he writes about people gathered around a "couch of pain" he was likely referencing his grandfather's painful death on what Lytle's mother had described as a "sick couch." In the second stanza he seemed to be referring to the death of his father in faraway New Orleans, where "stranger hands" may have smoothed down his father's pillow. He wondered if "the little stars" would "shine on some lone spot" where the "way-worn pilgrim" would die, "far from home and friends...." And he closed the poem with a question that seemed to haunt him all his life, "In the wide world, will none remember me?"

When the Long Shadows

When the long shadows on my path are lying,
Will those I love be gathered at my side;
Clustered around my couch of pain, and trying
To light the dark way, trod without a guide?

Shall it be mine, beyond the tossing billow,
'Neath foreign skies, to feel the approach of Death,
Will stranger hands smooth down my dying Pillow,
And watch with kindly heart my failing Breath?

Or shall, perchance, the little stars be shining
On some lone spot, where, far from home and Friends,
The way-worn pilgrim on the turf reclining,
His life and much of grief together ends?

Ah! Wheresoe'er the closing scene may find me,
'Mid friends or foemen or in deserts lone,
May there be some of those I leave behind me
To shed a tear for me when I am gone....

Yet when the thousand gales of morn are blowing,
Or when the bright moon gilds the solemn sea,
And the sweet stars their smiles on earth are Throwing,
In the wide world, will none remember me?[26]

There was some good news for the Cincinnatian. Colonel Lytle received official notification of his promotion to brigadier general, replacing Joshua Sill who had been killed at the Battle of Stones River. His commission was dated March 17, 1863, with rank from November 29, 1862.[27] The official commission read, in part, "Know ye, that reposing special trust and confidence in and the patriotism, valor, fidelity, and abilities of William H. Lytle I have nominated ... and ... do appoint him Brigadier General of volunteers.... Given under my hand.... By the President Abraham Lincoln."[28] The poet-soldier assumed command of the First Brigade, Third Division, Twentieth Army Corps, Army of the Cumberland.[29] "On April 9,

Chapter 15. The General and Mrs. Lytle

1863, Lytle officially accepted his promotion."[30] He finally had the dark blue shoulder straps with the silver star denoting his rank as a brigadier general.

Toward the end of April, Lytle confided to Josie that he did not know a single person in his new command. Lytle noted that this brigade comprised "western men" who were "full of fight."[31] Lytle's First Brigade, Third Division (Major General Philip Henry Sheridan commanding), comprised the Thirty-Sixth Illinois, the Eighty-Eighth Illinois, the Twenty-First Michigan, and the Twenty-Fourth Wisconsin.[32]

Born in New York, Philip Henry Sheridan moved with his family to Ohio when he was an infant and grew up in Som-

Portrait of Lytle as a brigadier general. His sisters thought this was very lifelike. The original hung in the Lytle mansion and has been passed down to the present generation. Another copy hangs in the museum at the Chickamauga visitor center (from the collection of Virginius Cornick Hall, Jr.).

erset. He graduated from West Point, Class of 1853, where his classmates included James McPherson, John Schofield, Joshua Sill, and John Bell Hood, all future Civil War generals. After graduation he served on the frontier. He began the war as a captain and quartermaster and was appointed colonel of the Second Michigan Cavalry in May 1862. From there he rose up through the ranks quickly and would end the war as one of the great leaders of the Union side.[33]

The Thirty-Sixth Illinois organized at Aurora and mustered in September 1861. They had campaigned in Missouri and Arkansas and fought at the Battle of Pea Ridge, then campaigned in Tennessee, Mississippi, and Kentucky. The Eighty-Eighth Illinois, or "Second Board of Trade Regiment" organized at Camp Douglas in Chicago and mustered in September 1862. They had campaigned in Kentucky and Tennessee. The Twenty-First Michigan organized at Ionia and Grand Rapids and mustered in September 1862. They campaigned in Kentucky and Tennessee. The Twenty-Fourth Wisconsin organized at Milwaukee and mustered in August 1862. They campaigned in Kentucky and Tennessee. All four regiments fought at Perryville and Stones River. The four regiments fought at Perryville in the Thirty-Seventh Brigade, Eleventh Division, III Corps. At Stones River they were under Joshua Sill in the First Brigade, Third Division, Right Wing, under McCook. The Eleventh Indiana Independent Light Artillery mustered in Indianapolis, Indiana, in December 1861. They had campaigned in Tennessee and Mississippi.[34]

Lytle also admitted to his sister that some officers' wives were confused about his relationship with Mrs. Lytle. Some of the visiting Northern ladies dropped by to call on his "wife." Colonel Joseph Burke's spouse found it somewhat difficult to convince the other women that Lytle was not married to Sophie and that she was simply a friend or distant relative.[35] In another letter home Lytle remarked that Mrs. Lytle was very pleased with her new wardrobe, which had been purchased by Lytle's sisters in Cincinnati since nice dresses were scarce in war-torn Tennessee. He commented on how pretty the "young widow" looked.[36] He also wanted to assure the home folks that Mrs. Lytle was on their side. "*Mrs. Lytle* is Union all over...." He wrapped up the letter once he heard his band begin playing. "You know how I love music."[37]

Lytle also wrote home about a pending presentation from the Tenth Ohio. They had collected funds from their ranks and contracted with a Cincinnati jeweler to create a token of affection for their former commander. Will was hoping the presentation would take place soon so that he could send the present home before the troops moved out again.[38] The gift was a special cross, and when it arrived a ceremony was planned, but the presentation was delayed because the Federal army was about to participate in Rosecrans's Tullahoma Campaign. Lytle's thoughts then turned to one who lived far away, and he closed his letter with this request, "When you write *Sed* say to her that I will never forget her, and if I survive the wars hope to meet her again."[39]

After the two-day battle along Stones River outside of Murfreesboro in December 1862, the Confederates retreated south and established a defensive line to protect their supply base in Tullahoma, Tennessee. Nathan Bedford Forrest and his cavalrymen anchored Bragg's left in Spring Hill and Joseph Wheeler's horsemen guarded the right of the line, near McMinnville. The main Rebel force was entrenched around Shelbyville, guarding the approaches to their supply depot.[40]

As Federal General U.S. Grant was tightening the noose around Vicksburg, Mississippi, Ambrose Pierce Burnside was about to march on Knoxville, Tennessee. Rosecrans's 60,000-man army then moved out from Murfreesboro to cut through the Rebel lines in middle Tennessee.[41]

This meant that General Lytle must say good-bye to Mrs. Lytle. Sophie's oldest son, Richard, later recalled William Haines Lytle's visits to the house. "I used to think what a fine-looking man he was, followed by old Guthrie, his faithful body servant...." Another Tennessee Lytle, referring to W.H. Lytle wrote, "He was a Lytle over and over, even to his walk, and the cleverest of his race, and the most distinguished man that she had ever known." Years later, a descendant of William Franklin Pitt Lytle, author Andrew Nelson Lytle, believed the visits to the Lytle house in Murfreesboro were never to see "cousin" Mr. Lytle, but to see Mrs. Lytle. She was "a beautiful woman" and "a fine horsewoman." Andrew Lytle imagined the poet reading "Antony and Cleopatra" to her and added, "One can only surmise, and yet one is impelled to think that she was more than cousinly polite."[42]

There was a dramatic scene in front of the Lytle house in Murfreesboro when the dashing Ohioan rode up to tell the beautiful Mrs. Lytle he was leaving. This would be the final farewell for the General and Mrs. Lytle. The young widow stood on the porch as the general, astride his charger, exclaimed to Sophie, "And you will never never forget me!" To which she replied, "Never! Never!"[43]

Lytle's brigade left Murfreesboro via the Shelbyville Pike on June 24.[44] During the next several days they moved out early each morning and made their way south. Despite a constant downpour, Lytle reached Manchester, via Beech Grove and Fairfield, on June 28.[45]

One man who participated in this march and experienced skirmishing for the first time was Dr. Henry A. Goodale of the Twenty-First Michigan, of Lytle's First Brigade. He recalled that the Federals ran into Confederate outposts not long after leaving Murfreesboro and, much to Goodale's surprise, as the shells whizzed overhead and exploded nearby, most of the Federal troops lounged in a wooded area. "Some of the boys were picking geese and poultry ... some skinning mutton, and all seemed unmindful of the impending danger around them...."[46]

The Confederates were uncertain where the Yankees were headed but once Bragg realized that Rosecrans was headed for Manchester and not Shelbyville he had to react quickly. Rosecrans reached Manchester which put the Yankees closer to the Rebel supply depot at Tullahoma than the Rebels were. Bragg moved south and managed to get his army across the Elk River, burning the bridge once they were across.[47]

Lytle's men marched to Tullahoma on July 1 and arrived at Winchester Springs on the Elk River on July 2 but since the bridge had been burned, they had to find another place to cross. On July 3 the Federals left their camp early and drove a detachment of Rebel cavalry away. Sheridan ordered Lytle to pursue the Rebels, but they were nowhere to be found. Lytle's command crossed the Boiling Fork of the Elk River about noon and arrived at Cowan at 4 p.m. having covered twelve miles. Lytle's brigade suffered no casualties. His only regret, he wrote, was "that the enemy was not met in force."[48]

Despite his belligerent tone and his war record to date, Lytle believed President Lincoln should declare amnesty to all Rebels who gave up the fight and pledged allegiance to the United States. He also believed the South would have been punished enough by the war and that a humane policy toward the Rebels would help ease the peacetime transition and encourage healing "between the sections."[49]

The war was far from over, however, and near the end of July, Lytle was in camp at Cowan where he enjoyed the fine climate and the delicious, cold, clear spring water. Lytle also reported that his old friend, Findlay "Fin" Harrison, had joined his staff, but was not behaving well. Lytle vowed to get rid of him as soon as possible. In the same letter Will told his sisters he would like to be with them on their upcoming trip to the East and reported an unfortunate incident during a recent march. Soldiers in the Twenty-First Michigan fired their Colt revolving rifles at a distant fence line where Rebels had been seen. One of the bullets struck and killed a little boy, the son of a Unionist. The boy's father swore revenge not on the Yankees but on the Rebels. Lytle also mentioned how tired he was and how he longed for rest. From the very beginning of the war Lytle suffered many sleepless nights tending to the various duties of his command. Lytle closed his letter home with a request for some books. He still loved reading but would not have much time to read in the coming days.[50]

Chapter 16

A Cross, a Speech, and a Bridge

At the end of July Lytle wrote to his sisters that he had been commanding the entire division for ten days. He also said he would give Findlay Harrison one more chance. Harrison pledged not to drink anymore, and Lytle believed Harrison could develop into a worthwhile and useful officer.[1] When they were in college Lytle had told Harrison, "Fin, I rank you first.... If I am ever in danger, I shall put you on the post of honor."[2]

On July 29 Sheridan ordered Lytle to send a regiment to reinforce Colonel Bernard Laiboldt in Bridgeport, Alabama, and to begin accumulating supplies at Stevenson to prepare the way to continue the push south.[3] To get at the Rebels they would need to cross the Tennessee River. At the beginning of August, Lytle moved with the rest of his command to Bridgeport where Confederates were visible on Long Island, in the Tennessee River, opposite the Federal works.[4]

The Tennessee River is the largest tributary of the Ohio River. After forming east of Knoxville, the Tennessee flows south before turning west just north of the Georgia line. It runs through Chattanooga then dips down into and runs across North Alabama. It continues west before turning north near the Alabama, Tennessee, and Mississippi borders, eventually feeding into the Ohio at Paducah, Kentucky.

Rivers allowed for the transportation of people and products. During the war they allowed for the movement of troops and supplies. Churning against the current, Federal gunboats and transports had utilized the Tennessee with success in their capture of Fort Henry. Using another Ohio River tributary, the Cumberland River, they also took Fort Donelson. U.S. Grant would use the Mississippi to capture Vicksburg. But at Florence, Alabama, there were the Muscle Shoals, which was a natural barrier to steamboat travel and movement upriver on the Tennessee was unpredictable and difficult if you wanted to continue eastward.

Before the war, the little community of Jonesville, Alabama, established a river port along the Tennessee but due to the fluctuating river levels found it was impracticable to depend on the river to move goods. They successfully lobbied for the Nashville and Chattanooga railroad to turn east at Stevenson and build a bridge across the Tennessee at Jonesville. Because there was an island, Long Island, in the middle of the river there, the railroad would only need to build two shorter bridges rather than one long one to cross the Tennessee River.

The railroad did just that in the early 1850s and the people of the area changed the name of the town to Bridgeport. Bridgeport, therefore, was a very important place to the Federal leadership wishing to cross the Tennessee and strike into the deep south. The northern section of the railroad bridge to Long Island had been burned by the Confederates and Federal troops would need to repair the bridge, build new roads, improve existing ones, erect defensive works, and unload supplies. But the distance they would need to span was less here because of that island.[5]

There was much hard work to do, but with this extended pause in the campaign, the time had come for the Tenth Ohio to present Lytle with the "handsome present" he had written home about recently: a Maltese cross, made by Cincinnatian Wilson McGrew. The cross was made of solid gold. There was an emerald in the center, and the piece was studded with diamonds. On the reverse side was an inscription:

> "EN TOYTO NIKA
> The officers of the 10th Ohio Vol. Inf.,
> To Their Colonel
> Wm. H. Lytle"

The inscription indicated that in this sign or cross would be found victory. Upon learning of the plan to present the cross, General Rosecrans placed a special train at the disposal of the presentation committee who arrived at 10 p.m. and were greeted by Lytle, Pirtle and other members of his staff. The ceremony would take place the next evening, August 9.

A correspondent wrote about Lytle's staff. He said that Lytle's orderly, Irish-born Joe Guthrie, was as well known in the army as Lytle himself, stating, "he is the General's right-bower, and dispenses his hospitality with a liberal hand." However, the reporter noted, on every march where the reporter had tagged along, Guthrie always made him take the loyalty oath "and that would ruffle the temper of a saint...." Lytle's staff were: James A. Grover, First Lieutenant, Tenth Ohio, Assistant Adjutant General; Alfred Pirtle, First Lieutenant, Tenth Ohio, senior aide-de-camp; Charles W. Eaton, Second Lieutenant, Twenty-First Michigan, aide-de-camp; James Findlay Harrison, Colonel, Ohio, state militia, aide-de-camp; John Turnbull, First Lieutenant, Thirty-Sixth Illinois, brigade inspector; Charles

Chapter 16. A Cross, a Speech, and a Bridge

Boal, First Lieutenant, Eighty-Eighth Illinois, topographical engineer; N.S. Banton, First Lieutenant, quartermaster, Thirty-Sixth Illinois. The correspondent added, "A more accomplished, active, friendly and courteous staff no General in the army can claim with any truth."[6]

On Sunday afternoon before the ceremony, Rosecrans ordered Lytle to allow a lady to cross the river to the Rebel-held island. Lytle sent Findlay Harrison and Lieutenant John Turnbull to represent the brigade, and Lieutenant Colonel William M. Ward to represent Rosecrans's headquarters. The lady they escorted was Confederate General Patton Anderson's mother. There, in the middle of the war, a mother wished to see her son and the Federals took her across the river under a flag of truce. Lytle also sent a bottle of fine champagne. Pirtle noted, "and by this generous act won the esteem of the gray-backs, who drank his health in a flowing bowl of the welcome beverage."[7]

That evening, the Tenth Ohio's presentation ceremony began at twilight near Lytle's headquarters. The band of the Thirty-Eighth Indiana played "The Conquering Hero Comes" as Lytle approached. Officers and men of the First Brigade formed a circle and Lieutenant Colonel William M. Ward stepped forward to make the presentation. Ward talked of the Tenth's history with Lytle and said that Lytle's old comrades, who had witnessed his "conspicuous gallantry in the field" as well as his "skill in council" wished to honor their former regimental commander. Having finished his speech, Colonel Ward pinned the cross on Lytle's chest.[8]

This is the Maltese cross presented to Lytle by the men of the Tenth Ohio. Colonel Ward pinned this on Lytle's chest (Colonel William H. Lytle presentation medal [2003.156.001]; Cincinnati Museum Center).

The fading light cast long shadows and the mountains' distinctive outlines began to blur and fade into the night. The men of the Tenth Ohio watched as Lytle strode to the center of the circle and began to speak. "Colonel, and Gentlemen of the Tenth Ohio Infantry—My old Friends and Comrades—I cannot tell you how deeply I am touched by this beautiful testimonial. I am very glad to learn that … you have not forgotten me; and I feel it also an honor that you have taken the trouble to visit me in our camp in the mountains to make me this present in the midst of a campaign.… Come what may to me tomorrow or in days beyond; … this token, from the cherished comrades with whom I entered the service, is secure."

Lytle reminded them of their beginnings in Cincinnati, of the marches through West Virginia, their baptism of fire at Carnifex Ferry, and the terrible battle at Perryville, which, he said, "added a new and glorious leaf to the somber annals of the Dark and Bloody Ground." He admitted a "sense of loneliness and isolation" when he first found out the Tenth would not be under his command, then thanked the men of his new brigade "for the warm and generous welcome they have awarded to a stranger." Turning once more to speak to the Tenth he said, "Gentlemen of the Tenth Ohio, you see around you … men from the Northwest, from the clans of the people who pitch their tents on the prairies of Illinois and Michigan and Wisconsin, and by the shores of the great lakes.…"

Lytle told them that they must see this terrible fight through to the end. And, when the war was finally over, it would be up to them, the victorious armies of the North, "To heal up the sores and scars, and cover up the bloody footprints that war will leave; to bury in oblivion all animosities against your former foe; and chivalrous as you are brave, standing on forever stricken fields, memorable in history, side by side with the Virginian, the Mississippian, or Alabamian, to carve on bronze or marble the glowing epitaph that tells us of Southern as well as Northern valor."

General Lytle then closed with these words. "That the day of ultimate triumph for the Union arms, sooner or later, will come, I do not doubt, for I have faith in the courage, the wisdom, and the justice of the people. It may not be for all of us here today to listen to the chants that greet the victor, nor to hear the bells ring out the new nuptials of the States. But those who do survive can tell, at least, to the people, how their old comrades, whether in the skirmish or the charge, before the rifle-pit or the redan, died with their harness on, in the great war for the Union and Liberty."[9]

The Cincinnati *Commercial* war correspondent noted, "While the sonorous tones of Lytle's voice made music along the wooded slopes of the Cumberland, and died in measured cadence far down the turbid bosom of the Tennessee … every man who heard him, mentally exclaimed that there was a leader.…"[10]

Chapter 16. A Cross, a Speech, and a Bridge

Pirtle wrote his mother that Lytle's speech was "the most beautiful thing of its kind of the war..." and "...at a grand reunion we had last night all united in pronouncing it the best yet delivered." The Kentuckian told his mother that Lytle's command "are becoming as enthusiastic in their admiration of him as was the 'Old 17th' of Chaplin Hills memory." Pirtle then made an ominous prediction. "Upon the hills of Georgia I think the 'Fighting First' will soon leave its mark, but I trust not with the terrible price of that 'Red Autumn day.'"[11]

One of the soldiers in the crowd that evening was Sergeant-Major Richard Realf of the Eighty-Eighth Illinois. Born in England, Realf was an accomplished and published poet himself, drawing the attention of Lord Byron's widow, who took him on as a protégé. Realf emigrated to the United States in 1854 after a "disagreement" with Lady Byron (most likely regarding the pregnancy of her 14-year-old relative). Once in America, Realf became a radical abolitionist and an associate of John Brown. He was arrested as a known accomplice of "The Meteor" but a Senate committee found he had no connection to the Harper's Ferry raid. After the Civil War began, he enlisted in the Eighty-Eighth Illinois. Realf was so moved by Lytle's speech that he wrote a tribute poem to Lytle immediately afterwards.[12] The poem was titled "Vates," which means a prophet or poet. "'Vates,' I shouted, while your solemn words, Rhythmic with crowded passion, lilted past..." wrote Realf. "Like this soul and this singing, shall not fail...." He pledged that "across the bloody gaps our blades must hold..." and that these men would follow Lytle to "The topmost heights of Being!" Realf implored Lytle to "Lead on, that we may follow..." and the future would be "Held by the steadfast shining of your brow!"[13]

In camp, Lytle and the Englishman became friends. The General provided Realf with books and their shared love of the written word no doubt enlivened campfire discussions. However, there was still work to be done. Lytle sent a message to Sheridan on August 12 stating that two deserters from the Forty-Fourth Mississippi reported there were five Rebel regiments on Long Island: the Seventh, Ninth, Tenth, Forty-First, and Forty-Fourth Mississippi, a battalion of sharpshooters and a battery of artillery (Patton Anderson's brigade).[14]

The two sides had an informal agreement not to fire upon one another, but Lytle continued to monitor activity along the Confederate side of the river. The Rebels finally burned the bridge on the south side of the island around 11:30 on the night of August 14.[15] Lytle had just fallen asleep when a soldier woke him to report that the bridge was on fire. Lytle walked up the hill near his tent and watched the magnificent scene unfold from the parapet of a redoubt. As a result of the conflagration the river could be seen for miles. Lytle ordered his artillery to fire at the island and the reports of the big guns echoed along the hillsides. Lytle wrote that the "scene was one of the grandest I ever beheld."[16]

Lytle wrote home to tell his sisters about the presentation of his cross and informed them that an article would be written and published in the Cincinnati papers about the ceremony and his speech. He hoped they would like the coverage and indicated that he had received praise for the speech from those who had heard him deliver it. Lytle was also happy to report that Findlay Harrison had not touched a drop of alcohol since they had left Cowan and was making friends. Lytle believed that Harrison could be redeemed. If he could succeed in bringing Fin around, Lytle felt he would have done a good service to the country. He was unsure where to send his cross since the sisters were not in Cincinnati. Then he closed the letter with thoughts of past loves. He asked the sisters to tell him about Sed Doremus and Lily Macalester when they saw them.[17]

Lytle sent 25 sharpshooters under the command of Lieutenant Jonathan M. Turnbull across the river where they met a small contingent of enemy horsemen and drove them off. Two days later the Ohioan sent another party of sharpshooters across the river to reconnoiter.[18] They were fired on by Rebel pickets. Lytle replied with artillery, causing, as one Federal noted, "much scatterment."[19]

Besides these forays, there was still work to be done on the bridge. Colonel William Innes and his Michigan engineers worked together with Lytle to complete the task.[20] On Sunday August 30, Rosecrans, who did not like to work on the Sabbath, had his men working and Lytle received a message asking if he had enough lumber to cover the bridge. He replied he had enough to cover 1,000 linear feet. Later that day Lytle was ordered to prepare the riverbank to render the approach easy. Another dispatch advised that a train loaded with pontoons was to arrive at 11 p.m. His men were to unload the material as fast as possible, then the train was to depart immediately to pick up another load and return before daylight. Lytle's Twenty-Fourth Wisconsin worked through the night unloading pontoon sections from rail cars.[21]

The next day, August 31, 1863, Lytle wrote to his sisters for the last time. He could not believe it had been a year since he had led his forces out of Huntsville. It did not seem that long ago. He hoped they were enjoying their time at the ocean and speculated that by the time the sisters read his long letter he and the Federal troops would most likely already be on their way to Chattanooga or Atlanta. Supply trains continued to steam into the depot and long wagon trains full of timber kept arriving for the bridge. His men were working hard and doing their best to complete the work so the army could cross the river and move south. Lytle sent his cross with

Chapter 16. A Cross, a Speech, and a Bridge   121

The pontoon bridge, not yet completed, is in the foreground. The ruined railroad bridge is behind it. Long Island is seen across the river channel. "Ruins of R.R. bridge across Tennessee River, at Bridgeport, Tenn. i.e. Alabama and pontoon bridge in course of construction. United States Alabama, ca. 1863" (Library of Congress).

Colonel Charles H. Larrabee who would deliver it to Pirtle's mother in Louisville.[22]

Lytle asked his sisters how they liked the pictures of himself he sent them. The photographs had been taken in camp recently and Lytle and his staff officers considered them to be "admirable likenesses." Lytle liked the pictures and said the photographer would not accept payment, because he already had orders for 800 copies of Lytle's picture. Lytle then closed his final letter home. He did not know where his next letter would be written since they were about to move. "*Do* write *when* ever you can…. God bless you Will."[23]

Rosecrans pushed Lytle to get the bridge completed and the poet-soldier replied that the crews were laying the stringers and planks as fast as possible. At 1:30 p.m. on August 31 Lytle was advised that the train that unloaded the night before had yet to arrive back where it was supposed to pick up the second load. Lytle was instructed to find out why "this criminal delay has occurred." Lytle replied that a detail unloaded the train the night before, but the train conductor said his orders were to return to Stevenson at five the following morning. Lytle showed the conductor a copy of the orders to return that night, but he still did not leave until the morning of the 31st.[24] In spite of the setback, the bridge was almost complete and soon the army would cross the river.

Chapter 17

JOHN BROWN'S BODY

On September 1 the pontoon bridge from the island to the south bank was completed.[1] The next morning an exhausted Lytle ate breakfast and consented to a group photograph with his staff.[2] Pirtle would later describe the people in the photo. Lytle looked "splendid I think, easy and natural." James Grover looked "so bold." Fin Harrison was "an old friend of Gen'l L… and a widower." Jonathan M. Turnbull was a "fine fellow … over six feet high and framed in proportion, dark hair & eyes and fine beard…" and "a Christian gentleman … universally highly esteemed by all his acquaintances." Lieutenant N.P. Jackson was about Pirtle's size, and "a good jovial fellow—rail road man of fair education—resolute and determined…." Jackson was "one of our funny fellows and when he and Lt. Eaton get started, we have a gay time." A Lieutenant Hartman was also in the picture and Pirtle thought he was in the Pioneer Corps. Lieutenant Charles T. Boal, from Chicago, was their topographical engineer and a "great help to Gen'l L in getting information about the country." He was about Pirtle's size, had blue eyes, dark brown hair, and heavy sandy whiskers. Lieutenant T.C.W. Eaton, another aide-de-camp was 21 or 22 and a former printer and editor. "Sharp as a steel trap and witty as comic paper."[3]

Lytle's command crossed the Tennessee River around noon on September 2. After they were across, a bridge section collapsed behind them and Lytle's brigade was cut off from their wagons, leaving the men without blankets, tents, or rations. When officers of the Fifteenth Kentucky came to see their former commander, Lytle informed the Kentuckians what had happened to their supplies. Ever the raconteur, Lytle's version of the unfortunate turn of events caused the Kentuckians to laugh and then invite him and his staff to dine with them. Just before sunset Lytle and Pirtle walked over to their camp. When the soldiers saw him approaching, they fell into line and gave him three hearty cheers. Lytle smiled and lifted his hat in acknowledgment.[4]

Pirtle recalled that time passed quickly as they talked about "old

The group photograph taken at Bridgeport. Pirtle describes some of the men in the picture. Turnbull is the second from the left. Pirtle is out front, arms crossed. Next to him is Grover, then Lytle, "Fin" Harrison, Boal, and Eaton. They would be with Lytle to the end (Infantry Soldier & Generals [outdoors—William H, Lytle], 1860s," SC#59—General Photographs Collection—Portraits—Lytle; Cincinnati Museum Center).

times, [and] the campaigns past and prospective...." When Lytle rose to leave the soldiers asked for a speech. Lytle obliged and talked "in touching terms" about "Pope, Jouett and Campbell and their glorious dead that had shed their blood in the campaign of '62." Lytle said he had not come to make a speech "but to say how much pleasure it afforded him to meet them again and at the opening of a campaign that promised so much...." Lytle concluded by saying "when the war was over they might meet without the restraint that military organization imposes...."

This was the last speech delivered by William Haines Lytle. From the "gem of the evening" in his youth, to this final farewell to fellow comrades, Lytle never disappointed. Pirtle later lamented, "Not anticipating that these brief, spontaneous but eloquent words would have such a peculiar interest for all of us as the last public utterance.... I deeply regret that I made no lengthy memoranda at the time...." Lytle and Pirtle returned to their camp at the foot of Sand Mountain in Hog Jaw Valley and waited for orders to march up the steep mountain road.[5]

By nightfall they still had not moved. Lytle used the pause to take a much-needed nap. Due to their delayed departure, they were present when the brigade's wagons finally arrived. They ate well that night.[6] The exhausted officers of Lytle's staff made their beds on the ground. As they lay down to sleep, Pirtle noted that not even the "Alabama feathers" or "as we call them rocks" could interrupt their slumber.[7]

On September 4 the brigade was still waiting for their marching orders. To pass the time the men lounged under the trees, sat on logs, leisurely ate their lunch, read newspapers, and smoked cigars. Pirtle, who slept until ten o'clock that morning, took time to engage in a pleasant conversation with the General. The brigade finally began their ascent later that day.[8]

On September 5 the brigade continued their march and around 11 a.m. the Federals entered Georgia. Since water was scarce, Sheridan moved his division to Trenton, Georgia, where there was a water source.[9] During this final march, Lytle issued orders to his brigade stating his beliefs and expectations.

> "Order 171:
> The Gen commdg Brigade desires to express his gratification at the soldierly bearing of the Brigade on the march the last two days. Soldiers & comrades let us remember that discipline is as important & essential as the drill. We do not war against women or non combatants. Respect their rights as defined by the laws of warfare among enlightened nations. If it becomes necessary to levy on the country for supplies let it be done by your commissaries & your Quartermasters— Genl Lytle desires to see you supplied with everything that conduces to your comfort. If necessary set an example to the Division & the army. Avoid straggling keep your ranks on the march, & when the day of trial comes write your names deep in history, as the fighting first."[10]

Sunday, September 6, was a bright and beautiful day. Two Ohio officers, Colonel Edward Augustine King of Dayton, and Colonel William Jones of Cincinnati called on Lytle and spent several hours in pleasant conversation. Here were three men, far from home, enjoying a lovely morning together. Two weeks later King and Jones would be killed at Chickamauga. At noon the brigade received orders to move out.[11]

The following morning the men were on the road by five.[12] Pirtle noted, "Gen'l Lytle takes the inconveniences of campaigning with his usual contentment. I never saw a Gen'l with as few fancies and who seemed to think as little of self." The young Kentuckian also recorded that none of them really needed camp comforts on the march anymore. They traveled with their blankets on their horses "cavalry style." He also described a useful item, a makeshift tent, known as a "shebang" which was a shelter consisting of "green boughs." The soldiers drove two forked sticks into the ground and placed a cross pole from one stick to the other, as a ridge pole.

Then the men piled the cut boughs on, one end resting on the ground, the other on the ridge pole. Pirtle said this made a "first-rate protection from the heavy dews of this climate." The men used leaves and small twigs as a base on which they placed their gum blankets and bedding.[13] Pirtle believed the war was "making practical abolitionists" of every soldier, writing "nothing can oppose the emancipation, at once and entire of the slave population.... Times change men rapidly, especially such stirring times as these." Looking up from his writing Pirtle noticed, "Gen'l L and I are writing at the same table...."[14]

In early September Rosecrans divided his force into three segments to flank Bragg out of Chattanooga. Federal Major General Thomas Leonidas Crittenden's XXI Corps advanced straight toward Chattanooga along the railroad tracks that passed through a canyon in Sand Mountain. Major General George Henry Thomas's XIV Corps crossed Sand and Lookout Mountains and entered McLemore's Cove on its way to LaFayette, Georgia. Major General Alexander McDowell McCook's XX Corps followed Major General David Sloane Stanley's Cavalry Corps across Sand Mountain and Lookout Mountain to the area around Alpine, Georgia. Bragg abandoned Chattanooga on September 8.[15]

On September 9 news reached Lytle's camp that Chattanooga had fallen, spreading joy throughout the ranks.[16] Two months earlier, Robert E. Lee's famed Army of Northern Virginia had smashed itself against a low stone wall by a copse of trees at Gettysburg on July 3 then retreated into the Old Dominion. U.S. Grant took Vicksburg the day after Lee's defeat. Ambrose Burnside's Federals drove Simon Buckner out of Knoxville in early September.[17] But upon hearing of the loss of Chattanooga, Confederate President Jefferson Davis wrote, "We are now in the darkest hour of our political existence."[18]

The attention of both sides focused on the hills of northern Georgia where the Army of the Cumberland would try to bring Bragg to bay.

Rosecrans assumed Bragg would retreat deeper into Georgia to regroup around Rome, but Jefferson Davis and his officers worked on a plan to gather as many Rebel forces as possible, concentrate them with Bragg, and smash Rosecrans. Two divisions from the Army of Northern Virginia, one under John Bell Hood and the other under Lafayette McLaws, as well as Colonel E. Porter Alexander's 26-gun artillery battalion, would be sent west under the command of Lieutenant General James Longstreet.[19] Before the troops left for the West, General Lee pulled Longstreet aside and said to his trusted officer, "General, you must beat those people out there." "Old Pete" assured his commander he would.[20]

On September 10, Lytle's troops marched early and that night they camped near a stream that cascaded down into a pool. The next day they reached the eastern slope of Lookout Mountain and Sheridan ordered Lytle to provide the rear guard for the transportation wagons of the division. From their new vantage point, Lytle and Pirtle enjoyed a "magnificent view" of Broomtown Valley.[21]

When Rosecrans learned that Bragg was concentrating his forces at LaFayette, Georgia, and not around Rome, he realized he had miscalculated and his army was vulnerable. He ordered McCook to join up with Major General George Henry Thomas.[22] On September 12 McCook forwarded two divisions of his corps to support Thomas and left Lytle in charge of overseeing the wagons for the corps, collecting and parking those trains at Little River, and finding the best place to protect them. General Stanley was to send a detachment of cavalry to help screen and guard Lytle's position from Rebel cavalry.[23]

Lytle received the brigades of Colonel Joseph Dodge and Colonel P. Sidney Post on September 13 to help guard the wagon trains. According to Pirtle, Lytle spent "an almost sleepless night, expecting to move this Command at any hour."[24] At 5:20 p.m. on September 13 Lytle reported, "Found heavy column of all arms [Confederate] marching rapidly on the road to Dirt Town."[25]

On September 14 McCook ordered Lytle to move the troops and wagons down into Lookout Valley then send the wagons on to Long Springs to find water. McCook expected to have the troops and wagon trains in the valley that night. Lytle then received new instructions to stay put, park the trains, and encamp at Little Creek. General Stanley had yet to send a cavalry force to cover his position.[26]

Pirtle set up a defensive position as troops and wagons passed throughout the day. That evening the men enjoyed a good supper and took a bath in Devil's Hole, the deep pool at the falls. Lytle and some of the officers received mail that night.[27]

On Tuesday, September 15, the brigade remained in camp as the wagon train of the cavalry passed all morning. Lytle's Brigade marched on the 16th toward their destination, McLemore's Cove. There was still no sign of the promised cavalry detachment.[28] Pirtle and the other officers worked late getting things in readiness for an early march.[29]

The Federals needed to make their way through the mountains. Lieutenant Charles Boal, topographical engineer of Lytle's staff, found a Southern civilian who knew a route to one such opening, Dougherty's Gap. They left at sunrise on the 16th and arrived at Dougherty's Gap at 11 a.m. Their camp was pleasant, but water was still scarce.[30] Because the cavalry had not arrived it was difficult to send dispatches. McCook ordered Lytle to move via the shortest route "with dispatch" to another opening, Stevens Gap.[31]

Lytle's brigade marched at 5:30 a.m. on September 17 for Stevens Gap. Pirtle noted, "It was the habit of General Lytle to insist that his Brigade should move at the hour ordered punctually, and the value of this habit was illustrated this morning...." On their march the brigade arrived at a point where the immense wagon train of Colonel Post's brigade was also traveling. The wagon train was ordered to halt and wait for Lytle's brigade to pass. Had they been a half hour later the train would have been on the road in front of them and they would have had to wait in the heat and the dust with little water. As it was the nearly twelve-mile march in the heat of the day was still grueling. They arrived at last at McLemore's Cove that evening where Sheridan and his staff "were delighted to see us." Pirtle noted the exhausted men slept "soundly" that night.[32]

James Patton Anderson, a hard fighter, was moved that Lytle let his mother cross the river to see him. There would come a day when Anderson would repay Lytle's act of kindness. "Maj. Gen. James Patton Anderson" (Library of Congress).

The next morning, September 18, they were on the road again. Due to the recent lack of rain, dust clung to every object it touched, and in some places was at least six inches deep. Around noon the brigade halted and made camp. It was a cloudy day and the high temperature reached 62 degrees. Lytle had developed a severe cold on the march so Guthrie made a place for Lytle to lie down under a tree. Pirtle carefully placed a blanket over Lytle and encouraged his friend and commander to sleep. Instead, Lytle pulled out the letters he had received recently and read excerpts to Pirtle. One of the letters was from his sister Lily.[33]

Dated September 2, 1863, Wednesday, from Rye Beach, her letter began, "How anxious we have felt about you ever since we received your splendid long letter to me from Bridgeport." (Lily noted that Josie said it was her letter, too.) The sisters had seen in the papers that Rosecrans had been shelling Chattanooga. They supposed Will "was the advance."

Chapter 17. John Brown's Body

Josie had been ill and her husband, Dr. Foster, did not think she was well enough to go swimming in the sea. Lily had gained weight recently. She and Josie had been in a carriage accident. Lily was driving when a conveyance full of women approached from the other direction. She gave them a "wide berth," but the other horse got scared and ran right into their carriage. Workmen had to free the vehicles.

Lily described their upcoming travel plans. Then she told him, "All of your friends … inquire about you constantly…." Lily said when his friends ask about him, they find out that that is "the pleasantest theme to Josie and me." Emma Shonberger was going to marry one of Will's friends this winter—had he heard about that? Then she closed the letter with these words: "Dear Sister sends bushels of love, in which Dr. & Sam most warmly unite & more than all from your loving Bessie." Then she added a postscript.

Lytle did not particularly care for his expression in this photograph but overall was pleased. He was also grateful to know the photographer, who took no payment for the pictures, already had orders for 800 copies (oval portrait, William H. Lytle [Military regalia], 1863." SC#59—General Photographs Collection—Portraits—Lytle; the Cincinnati Museum Center).

"It seems to me I never longed to see you dearest Brother as I do today—I actually hate to bid you good bye … but as they are all waiting for me I shall have to go—so again good bye. Lily"[34] After reading the letter Lytle put it in his coat pocket, laid down, and went to sleep.

The soldiers, having completed their march, figured they would stay where they were for the night, so they built fires in preparation for making supper and coffee. Lytle received orders, though, to put his brigade in motion just after dark. Lytle's men filed into line then waited for the troops ahead of them. After two or three hours of waiting, Lytle and Pirtle rode ahead to see what was causing the delay.

Laiboldt's brigade had yet to move so Lytle and Pirtle rode back and made themselves comfortable by a watch fire and began to talk. Soldiers who were nearby listened "with great respect and rapt attention to the General's conversation...."

The discussion began as "lively, genial, and full of fun," and the eavesdropping soldiers enjoyed listening but once the talk "took a more serious turn" the men left Lytle and Pirtle alone. The General talked of home and his friends as well as his sisters. He reminisced about his visits with the elite of Louisville and recalled the people and places of his past. "Louisville seemed always to have had great attractions for him, and he spoke to-night as he often had of the wit and beauty he had met assembled at our parties." Lytle sat on a rail fence, and the firelight glanced "from his sabre, illuminating every feature. I remember his high-top boots, his overcoat with his belt outside, his hat with the gold cord glistening in the light...." Their pleasant conversation was interrupted when an aide rode up and said the road was clear and they could continue their march.[35]

Before returning to the road, Lytle pulled Pirtle aside and made a request. He told the Kentuckian about "the lady of his heart..." and asked Pirtle to deliver a message if he ever met her. Tell her, "that never was [k]night truer to his lady love than I am to her. Never have I thought of another woman. That I shall go on loving her, always the Same." Pirtle assured his commander that if he ever met the lady, he would deliver the message.[36]

Sometime after midnight Lytle said he would like to have something to eat and Pirtle dug in the skirt pocket of his coat and pulled out some food for his commander. As he withdrew his hand from the pocket, his seal ring slipped off and fell into the dusty road.[37] It was a fine gold ring, with his initials engraved in script on a piece of bloodstone. Pirtle halted the men behind him, dismounted, lit a candle and after a few minutes found his lost treasure. He triumphantly rode up to General Lytle who asked if he had found his ring. Pirtle replied he had found it and then handed Lytle the food. Lytle laughed and said, "a man who can lose a ring at mid-night and find it in six inches of dust, on as dark a road as this, is not going to be hit in the coming battle."[38]

It was very cold that night. Scouts rode ahead of the column and set fences ablaze to light the way. When soldiers marched during the day, they would sometimes talk and joke to help pass the time. At night, the marches were almost always silent. Almost always. This night would be different. Pirtle recalled that after midnight, as they marched along "the dusty, smoke laden road," a fine baritone voice broke the silence, singing a song well known to the men, "John Brown's Body." The singer began quietly, almost to himself. The other soldiers "listened with perfect quiet" until the chorus, when suddenly the other soldiers joined in, marching in time with the cadence of the song.

For the second verse, the soldiers again grew silent, and the lone voice sang with more intensity "as he seemed to be filled with the aroused feelings of his thousand hearers who hung upon every word...." At the chorus the men once more joined in and repeated the same for the third verse. "It is not possible to tell the effect on the column, of this song, for all had caught the inspiration of the words.... The memory of that marching to the tones, lingers with me still, and I recall the total silence save of the singer's voice, the absence of a foot fall, the anticipation of each line as it came in the song, and the story that was underneath it all, united to make a scene never to be forgotten."[39]

Chapter 18

OLD PETE ARRIVES

At Carnifex Ferry, the two sides had fought for control of a key river crossing. At Perryville the combatants were looking for water. At Chickamauga the Rebels and Yankees more or less stumbled into each other.

Due to Rosecrans's miscalculations regarding the whereabouts of Bragg, the irascible Rebel commander saw opportunities to strike the vulnerable Federals while their corps were dispersed. Unfortunately for Bragg, the generals he entrusted with carrying out his plans, Thomas Carmichael Hindman and the "Fighting Bishop," Leonidas Polk, were unable or unwilling to obey his orders. (Hindman actually had two chances to hit the Federals but balked at both. One of Hindman's own brigade commanders, Arthur Manigault noted that Hindman "was not up to the work, it being far beyond his capacity as a general. Had there been a proper man to manage for us, I have little doubt but that a most brilliant success would have been achieved.")[1]

Disappointed but not defeated, Bragg decided to wait at LaFayette for promised reinforcements. As Bragg waited, Rosecrans gathered his troops together to defend Chattanooga.[2]

A few miles to the north of Lytle's position, on September 18, Bragg formed a plan to get his army across Chickamauga Creek, sweep south, and drive the Yankees towards McLemore's Cove. Determined stands by Federal troops delayed the Rebel crossings but by late in the afternoon of the 18th, the Rebels had captured Reed's Bridge and proceeded southward toward the LaFayette Road. They also had fought their way across Alexander's Bridge where they suffered heavy casualties and they failed to take the main north-south highway. Federal Major General George Henry Thomas moved his troops to counter the creek crossings by the Rebels.[3]

On the morning of September 19, Thomas sent a single brigade from Brigadier General John Milton Brannan's Division to destroy what he thought was a single Rebel brigade. The Federals instead ran into Butternut cavalrymen. Both sides seemed surprised as they encountered unexpected enemies in their front, and fed troops into the growing conflict. The famous Confederate cavalryman Brigadier General Nathan Bedford Forrest encouraged his dismounted troopers as they battled Yankee infantry. "Hold on, boys," the Tennessean told his troopers, "the infantry is coming...."[4]

Pirtle awoke at 5 a.m. on the 19th, having slept only about two hours by the roadside. An hour later he wrote a letter to his folks. "Gen'l Lytle has caught a very bad cold, but it is improving this morning.... He is in excellent spirits—enters into the campaign with the ardor of youth and the discretion and discrimination of a veteran and statesman."[5]

Lytle's troops were at Pond Spring, south of the battlefield, near General McCook's headquarters. They could hear the battle raging. Sheridan's Division moved toward the sound of the firing with the Third Brigade in the lead, followed by the Second and then Lytle's First Brigade.[6] Men were given extra ammunition, then marched a mile at the double-quick to Lee and Gordon's Mills, on Chickamauga Creek, where they halted around 4 p.m. Lytle's Brigade was the extreme right of the Federal line. The other two brigades continued marching north.[7] Pirtle recorded that Lytle was constantly in motion, "riding up and down the lines stationing his troops; inspecting their positions and attending to the minutest details."[8]

Lytle ordered the Twenty-Fourth Wisconsin to send out skirmishers along the edge of the creek to watch for Rebels. Around 5 p.m. an enemy cannon fired at them but did no harm. After dark, Lytle ordered the skirmishers to pull back into the woods where they spent the night.[9] The Eighty-Eighth Illinois, the Twenty-First Michigan, and two sections of the Eleventh Indiana artillery battery were posted on a ridge near the mill to guard the ford. The Thirty-Sixth Illinois, the Twenty-Fourth Wisconsin, and another section of the Eleventh Indiana artillery were about one quarter of a mile to the left. Lytle rode over to be with his troops on the left while Pirtle stayed on the right.

Lytle visited Pirtle around 10 p.m. and inspected his deployment. The General told him rations would be there in a few hours and to be alert because the enemy was in their immediate front and might attack at daybreak. Lytle returned to his headquarters. The men slept on their arms. Wagons continued to pass throughout the night.[10]

The Rebels controlled the LaFayette Road until the Federals brought up reinforcements and retook the thoroughfare by the end of the 19th. That night Thomas strengthened his position on the Federal left and McCook withdrew slightly to bring in the right of his line. Sheridan requested that Lytle be relieved from his position at Lee and Gordon's Mills and allowed to join the rest of his division. His pickets had been hearing the rumbling of carriages from the Rebel side and Sheridan believed he would need his entire division on the 20th.[11]

Meanwhile, Confederate Lieutenant General James Longstreet reached Catoosa Platform near Ringgold, Georgia, at 2 p.m. on September 19. "Old Pete" and two of his aides stepped off the train expecting to be greeted by someone to guide them to Bragg's headquarters. One of Longstreet's aides, Colonel Moxley Sorrel, noted, "It would appear that if Bragg wanted to see anybody, Longstreet was the man. But we were left to shift for ourselves." After waiting for their horses to arrive on the next train, the trio followed the sounds of the distant battle, toward where they thought Bragg must be, all the while dodging wagons, stragglers and wounded on the same road. They did not arrive at Bragg's headquarters until around 11 p.m. of the 19th.[12] Tired and frustrated, Longstreet and his aides were at least glad to be able to get out of the cold.

Federal commander William S. Rosecrans sent a telegram to Major General Henry Halleck, General in Chief, in Washington, D.C., informing Halleck of the day's actions. "We have just concluded a terrific day's fighting, and have another in prospect for tomorrow."[13]

Chapter 19

THE THIRD FALL: CHICKAMAUGA

Sunday, September 20, 1863.

In the early hours of September 20 William Haines Lytle rose and dressed for battle. He wore plain dark pants and a single-breasted fatigue blouse with his brigadier general shoulder straps. His orderly, Joe Guthrie, helped him pull on his high-top boots. After buttoning up his overcoat, Lytle fastened his sword belt around the coat and placed his military hat with the solitary gold braid on his head.[1] As he dressed, he admitted to Guthrie that he was exhausted, and his orderly begged him not to go into battle, but the Cincinnatian would have none of that. "No, Guthrie, I never shrunk from my duty but if I fall I want you to carry me off the field—and take care of my poor horse."[2]

When rations arrived in Lytle's camps, he told his men to eat quickly because they had been ordered to move out.[3] They did not depart until around 3:30 a.m. and by sunrise they would occupy a strong position near the Widow Glenn's house. Rosecrans, McCook, and Sheridan were already there.[4]

The sun rose at 5:47 a.m. "red and sultry" as one soldier described it. A heavy fog shrouded the battlefield like a blanket for the dead. Temperatures had plunged into the 30s the night of September 19 and on the morning of the 20th frost covered the ground.[5]

Bragg organized his Rebel army into two wings. Polk would command the right wing and Longstreet the left. Bragg's battle plan for the 20th called for an attack to begin at dawn with Polk's wing and move right to left, north to south, to flank the Federals away from Chattanooga. Each brigade was to advance as soon as they saw the brigade to their right move forward, hitting the Federal lines with a series of hammer strikes.[6] But the "Fighting Bishop" did not move as ordered and the attack did not begin at dawn. The Confederate attack would not begin until much later that morning.[7]

As the Federals waited for the expected onslaught, Rosecrans,

Sheridan, and McCook all rode off to prepare for the coming battle. Rosy told the soldiers as he passed, "Boys, I never fight on Sundays, but if they begin it, we will end it." Sheridan's division was deployed in a line running south from the Widow Glenn house. The Second Brigade under Colonel Bernard Laiboldt and the First under Lytle were in position and Colonel Luther Bradley's Third Brigade (now led by Colonel Nathan Walworth since Bradley was wounded the night before) was in reserve. A soldier noted that Lytle "sat calm and dignified at the head of the brigade, to all appearances unmoved by the circumstances, though comprehending all the gravity of the situation."[8]

Pirtle described the Glenn house as "a little log weather boarded cabin, two rooms, one on each side of a passageway, and a small room opens on a back porch." It fronted a road which was about one hundred paces west. East of the house the land sloped downward. There was a forest and beyond that for several hundred yards was a large cornfield which was several hundred yards long, north and south. The longest side of the field was the most distant, where it joined dense woods.

Lytle deployed his regiments in the standard two regiments up, two regiments back with the Eighty-Eighth Illinois and Twenty-First Michigan up and the Thirty-Sixth Illinois and Twenty-Fourth Wisconsin

This is how Lytle would have been dressed on September 20, 1863. Note the gold braid on his hat, the belt fastened around his coat and the sword at this side. "Brigadier General William Haines Lytle of the 10th Ohio Infantry Regiment and U.S. Volunteers Infantry Regiment in uniform with sword/Schwing & Rudd, Photographers, Army of the Cumberland" (Library of Congress).

back. Federal artillerists stood ready in the yard to rake the cornfield in case the Confederates decided to strike there. Northern skirmishers were thrown out in the field far enough to monitor the woods and prevent surprise. Two other regiments formed at right angles to prevent their flanks from being turned if the Rebels advanced up the road.[9]

Lytle's First Brigade would go into action with the Thirty-Sixth Illinois commanded by Lieutenant Colonel Silas Miller, the Eighty-Eighth Illinois under Lieutenant Colonel Alexander S. Chadbourne, the Twenty-First Michigan under Colonel William H. McCreery, the Twenty-Fourth Wisconsin under Lieutenant Colonel Theodore S. West, and the Indiana Light Artillery, Eleventh Battery, Captain Arnold Sutermeister commanding.[10]

Rebel prisoners were brought into the area near Lytle's position and one of the captives told the Yankees, "You fellers will catch hell this morning."[11] The Rebels were guarded by a contingent from the Tenth Ohio. When Pirtle informed Lytle that members of the Tenth were nearby Lytle said they must go and "see the boys." The General shook hands and spoke with each one individually. As the men moved off, they all wished Lytle well. One said, "Take good care of yourself, General." Another said, "Goodbye, Lytle." Pirtle was taken aback by the seemingly disrespectful tone of the last well-wisher and asked the General if he knew the young soldier. Lytle replied, "Yes, it is Billy Sullivan."[12]

Captain Howard D. Greene, Company B, Twenty-Fourth Wisconsin, approached Lytle and offered his services for the battle as a volunteer aide. Lytle consented and continued overseeing preparations for the upcoming fight. Once everything was in order, the Ohioan reclined at the foot of a tree to rest, and Guthrie brought him some breakfast. Lytle's cold seemed better today but he had suffered during the night and slept very little. He knew a battle was imminent but was calm. Pirtle believed Lytle was, "if possible more quiet than usual." Lytle called Pirtle over, put his arm around him and said, "My boy, do you know we are going to fight two to one to-day?" Lytle said Longstreet had undoubtedly joined Bragg. "He wanted me to promise to stick to him to the last, and that we would do our duty like men." Pirtle said he would. "We did not talk much more for every man on the eve of battle communes with himself."[13]

The History of the Thirty-Sixth Illinois claims that before the battle Lytle called over Lieutenant John Turnbull and told him he believed he would be killed in the upcoming battle. According to the story Lytle said, "Turnbull, I want you to stay with me today." The tall lieutenant responded, "General, if you wish while I live and you live we will be together."[14]

To the left, or north, of Lytle's position was the center of the Federal line. Brigadier General Thomas Wood's division fronted the LaFayette Road, supported by the division of Brigadier General Jefferson Davis. To

Wood's left was Major General James Negley's Division and to the left or north of Negley were the divisions of Brigadier General John Brannan and then Major General Joseph Reynolds. The Federal left was held by the loyal Virginian, Major General George Henry Thomas.[15]

When the Rebel attack finally began the Butternuts first slammed into the Union left. Thomas began calling for more and more reinforcements.[16] Pirtle heard the distant fighting and recorded, "I never listened to more awful musketry in my life."[17] At 10:10 a.m. Brigadier General James Garfield, Rosecrans's chief of staff, sent orders to Major General Alexander McCook to prepare to move to support Thomas. "The left must be held at all hazards." Five minutes after McCook received that message he received orders to send two of Sheridan's brigades to assist Thomas, and then send the third brigade once "the lines can be drawn in sufficiently."[18]

In the confusion of the developing battle, a gap developed in the Federal line. Brigadier General Thomas J. Wood received an order to "close up on Reynolds as fast as possible to support him."[19] The wording was confusing because if Wood "closed up" he would need to move left and *connect* with Major General Joseph J. Reynolds's division. If he "supported" Reynolds he would have to move his troops *behind* Reynolds's position. Wood asked for clarification and was going to wait for a response but the commander of XX Corps, Major General McCook rode up and insisted "there was no time to lose" and reminded Wood, "You could be court-martialed for not obeying it."[20] When Wood obeyed the order around 11:00, he moved out of line and marched behind Brannan before joining Reynolds. This left an opening in the Federal position.[21]

McCook ordered Brigadier General Jefferson C. Davis's division to fill the gap. Colonel Laiboldt's Second Brigade moved to support Davis. The Third Brigade took Laiboldt's place in line near the Glenn house. Sometime between 10:45 and 10:55 a.m., Major General Sheridan and his staff rode up to the Widow Glenn house and spoke with Lytle for a few minutes. Lytle was showing Sheridan the disposition of his troops when Lieutenant Colonel Thruston P. Gates, chief of staff to McCook, rode up and delivered orders for Sheridan to move with his remaining two brigades to help Thomas as quickly as possible. Sheridan expressed surprise and Gates repeated the order urging the necessity of haste.[22] Sheridan turned to Lytle and said, "You have heard the order General, put your Brigade in motion at once."[23]

Pirtle noted that the brigade moved forward with the Eighty-Eighth Illinois leading the way followed by the Thirty-Sixth Illinois, then the Twenty-First Michigan, then the Twenty-Fourth Wisconsin, and then the artillery. Lytle assigned Pirtle the artillery, which went last because the road in front of the Widow Glenn house was too narrow for the artillery

Chapter 19. The Third Fall: Chickamauga 139

to take its place in the center of the march. Pirtle directed the artillery to keep close. (The history of the Thirty-Sixth Illinois states that the artillery was placed in between the first two and last two brigades.) The brigade moved left along the Glenn-Kelly Road to support the Second Brigade around 11:30.[24]

Lytle's skirmishers were still at the edge of the woods about 75 yards down the slope from the rest of the line. As his brigade prepared to move out, Lytle sent Lieutenant Turnbull to the skirmish line to check on the men. When Turnbull arrived at the rail fence, he distinctly heard several Rebel officers ordering their men to "halt." Turnbull moved the Yankee skirmishers to the left and then rode back to Lytle to report.[25]

As Lytle and the other Federal troops were moving toward Thomas, Turnbull rode up and advised his commander, "We should move into line of battle for the enemy [is] close." One of Rosecrans's aides, who was overseeing the movements with Lytle, laughed and said Turnbull was just scared. Turnbull was not scared. He was right. At that very moment, Brigadier General Arthur M. Manigault's Brigade was headed directly for Lytle's column.[26]

The left wing of the Confederate advance, which Lytle would soon face, was under the overall command of the recently arrived Lieutenant General James Longstreet. Major General Thomas Hindman's Division, which would hit Lytle's position, was on the far left of the Rebel left wing. Brigadier General Patton Anderson, Lytle's counterpart at Bridgeport, commanded his Mississippians, and Brigadier General Zachariah C. Deas led his Alabamians. Brigadier General Arthur M. Manigault's brigade comprised Alabama troops and a South Carolina regiment.[27]

At 11:10 a.m. Longstreet's grand column exploited the gap in the Union center near the Brotherton cabin along the LaFayette Road and broke through the Federal defenses. The gray line moved forward right to left and around 11:20 Zach Deas ordered his men to advance. Manigault was to Deas's left and Anderson two to three hundred yards behind, in support.[28]

Laiboldt's Brigade had taken up a defensive position just down the slope from what would later be known as Lytle Hill, in support of Jefferson Davis's Division. With Confederates fast approaching, McCook rode up and ordered Laiboldt to charge the approaching Rebels. Laiboldt moved forward in columns of regiments, meaning they would be stacked up one after another, rather than forming a long line. This would limit the number of troops coming into battle against the Rebels. Laiboldt recognized his error before starting the advance and asked for time to redeploy. McCook replied, "No, charge as you are." Moving down the gentle sloping hill he ran into Deas's Alabamians who fired into the bunched bluecoats and overlapped their flanks. Manigault's Rebels appeared and moved toward the rear of the Federals. The overwhelmed Northerners began falling back. Fortunately for Laiboldt's men, just as they were launching their ill-fated attack, Lytle's Brigade was diverted from moving toward Thomas and instead were moved into position at the crest of the hill behind them.[29]

As Lytle's column had continued to the left, orders were barked to "double-quick."[30] Pirtle recalled, "The firing now was tremendous and at the first open woods we came to, not more than a quarter of a mile from our chosen position, we were turned off to the right of the road, still at double quick.... The regiments had been marching as usual, by the flank [four men abreast, as they would march 'through a city' Pirtle recalled in his journal] and then the order 'by companies into line' was given while the men were falling from the enemy's fire." As they moved to their right they marched right into the battle. Lytle shouted, "Forward into line'" and the Eighty-Eighth Illinois rushed forward to occupy the crest of a hill. Led by General Lytle, they fired into the approaching Rebels, driving them back.[31]

Having gained the crest, the Midwesterners now beheld a terrible, awesome scene. The large field before them, Dyer Field, sloped away to the Glenn-Kelly Road at the base of the hill. There were woods on the other side of the Glenn-Kelly Road and on the other side of those woods was the main area of fighting, now moving toward Lytle. Dry grass and old logs had caught fire due to the bursting shells. A thick cloud of smoke, almost head high hung in the air. But through and below the smoke the Midwesterners could see masses of men moving hurriedly toward their vulnerable position.[32]

Lytle's men also saw Laiboldt's Brigade falling back, hotly pursued by the Rebels. The sight of these veterans breaking and running for the rear sent a thrill of terror through the men in Lytle's Brigade. One of the Illinois soldiers noted that Laiboldt's "brigade was the best and largest in our div[ision] composed of old troops ... and until then had never been repulsed."[33]

Rosecrans appeared and rode along the hilltop through Lytle's men shouting, "Fix bayonets—Forward—Double-Quick—Charge!" One of Lytle's Illinois officers recalled, "They took us into a very hot fire. We double-quicked to gain a ridge and form our line to meet the shock." Another said, "...bullets began to whiz and the men commenced falling."[34]

After placing the Eighty-Eighth in line, Lytle positioned the Thirty-Sixth Illinois to the right of the Eighty-Eighth. Lytle rode along the line and encouraged the men, "Stand firm boys, stand like iron: never let the name of the 'Old First' be disgraced."[35] Lytle then ordered Turnbull

Chapter 19. The Third Fall: Chickamauga

Taken from the Lytle monument, this is the landscape the First Brigade encountered when they reached the battlefield. The Rebels attacked across that open field in the distance (photograph by Randy Duncan).

to bring up the Twenty-Fourth Wisconsin and the Twenty-First Michigan and extend the battle line to the right of the Thirty-Sixth Illinois.[36] The brigade formed a line down the slope from the crest of the hill.

When the Twenty-Fourth Wisconsin surged over their corner of the hill, they ran into Rebels that one Wisconsin soldier recalled were "only two musket lengths away." The Badgers broke the Confederate advance. Lytle rode in front of the Federal lines, waving his hat and sword and cheering on the men. A Wisconsin soldier observed, "Oh! It was a glorious sight to see that line of men charge up the hill and scatter the first line of rebels to the four winds."[37] Then the Twenty-First Michigan "came into line as handsomely and steady as if on battalion drill," recalled a Michigan soldier. Colonel McCreery ordered his Twenty-First Michigan to lie down as the remnants of Laiboldt's Brigade streamed past to the rear. Once they passed, McCreery ordered his men to rise up, aim, and fire and the Wolverines poured a withering volley into the approaching Confederates. One group of Rebels worked their way around the right of the Twenty-First, but Company A of the Michigan troops, armed with Colt Revolving Rifles, drove the Butternuts back with nearly constant fire and good aim.[38]

Lytle stationed himself thirty paces behind the Badgers, near their colors and shouted, "Brave boys, brave 24th!" He also exhorted them with "Boys, if we whip them today, we will all eat Christmas dinner at home." Turning to his staff the General commented, "All right men, we can die but once. This is our time and place...."[39] He then pulled on his gloves and remarked, "If I must die, I will die as a gentleman."[40]

The Rebels reformed and charged again. Advancing up the slope, Deas's men were hit with canister from Sutermeister's guns.[41] Captain Harry Toulmin of Alabama noted that Lytle's Brigade was "obstinately contest[ing] every foot of ground...."[42] Lytle's Brigade might have broken Deas's charge completely, but the bulk of Thomas Hindman's Division was about to come into action. Arthur Manigault's Brigade was the largest in the division with 2,025 men. They formed in a single line that stretched nearly 500 yards. A Confederate said that once they raised the famed Rebel yell the Federals "fled as if Old Scratch had been after them." However, in the confusion Manigault's large brigade also became scattered and the Tenth/Nineteenth South Carolina encountered the Twenty-First Michigan.[43] The South Carolinians were soon forced to retreat.

Seeing the damage done by Sutermeister's artillery, Patton Anderson sent two of his regiments to charge the Yankee guns. The Mississippians ran straight toward the threat and fired a volley that killed 19 of the artillery horses, wounded five drivers and the section commander. The Yankees fled and left behind two 3-inch rifled cannons. With the arrival of the Mississippians the Confederates pressed forward.[44]

Major Chase of the Twenty-First Michigan noticed a mass of Rebel infantry on his right flank. Within minutes, the right wing of the Michigan regiment began to crumble and retreat. Sergeant John C. Taylor, Company K, recalled, "...we did not linger, and on the order ... the men broke and moved back with speed." The Twenty-First's Lieutenant Colonel Wells was shot.[45]

To the left of the Twenty-First Michigan, the Twenty-Fourth Wisconsin stood fast. To their left, or north, the Illinois regiments were being hammered by Deas. As Lytle predicted, here the Confederates enjoyed nearly a two-to-one advantage with 1,500 Confederates going against 800 Illinois troops. When Deas resumed his attack, the Eighty-Eighth Illinois had nothing on their left to stop the Confederates, so they fell back to the base of the hill, on the backside of the slope. Because the Thirty-Sixth Illinois's left flank was exposed, they too headed back beyond the crest to the other side of the hill.[46]

As the battle raged, Lytle sat on his horse, facing south, his left side to the enemy, grasping the reins with his left hand. His sword was drawn with the hilt resting on the reins, sloping across the front of his body. His hand was low, and the point of the saber was about the height of his shoulder.

Chapter 19. The Third Fall: Chickamauga

Pirtle recalled that Lytle's face was lit with "battle-fire, a spirit of enthusiasm brought on by the tremendous excitement of conflict, which irradiates every feature, sparkles from his eyes, marks with sharp outline the curves of the nostrils and seems ready to leap forth in words from his parted lips. His very beard seems electrified, and his superb mustache which he has twisted and curled with his impatient fingers, adds a determined cast to his whole countenance."[47]

Captain Howard Greene was a few paces to the rear, to Lytle's right. Lieutenant Boal was about the same distance, to his left. All were facing south. Pirtle was between Lytle and the guns facing him. Their horses were close together when Lytle calmly leaned over to Pirtle and said, "Pirtle, I am hit." Pirtle asked, "Are you hit hard General?" Lytle replied, "In the spine, if I have to leave the field, you stay here and see that all goes right." Pirtle replied, "I will, General."[48]

Pirtle asked if he should bring up more guns and Lytle replied, "No, we have more now than we can take care of." Lytle saw the Twenty-First Michigan breaking for the rear. He turned to Boal and shouted, "For God's sake bring up another regiment!" Boal did not hear the order, but Pirtle did and decided to act. Pirtle told Lytle "good-bye" and rode down the back of the slope to the foot of the hill, away from the intense firing. There he found the Thirty-Sixth Illinois and gave Colonel Miller the order and they rallied the shattered regiment. Fire poured in from the left. As the Thirty-Sixth advanced back up the hill the Twenty-Fourth Wisconsin began to waver. Four shells burst near Pirtle causing his startled horse, *Old Starry*, to throw the Kentuckian and run off, leaving Pirtle on foot.[49]

Lytle had just turned to give Greene an order when he was struck in the head. The bullet caused the poet-soldier to reel in his saddle. Greene jumped off his horse and caught his commander by the head and shoulders and gently pulled him to the ground. Lytle tried to say something but could not. According to the young officer, "The ball struck him in the left corner of the mouth, passed through his head and came out near the right temple so that the blood welled up into his mouth so rapidly that he was unable to speak." Because the horses had run off the only way to remove Lytle would be by carrying him.[50]

Captain E.B. Parsons, commander of Company K, Twenty-Fourth Wisconsin Volunteers, remembered Lytle "was close behind our regiment" when he was hit. Lytle and his staff "rode right behind the center of our regiment, and he remained there until he was shot. Almost the last words he uttered were, 'Brave, brave, brave boys!' As I was looking into his face, a ball struck him, and it seemed to me must have struck him in the face or head, for the blood flowed from his mouth."[51] Members of the Thirty-Sixth Illinois remembered that Lytle had just ridden up to their regiment and drawn his sword "close by our colors and was apparently about to give orders to charge, when he was struck in the head with a bullet and fell into the arms of one of his aids [sic]."[52]

Greene called out for two of Lytle's orderlies, Passmore and Sillcox, and they began trying to move him to safety. Colonel Findlay Harrison, the former hard drinker to whom Lytle had given a second chance, then came "up with a Regiment he had been rallying. As soon as he saw us he jumped off his horse and helped us carry off the General." The quartet had not gone far when Sillcox was shot and killed. The brigade broke for the rear and "It was just at this time that Lytle opened his eyes and tried to speak but could not. I asked him if he wished to lie down, and he nodded." Harrison now took charge and responded, "No, carry him or we will all be taken Prisoner." Lytle tried to speak again but finding he could not, "threw his arms out convulsively," caught hold of Greene and "gave me one embrace which I think was his death struggle." Greene noticed, "… his limbs immediately relaxed, his eyes rolled up into his head, and he fell limp and lifeless." Greene told Harrison he thought Lytle was dead. Harrison mounted his horse and rode off to rally the troops.[53] (Greene would soon give his life, at Missionary Ridge, in November.)[54]

Colonel William McCreery was the next man to find Lytle. The Cincinnatian was still alive when McCreery reached him. Lytle gave his sword to David Hunter, a private in Company A, Twenty-Fourth Wisconsin.[55] McCreery and some other men tried to move their wounded commander. Lytle tried to wave them away. One of the men who responded to McCreery's call for help to move Lytle was Edward "Sandy" Glenn, who was then shot in the side. McCreery was also hit. They had to leave Lytle and save themselves.[56]

His face was toward the sky, but his eyes did not see. His mouth was open, but he did not speak. His ears did not hear the foeman's cry. His last deep breath had flown. There, on a lone spot far from home and friends, on the turf reclining, the poet-soldier died alone.

Rosecrans, looking "distressed," ordered Pirtle to tell the men to fix bayonets and charge, but there were no men to order. Pirtle saw Lytle's riderless horse gallop past, down the hill. His first thought was perhaps Lytle was dismounted by his wound. "I cannot describe what my feelings were, but a thousand conflicting emotions filled my breast."[57] Pirtle kept moving toward where he left Lytle, but Rebels were everywhere, and he was forced to "sadly turn and fall back toward the road."[58]

Pirtle tried to run away from the Rebels, but he was exhausted. He was about to give up and be killed or captured when James Findlay Harrison rode up. Pirtle shouted to Harrison, "Tell my father you saw me, and my address will be Libby Prison." Fin shouted back, "Not by a damned

Chapter 19. The Third Fall: Chickamauga

Taken from the Glenn-Kelly Road at the bottom of what is now known as "Lytle Hill," this is from the attacking Confederates' point of view, looking up at where the Federals tried to hold the line (photograph by the author).

sight!" Harrison dismounted, got his friend into the saddle, and ran alongside as they got away from the danger.[59]

As the victorious Confederates overran the Federal lines, a wounded Federal officer limped up to Confederate Captain Douglass West and asked him to save his fallen general from nearby fires. West asked, "Who is your General?" The Federal replied, "General Lytle." West asked if Lytle was the officer riding a small, dark horse, trying to rally his men. The Federal replied, "Yes." West instructed the Yankee officer to pick four or five men and lead him to the spot. When West arrived at the location, "we found the body lying in the leaves. His face was upwards.... He was dressed in full regulation uniform, but was minus his sword, his scabbard and belt still being on his person. My first exclamation on looking down upon his graceful and manly form, so perfectly dressed and accoutered was, 'I am dying, Egypt, dying.'"[60]

A courier advised General Anderson that a Federal general was dead on the hill. Anderson went to the spot and recognized his thoughtful adversary from Bridgeport. Anderson ordered a guard placed over the body.[61] Major West found an ambulance passing by and directed it to take

Lytle's body from the battlefield, but it was already transporting a mortally wounded Confederate officer, Captain Deas Nott of the Twenty-Second Alabama. West told Nott that Lytle had been a "war Democrat and friendly toward a proper conduct of the war" and asked if it would be acceptable if they put Lytle's body in the ambulance. Nott replied, "Certainly."[62]

At Chickamauga, J. Stoddard Johnston was assigned to the staff of Simon Bolivar Buckner and did not see Lytle fight or fall, but his brother, Captain Harris H. Johnston, an aide to Brigadier General William Preston (also a native of Louisville) did. Harris saw Lytle on a black horse and waving his sword when he was shot down. When Preston reached the spot where Lytle fell, Major Miller Owen, another member of Preston's staff, and former resident of Cincinnati, identified the body as that of William Haines Lytle. Preston asked, "What? Is it the son of my old friend Bob Lytle?" Owen replied. "Yes. It's General Lytle of Cincinnati." Preston then said, with much feeling, "I am very sorry—very sorry that Lytle is dead."[63]

After Lytle's death the Confederates pushed north, to their right, toward Snodgrass Hill where Thomas, who had incessantly called for and received reinforcements all day, held the Federal line. Thomas and his soldiers stopped the Rebel advance and for this he earned the sobriquet, "The Rock of Chickamauga." The exhausted Confederates failed to take the hill and the Federal army, still intact, withdrew to Chattanooga where they began to fortify their position. Bragg's shattered army was spent.

When the Confederates went into their camps, Captain West and others read the letters and scraps of poems they had found in Lytle's pockets. One item removed from his pocketbook was a printed poem titled "Co. K." There is no indication Lytle wrote that short piece or where he had gotten it. The letters "appear to have been written by his sister … it was painful for us to think that we had assisted in putting out so brilliant a light. We talked of the poem that gave him his great celebrity.…" General Anderson asked to send Lytle's effects to the family, telling West, "Major, you will do me a great favor if you will allow me to do this, as General Lytle had placed me under peculiar obligations by having sent my old mother through the Federal lines."[64]

The Confederates covered the wound on Lytle's face with green leaves, then with lace-net and a fine cambric handkerchief.[65] Confederate Assistant Surgeon Dr. E.W. Thomason clipped a lock of Lytle's hair. An untitled and undated newspaper article in the Broadwell scrapbook in the Lytle Papers, written after Lytle's death, refers to Thomason as "Thompson" and states that Thomason had been captured earlier in the war and met Lytle in Louisville and Murfreesboro. Lytle had treated him so kindly then that Thomason felt obliged to return his acts of kindness now. A Confederate wrote Lytle's name on a piece of paper and pinned it to his shirt.[66]

First Lieutenant B.L. Archer, Company D, Nineteenth Alabama, of Deas's brigade was ordered by Dr. Thomason to get some men and bury Lytle, which they did about forty yards from Deas's hospital tent. Archer said they "wrapped him in a United States blanket and laid him in the grave near Chickamauga Creek." The Rebels marked his grave with a slab.[67]

Chapter 20

The Rain on the Tent

Lytle's First Brigade fought bravely at Chickamauga. The Thirty-Sixth Illinois entered the fight with 358 soldiers and lost 20 killed, 101 wounded and 20 missing (39.4 percent casualty rate). The Eighty-Eighth Illinois started the battle with 449 men and suffered 12 killed, 62 wounded, and 14 missing (19.6 percent casualty rate). The Twenty-First Michigan took 299 men into the battle and lost 16 killed, 73 wounded, and 17 missing (35.5 percent). The Twenty-Fourth Wisconsin began the battle with 487 men and lost three killed, 73 wounded, and 29 missing (21.6 percent). The brigade totals were 52 killed (the fifty-second fatality was Lytle), 309 wounded, and 80 missing for an overall casualty rate of 27.7 percent.[1]

The day after the battle Rosecrans sent a flag of truce to inquire about Lytle but the Rebels were in no mood to receive it. With Sheridan's permission, Pirtle and Grover rode into Chattanooga to see Rosecrans who, despite all his other pressing obligations, received them. Pirtle and Grover wanted to retrieve Lytle's body if he were dead and Rosy, "laid aside all business and talked most affectionately about the loss of the General, and promised us as soon as the enemy would receive a flag, he would communicate with them on the subject."[2]

Returning from the East Coast, Lytle's sisters waited for news of their brother. The September 23, 1863, *Cincinnati Enquirer* reported hopefully, "General Lytle was not killed, as reported, but was wounded and taken prisoner." However, the Cincinnati *Catholic Telegraph* stated, "Among general officers killed are Gen. Lytle."

That same day Pirtle wrote home, "poor Gen'l Lytle was badly wounded and left on the field.... I am suffering great anxiety for fear we may not get his body.... I have not been myself at all since that awful moment when I saw his horse gallop riderless past me.... How I did love Lytle! ... Gen'l Rosy feels with us ... he saw our gallant Gen'l just before he fell, in the thickest of the fray."[3]

On September 26 Pirtle wrote that he was "almost positive" Lytle was dead. Pirtle sent Lytle's sword, horses and effects home with Joe Guthrie and Fin Harrison.[4] The next day Pirtle wrote home, "He and I were as two brothers, so kind and confidential was his bearing toward me from the commencement of our military companionship...."[5]

Dr. Goodale of the Twenty-First Michigan, who was captured while caring for the wounded, inquired as to the whereabouts of Lytle's body. He was told by General Patton Anderson, "General Lytle was buried about one and a half miles below Lee & Gordon's Mills, about one hundred yards below Hunt's Ferry on west bank of West Chickamauga, at or near General Davis's [Deas's?] Confederate Hospital." Goodale said a Captain West added, "General Lytle was buried at Hunt's [Dalton] Ford on the Chickamauga creek on the Chattanooga side of the river, left hand side of road going from Chattanooga."[6]

William Starke Rosecrans, whose brilliant Tullahoma Campaign was overshadowed by the loss at Chickamauga, liked Lytle. He was with Lytle at the beginning, at Camp Dennison, and at the end, when Lytle saluted him a final time at Chickamauga. "Portrait of Maj. Gen. William S. Rosecrans, officer of the Federal Army" (Library of Congress).

Even Sheridan asked Rosecrans to inquire about Lytle's remains after the battle. The Rebels finally informed the Northerners that Lytle was killed during the battle, and they had carefully buried him and marked the grave.[7]

The September 29, 1863, *Cincinnati Daily Gazette* reported the terrible news under the headline "Death of General Lytle." His sisters had received a dispatch from General Sheridan advising them of the death of their brother. A newspaper writer opined, "He was brave, even to rashness." That comment did not sit well with the Lytle family. An officer named Trowbridge (perhaps Sergeant W.E. Trowbridge of the Twenty-Fourth Wisconsin) wrote to the sisters to let them know their brother "acted most gallantly & bravely—but not in the least rashly."[8]

Colonel Silas Miller, who assumed command of the brigade after

Lytle's death, in his official report of the battle included a tribute to his late commander. "No words or eulogies of men can add any luster to his deeds of heroic daring or render more honored and revered among men the name and memory of William H. Lytle." Miller also recognized the contributions of Lytle's aides and staff and said that James Grover was always in the "thickest fire" and where he was most needed and James Findlay Harrison, although wounded, "seized a stand of colors, and under the influence of his example, the men rapidly went forward, again forming under a terrible fire."[9] Sheridan reported that Lytle "was three times wounded, but refused to leave the field. In him the country has lost an able general and the service a gallant soldier."[10]

Laying aside official decorum, Major General Rosecrans wrote:

> "As Brig. Gen. William H. Lytle fell leading a gallant charge against the foe, advancing on our retreating troops, I may be excused from departing from the strict rule of mentioning those officers whose good conduct could be properly officially noticed by the general commanding only. This brave and generous young officer, whose first wounds were received while fighting under my command at Carnifix Ferry, where he fell desperately wounded at the head of his regiment, was also badly wounded and taken prisoner at the battle of Perryville, where he repelled a desperate onslaughter [sic] of the enemy.
>
> On joining the Army of the Cumberland with his well-earned rank of brigadier, he was assigned second in command to General Sheridan. When he fell gloriously on the field of Chickamauga, Ohio, lost one of her jewels and the service one of its most patriotic and promising general officers.
>
> W.S. Rosecrans
> Major General"[11]

On October 1 Pirtle wrote to his mother from Chattanooga. He was back with the Tenth Ohio and in charge of one of the two German companies, noting, "A citizen of Kentucky, in an Ohio Reg't known as an Irish organization and Lt. in a Dutch Company—laughable ain't it?" But his thoughts turned once more to his dear friend. "Words, cold formal words, do not convey what I feel. I am continually thinking of my loss—the first real one I have ever had to bear. I have had many friends I prized highly, but none compared with Lytle.... My eyes are filled with tears and I must stop."[12]

The Cincinnati *Commercial* of October 3, 1863, reported that Lytle's family had received word that his body might be recovered from the Rebels under a flag of truce. The sisters sent a metallic coffin to Chattanooga. Pirtle wrote home, "We learn that Gen'l Lytle's body was carefully buried ... by the staff of Brig Gen'l Patton Anderson, with whom we exchanged courtesies at Bridgeport. Gen'l A. as soon as he heard of our General's death, took steps to find the body and remarked that he had been kind and gentlemanly in every respect toward his mother and that all care should be taken with Gen'l Lytle's remains.... How gratifying to know that even among his enemies he was honored for his noble qualities."[13]

Lytle's friend and fellow soldier, Richard Realf, the poet who had fled England and Lord Byron's disapproving widow, sent a tribute to the Cincinnati *Daily Commercial* which they published on October 9, 1863. The Englishman wrote in his introductory letter that Lytle had "honored me with an especial friendship. I loved him greatly and I think your citizens should know how brave and noble he was."

Realf said that Lytle was "a representative man" and stood for the "truest and loftiest expressions" as a "Soldier, Poet, Statesman, Orator, or Scholar." Realf said that "once or twice in a century ... there is found a man who gathers unto himself and develops in his own life the conscionable excellence of all these separate departments of rare endowment and noble being...." Realf said Lytle "in the highest realm of literature—the domain of poetry—occupied a position of no common order...."

The Englishman pointed out that the first reports of the battle included this comment: "Lytle fought a most terrible battle and damaged the enemy badly." He understood that when describing monumental events it is often necessary to condense much into "a single phrase...." Realf had witnessed acts of heroism committed by men who were inspired by Lytle's example. These soldiers, "men of low esteem, whom no poetry will celebrate, and of whom renown will be mute..." will remain unknown. Lytle, on the other hand, should be remembered not only as a brave soldier but also as a poet.

And then, Realf declared, "But, after all, his life was his best poem. It is nobler to be than to seem, better to do than to desire; and through all the moments of our leader's days there ran even a higher strain of the eternal music than along the chords of love and passion, which he struck so reverently and well."[14]

Rosecrans appealed directly to Bragg to return Lytle's remains. On October 11 Bragg replied that they would receive the metallic coffin sent by Lytle's family and "Col. J.P. Jones, of my staff, will meet the conveyance at 9 o'clock tomorrow morning, on the Chattanooga and LaFayette road. The remains of Brigadier-General Lytle will be returned to the same point as soon as practicable."[15]

Rosecrans responded, "On behalf of General Lytle's friends I thank you for the courtesy of sending his remains to our lines."[16] The Yankee wagon carrying the empty coffin proceeded through the no-man's land to the Confederate pickets. The Federal driver handed over the wagon and waited as Confederates drove it into their lines to pick up the body. Confederate Assistant Surgeon Dr. E.W. Thomason wrote a hasty note to accompany the body. Dated October 10, the doctor stated he was sending the lock of hair to return a favor for a gentleman named L.P. Thompson (to whom the letter was written) who had shown him kindness years before in Baltimore, "I send you a lock of his hair cut from his head after he was killed." Thomason, a surgeon, said that it appeared that Lytle had received two wounds in his face, and one in his neck. The doctor concluded, "he must have died instantly."[17]

A Confederate officer recalled that Lytle "was known to the gentlemen of the Southern army to be a gallant and chivalrous soldier, as well as the author of the beautiful poem, 'Antony and Cleopatra,'" and "all were sincerely grieved at his taking off." When Lytle's remains passed by "the road was lined with officers and men, who testified their respect for the dead General by removing their hats and looking on silently."[18] Another Confederate remembered that, as the coffin passed through the Rebel camp someone asked, "Whom have you there?" Another Confederate replied that it was the body of General Lytle. "Almost before one could think, a soldier of the South had raised his hat, and with bowed head and subdued voice he began to recite, 'I am dying, Egypt, dying.' The effect was electrical ... every soldier's cap was raised as the mellow cadences of their comrade's voice welled out the splendid sentences of the dead general's immortal poem."[19]

Lieutenant Colonel Ward received a package containing items found on the body of Brigadier General Lytle as well as "a certificate as to the identity of the body received to-day by flag of truce."[20] The effects sent to Ward included the personal papers of Lytle, a pocketbook, a penknife, and buttons from his coat.[21]

The Federal Honor Guard, who would receive, guard and transport Lytle's remains were selected from the Tenth Ohio. They met the ambulance carrying Lytle's remains at the Union picket line.[22] Major John E. Hudson of the Tenth Ohio reminded the men of the importance of their duties. He told them that they were to show the people at home "that the lessons taught them by their General, whom they had all so much loved, had been well learned. When they were on post as sentinels, they were to stand at 'attention' and motionless as they would be were he speaking to them, for they were in his presence."[23]

The October 23, 1863, Chicago *Tribune* listed Lytle's honor guard. Lieutenant Joseph Donohue (from Company D) led the group. Corporal Frederick Englehart, Company G; Corporal Frederick Baum, Company K (actually he was a private); Thomas Dolan, Company A; Ernest Mirer, Company B (they may have been referring to Ernst Mathies); John S. Pierce, Company C (he was a corporal); John Cunningham, Company D (also a corporal); David Butler, Company E (listed as Nicholas Butler,

Chapter 20. The Rain on the Tent

private); Frank Sutter, Company F (listed as Franz Sutor on the official Roster); Patrick Finigan, Company H; and William "Billy" Sullivan, Company I. Billy was the soldier who had said "Good-bye, Lytle" the morning of the battle.[24]

A contemporary once described the Tenth Ohio as "the most unpoetic people who ever paraded on the field of glory, or elsewhere. On the contrary, they were full of jokes of the rudest character; they really indulged in everything that would bring on a row." The writer was amazed that someone as refined and cultured as Lytle would have been called on to lead this rowdy bunch.[25] The Tenth prepared to receive Lytle's body in their camp on a hill just outside of Chattanooga.

Carpenters from the Tenth built the dais on which Lytle's coffin was placed. The platform was in a large hospital tent, in front of their regimental headquarters. A newspaper reporter wrote, "Had Lytle's own family been here, his bones could not have been received with more affection or respect than that shown to them by his old comrades of the Tenth Ohio Infantry." The correspondent, though sick, had gotten out of bed to see this and was not disappointed. He marveled at the little memorial the Tenth erected for their beloved leader. "Emphatically the prettiest thing of the kind I have ever seen in camp was the temporary resting place of the corpse while here." Over the coffin were stacked the colors of the regiment and a light screen of weeping willows "which flowed gracefully over the corpse like ringlets over a maiden's shoulders." Four sentries stood guard. "In short, nothing that taste could suggest or money procure was omitted by the officers and men of the brave Tenth to complete this, their last testimonial of esteem for their first colonel."[26]

It was an emotional day in the camp, but Lytle was with them once more. That night it began to rain. Around midnight on the 12th, a solitary figure approached the tent. Entering the shrine, Alfred Pirtle noticed in the dim candlelight the four sentinels on duty, white-gloved, motionless, and silent as statues surrounding the casket. Pirtle stood alone with his thoughts. Except for the steady beating of the rain on the tent "not a sound disturbed the sublime silence of the hour."[27]

Chapter 21

SHE REMEMBERED

Lytle's body remained in the camp of the Tenth Ohio throughout the 13th. Pirtle noticed that the rain and storms could not keep away "crowds of old friends and admirers" who came to pay their respects to General Lytle. Pirtle was given ten days' leave to accompany the body back to Cincinnati.[1]

On October 14, the rain finally relented for several hours allowing the memorial ceremonies to proceed in Chattanooga. Father O'Higgins addressed the men and then Lieutenant Colonel William M. Ward of the Tenth Ohio made his remarks. Ward said they had come to pay their "last sad tribute of respect" to Lytle before his body would be sent home to its "last resting place near the graves of his fathers." Ward talked about "that indefinable something" about Lytle that caused people to develop "a fond love of him." The Ohio officer reminded the men how Lytle had fallen the first time on the "blood-stained field" near the "rushing Gauley." Then, the next autumn, he fell "on Kentucky's dark and bloody ground." Then, "the red and gold of another autumn had scarce begun to dye in beauty the forests of Northern Georgia ere the enemy's fatal bullet struck thee down in thy prime. But you died a soldier's death...." Ward then exhorted the men to finish the fight and win the war so that their commander "did not die in vain."[2]

The casket was placed in a wagon by the Honor Guard. The band of the Tenth Ohio led the procession to the bridge. Near the river the column of soldiers halted, wheeled into line, presented arms, and opened their ranks to allow the funeral wagon and guard to pass onto the bridge. Flags were lowered, drums rolled, and the Tenth Ohio said a silent good-bye to their beloved commander. The Honor Guard crossed the Tennessee River and began their march for Stevenson, Alabama, where they would place the casket onto a train for shipment to Nashville.[3]

Along the route the sun came out and played on the distant mountainside of Walden Ridge. Pirtle saw this as a good but sad omen. "This beautiful and sublime scenery awakened sad thoughts, as I realized the many happy moments spent with the General gazing on the beauties of nature."[4]

The funereal odyssey was marred by rainstorms, high water in the rivers, and sniping Confederate guerrillas. Because the roads were so muddy, the group decided to change their destination and go to Bridgeport, which was closer, where they arrived after dark. Pirtle noted, "Every spot here was so sadly associated with the memory of General Lytle that I did not regret that a train was expected in a few hours, on which we could leave." Donohue and the guard would take the remains to Nashville by the night train. Pirtle would leave later. He telegraphed friends in Cincinnati and Louisville that they were on their way and would be home soon.[5]

Pirtle reached Nashville late in the afternoon of October 18 and met with Lieutenant Donohue.[6] The following morning, they left for Louisville and arrived after dark. They spent the night in the River City and planned to place the casket on a steamboat the next morning.[7]

The body was moved to an undertaker on Seventh Street. Lytle's brother-in-law, Dr. Nathaniel Foster, and an undertaker named E.P. Jenkins arrived from Cincinnati to help verify the identity of the body. In life he had been handsome and well-groomed, as befits a gentleman. What was left of him now was, as described by one newspaper account, "so badly decomposed as to be hardly recognizable...." The body had been stripped to the undershirt and gloves. Pirtle, Foster and Jenkins agreed it was Lytle's body and decided that once the remains were placed in the burial casket it should not be opened again under any circumstances.[8]

On October 20 Pirtle boarded the mailboat *Nightingale*. Lytle's coffin was placed on the bow of the boat. An American flag was draped over it. The Honor Guard stacked their arms at the head and foot of the casket. The flag of the steamer was lowered to half-mast. Pirtle recalled, "as the band softly played, we moved slowly from the shore, and the for the last time, the Noble and Gallant Lytle left Kentucky, the state he so much loved, and where he is deeply mourned."[9] Mr. Burcaw, the clerk of the *Nightingale*, telegraphed Cincinnati to let them know they were leaving Louisville and would be in Cincinnati in the morning.[10]

More than sixty years before this journey, Zadok Cramer added his comments about traveling on The Beautiful River in the fall, at night, in his *Navigator* book. The sycamore, Cramer wrote, is the "king" of the trees along the Ohio and "In the fall of the leaf ... the rays of the bright moon playing through their white branches, form a scene uncommonly brilliant, and quite cheering and amusing to the nightly traveler."[11] The scene would not have brought cheer or amusement to the mournful Pirtle.

The Queen City prepared to honor her fallen son. The Seventh Ohio Militia would escort the body from the wharf to the courthouse where it would lie in state for the remainder of the day. In the evening the body would be taken to the residence of Samuel and Lily Broadwell at the corner of Third and Broadway. Many leading merchants suggested suspending business on the afternoon of the 22nd so people could pay their respects. School superintendent Mr. L. Harding announced that in order "to enable Teachers and Pupils to witness the funeral ceremonies" schools would close at noon.[12]

His lawyer friends, from the Bar of Hamilton County, who had presented him with a sword and sent him off to war, met to remember him. They said that his "genius shed luster upon literature and law." Several members shared their thoughts and then a man named Judge Johnson spoke. Johnson said he had believed Lytle was known only in Cincinnati but a recent trip across the country showed Lytle was known throughout. He advised the members of the Bar, "not to view his death with unmixed regret, because this gentleman had accomplished his destiny. He died well...."[13]

When the mailboat reached Cincinnati, Dr. Foster took Pirtle to breakfast and then to the home of the Broadwells. Lytle's sisters had wanted privacy but agreed to let their brother's remains be shared with the public at the Courthouse for one day. Josie wrote, "a few hours there would gratify his many friends and ensure us quiet & privacy when brought home—so that finally we yielded for the first day."[14]

The Seventh Ohio Militia placed the casket, covered in fine black silk, in the courthouse rotunda. A large American flag was draped overhead and acted as a canopy under which people came to pay their respects. The gas lights in the room flickered and cast a dim, soft glow over the coffin and the mourners.[15] After lying in state throughout the day, Lytle's casket was moved to the Broadwell house where family and close friends had gathered. Among the mourners was Alfred Pirtle, who had a promise to keep.

A little more than a month before, Lytle and Pirtle sat beside a fire and reminisced about the old days. They talked about their families and friends. Before resuming their march that night, Lytle told Pirtle about his one true love and asked his friend to deliver a message to her. Tell her, he said, "That I shall go on loving her, always...." As Pirtle entered the still, dark room where Lytle's body reposed, he saw the woman Lytle had identified as "the lady of his heart." She sat silently beside the casket, alone. Pirtle quietly moved over beside her and delivered the message from his friend. Sed Doremus murmured a few words of acknowledgment. Pirtle then left her. She kept her silent vigil "in solitary grief, til the household awakened."[16] For the rest of that long night, and the rest of her life, she remembered.

Chapter 22

The Funeral

The funeral of William Haines Lytle was conducted on Thursday, October 22, 1863. It was a beautiful day in the Queen City. The air was warm. The fall colors were near their peak. Pirtle noticed the beauty of the leaves and thought about how his friend "would have appreciated all their magnificence in their autumnal robes."[1]

The 14 pall bearers, including future president of the United States James Garfield, received their sashes and walked over to the Broadwell house where the body lay. A little before two o'clock the Honor Guard from the Tenth Ohio brought out the body and placed it in the hearse. Six milk white horses, each with a black ostrich feather on its head, were harnessed to the hearse. The coffin was covered with the American flag, a hat, sword, wreaths, and flowers. On either side of the hearse were the pall bearers in full military dress. The procession moved to Christ Church Cathedral on Fourth Street where the service would take place.[2]

Once the church doors were opened, at first only ladies were permitted to enter to prevent overcrowding. After they had taken their seats, dignitaries and others entered. The mourners could hear the band playing a dirge as it approached from the outside. The church organist began to play and added the organ's deep tones to the somber scene. Bishop Charles Pettit McIlvaine (who had consecrated Leonidas "The Fighting Bishop" Polk here years before) and the Rev. John W. McCarty met the cortege at the front entrance of the church and led them into the chancel. The congregation silently rose and remained standing as they passed.[3]

The casket was placed at the front of the church as Miss Josephine Ayers, the church organist, played Handel's beautiful and majestic "Dead March" from the oratorio "Saul." Will loved music. His sisters knew that. He used to sing to them. Now they would sing to him. The choir, augmented with additional local singers, sang the anthem "Come Ye, Disconsolate." Bishop McIlvaine read the opening service for the burial of the dead. The choir sang William Muhlenberg's "I Would Not Live Alway." The service concluded with prayers and a Mozart funeral anthem.[4]

Chapter 22. The Funeral

This is the interior of the beautiful Christ Church Cathedral in Cincinnati, as it might have appeared when Lytle's funeral service was conducted there (courtesy of Christ Church Cathedral, Cincinnati, OH).

When the casket was carried out the front of the church to the street, the pallbearers and other mourners beheld an incredible scene. All along the route of the funeral procession, thousands of people stood, silently, waiting for the moment when the body of William Haines Lytle would pass by for the last time. The *Cincinnati Enquirer* recorded, "Every window and doorway swarmed with human beings, while, as far as the eye could reach draped flags and the symbols of mourning betokened that a distinguished military citizen had departed, and the last act of respect to his remains was about to be performed."[5] The *Cincinnati Commercial* noted, "We have not often seen the time when the grief for any public man has been so widespread and so sincere. Our city has lost one of her proudest jewels...." The *Catholic Telegraph* stated, "Such a scene as the streets presented on this day, was never before witnessed in this city."

The funeral procession left the church at 3 o'clock precisely and took thirty minutes to pass the corner of Fourth and Vine Streets.[6] The *Cincinnati Commercial* reported, "So crowded were the streets that at certain points it was with difficulty that the procession moved at all.... Every window and balcony were filled with ladies and children." The article stated, "The sorrow felt for the untimely death of General Lytle has pervaded all classes...."[7]

Elias Haines's burial crypt at Spring Grove Cemetery. This was the second burial plot for Lytle and where his funeral service concluded the evening of Thursday, October 22, 1863, when a final farewell was said in the unsteady light of a single flickering candle (photograph by the author).

A friend would later write to Smith Haines about the day. "His funeral was the largest by far that I have ever seen. From Trinity Church to Brighton the streets were crowded. Barely room was left for the procession to pass. Many of the houses along the entire route had flags hung out draped in mourning."[8]

The line of march was Fourth Street to Race, then north to Seventh, west on Seventh to Plum, north on Plum to Ninth, west on Ninth to Central Avenue, north on Central to Richmond Street, west on Richmond to Baymiller, north on Baymiller to Court, west on Court to Freeman, north on Freeman to Central Avenue. The escort was dismissed at the corner of Freeman and Central and the family continued to the cemetery.[9]

It was nearly dark when the funeral procession reached Spring Grove Cemetery. Soldiers carried the coffin up the little rise to the door of the crypt of his uncle, Elias Haines, where Lytle would be interred beside other family members. The Reverend Mr. McCarty concluded the service by the light of a single candle and then "the doors closed upon all that is earthly of that true orator, poet, gentleman, soldier and leader, William Haines Lytle."[10]

The long shadows had crossed his path for the last time, but as shadows always do at day's end, they pointed toward the dawn.

Epilogue

The fighting did not end after Chickamauga. The war continued and many more men died for their countries. But in the end, as Lytle predicted, the Union was preserved. Not long before the end of the war, on October 24, 1864, Nathaniel Foster and Samuel Broadwell bought for $7,500 the lot where the Lytle monument now stands in Spring Grove Cemetery. On June 15, 1865, all the Lytles whose bodies were in the Haines vault were moved to and buried around the newly completed and installed Lytle Monument. William Haines Lytle is buried in front of the bas relief of the Battle of Chickamauga. As one faces that panel to the right are buried Uncle William Henry Lytle (who was the youngest of William and Eliza's children to die, at age 23), Grandmother Eliza Lytle, and Grandfather William Lytle. To the left of the front of the monument are buried Margaret Lytle, Elizabeth Lytle, and Robert Todd Lytle.[1]

The sisters would never fully recover from the loss of their brother. They had braced themselves each time Will was in a battle for the message that would indicate their worst fears had been realized. The first two falls, although the original reports were bad, ended happily enough with the news from the front that he was still alive and coming home. When the news of his death did come, from Philip Sheridan himself, there was shock. Josie and Lily could not have been prepared for that final message that their loved one was gone.

The sisters did take some comfort in the fact that so many people, some of whom they would never know, wrote to express their grief and offer their condolences. Letters, cards, and tribute poems continued to arrive. One letter, however, that arrived in November of 1864, expressed more than grief. It was also a request.

Emily Perkins of Franklin, Tennessee, wrote to Lily Broadwell and asked for the return of letters between Lytle and Emily's sister, Sophie Lytle. Sophie Ridgely Dashiell Lytle, after the deaths of her husband and General Lytle, visited the Federal camps in Murfreesboro and caught the

The beautiful Lytle monument in Spring Grove Cemetery. Once you enter the cemetery from the Spring Grove Avenue, main gate entrance side, and drive under the railroad archway, the first monument you will see to your left is this. Lytle, his parents, grandparents, and one great uncle are buried around this stone memorial (photograph by the author).

eye of another Ohioan and Hamilton County native, Carter Bassett Harrison (younger brother of Benjamin Harrison). Though he was 14 years younger than Sophie, they married the following June. Carter Harrison found a locket with Lytle's hair in her possession and became enraged. (Emily described Carter Harrison as a "fiercely jealous man..." and said Sophie had constantly worn and treasured the locket before her marriage.) Sophie would be in Cincinnati soon but was afraid to stop by to meet the sisters so would Lily please send the letters to Mrs. Perkins? Mrs. Perkins ended her letter to Lily with this postscript: "I can't but reiterate my request that you will let no one know of this matter. I wish I could explain more fully."[2] Sophie survived that marital setback and lived a long life, passing away on August 4, 1927. She is buried in Murfreesboro beside Carter Bassett Harrison.[3]

After their terrible loss, Lytle's sisters kept their brother's memory alive. Elizabeth "Lily" Haines Lytle Broadwell stayed active in voluntary charity activities and worked to put together a tribute book memorializing her brother. She also assembled a scrapbook full of newspaper articles and letters about her brother stretching all the way back to when he was in school, and his speeches began attracting attention. One of the letters in the scrapbook is the last letter she wrote to him. It was found on his body and returned by the Rebels. She wrote a note in the scrapbook above the copy of the letter that reads, "This letter was in my precious Brother's pocket when he was killed. 'I hate to say good-bye' as it proved my last!" Lily and Sam Broadwell had no children. She passed away at home on January 10, 1890.[4]

Josephine Roberta Lytle Foster, "Josie," was widely

Elizabeth "Lily" Lytle Broadwell, Lytle's beloved little sister. Although close with Josie, Lytle seemed particularly attached to Lily. Her letter was the last one he read from home (from the collection of Virginius Cornick Hall, Jr.).

beloved and known for her charitable work for Christ Episcopal Church. She collaborated with William Henry Venable to assemble and edit a collection of her late brother's poems, *"I Am Dying Egypt Dying," and Other Poems*. Josie dedicated the book "To the Memory of a Beloved Sister Mrs. Elizabeth Haines Broadwell with the hope that in its accomplishment her cherished wish has been fulfilled." Josie passed away at home on December 21, 1898, and was buried in Spring Grove Cemetery. She and her husband had five children: Elizabeth (who died in infancy), Anna Haines Foster, John Moorhead Foster, William Lytle Foster, and Lily Lytle Foster Livingood.[5]

Letters and poems continued to arrive in Cincinnati for many years. An Alabamian named Dr. Hamilton Moore Weedon wrote a poem and sent a copy to the family of General Lytle in 1903. Dr. Weedon's poem described the battle of Chickamauga and near the end Weedon focused his attention on one participant.

> One face was turned toward the stars,
> Who sang of love, and not of wars.
> No arms of queen enfolded there,
> No queen to gently bend her ear;
> The crimson life-tide ebbed away,
> And left but cold and lifeless clay.
> And Lytle's soul that sang so sweet,
> Had placed the stars beneath his feet.
>
> Set in the boundless realms, they say,
> There are fixed stars, so far away,
> That if some power should veil their face,
> Their light would still shine on through space,
> And none on earth would ever know
> That the star had ceased to glow.
>
> So with the poet and his lay;
> His soul the light, his song the ray;
> His soul ere long will take its flight,
> But his song will shine forever bright.[6]

Not all the "tributes" were of such a solemn tone. The *Confederate Veteran*, Volume 3, 1895, ran a parody of "Antony and Cleopatra" on page 243. "I'm Conscripted Smith, Conscripted!" By "John Happy—not by Wm. B. [sic] Lytle or any other man." ("John Happy" was actually a Tennessean named Albert Roberts, president of the American Newspaper and Publishing Company.)[7] Here is the first stanza of "Mr. Happy's" poem:

> I'm conscripted, Smith, conscripted—
> Ebbs the subterfuges fast.
> And the sub-enrolling marshals

> Gather with the evening blast—
> Let thine arms O Smith! support me,
> Hush your gab and close your ear,
> Conscript grabbers close upon you,
> Hunting for you far and near...

Two years later the *Confederate Veteran* did print Lytle's version of "Antony and Cleopatra" with this note: "He was buried with honor by the Confederates, and these verses obtained a wide circulation in the Southern press, with honorable mention of his name."[8]

When the national military park at Chickamauga and Chattanooga was dedicated September 19 and 20, 1895, aging veterans gathered on that now peaceful ground. General Rosecrans attended the ceremony. Rosecrans said, "I was standing here with my staff when Lytle came up at the head of his brigade. He saluted as he rode by, and in less than fifteen minutes his horse came galloping back without a rider." A pyramid of cannonballs marked the spot near where Lytle fell.[9]

James Findlay Harrison was a widower at the time of the Battle of Chickamauga. His wife, Caroline, died in the spring of 1863. Lytle's faith in his friend was justified by Harrison's heroic actions at Chickamauga, including saving Alfred Pirtle from certain death or capture. After the war Harrison remarried and moved to Linn County, Kansas, where he was the county surveyor for many years and was well liked by those who knew him. He died February 14, 1907, and was buried in Mound City, Kansas.[10]

Joseph Guthrie, Lytle's aide and "right-bower," served in the Tenth Ohio until June 1864 when the Tenth mustered out of the service. He then moved to Meigs County, Tennessee, and settled in a community known as Ten Mile Stand where he became a United States postmaster in 1866. Guthrie was at the dedication of the Chickamauga National Battlefield in 1895. He died August 26, 1909, and was buried in Ten Mile Stand Cemetery. He was remembered as "a most prominent citizen of Ten Mile" by the local papers.[11]

Sarah Du Bois "Sed" Doremus, "the lady of his heart," continued the work begun by her mother, Sarah Platt Haines, who had founded the Woman's Union Missionary Society of America. Sed traveled the world to help women and wrote numerous articles and pamphlets about her work as well as books about art. Sarah Du Bois Doremus died at her home on January 24, 1915, in New York City. She specifically asked that no memorial of her be printed. A friend of Sed's wrote, "After the terrible shock of his [Lytle's] sudden death she never married...."[12]

Alfred Pirtle continued to serve in the army until poor health caused him to resign his commission in April 1864. Pirtle went home to Louisville and worked in the insurance industry for the rest of his life, founding the

Pirtle, Weaver and Menefee Insurance Company. He married Fannie Nold in 1869 and they had three children. In addition to his insurance work, Pirtle authored more than a dozen papers for the Filson Historical Society in Louisville. He was secretary of the Filson from 1905 to 1917 and president from 1917 to 1923. He died February 2, 1926, and was buried in Cave Hill Cemetery in Louisville. His epitaph simply reads, "He was a soldier of the Union."[13]

The *Chattanooga Sunday Times* on September 13 and 20, 1936, printed a two-part article by Robert Sparks Walker, "The Pyramids of Chickamauga." Walker opened with a description of Lytle Hill, talked about Lytle's life and works, and the battlefield monument, marking the spot where the veterans said Lytle fell, which was a pyramid of cannonballs. "In the hearts of the American people," Walker wrote, "stands another pyramid of a different kind. It is composed of inspiring poems marking the place where William Haines Lytle the poet lives ... there are still tears shed for him, as well as grateful thoughts for the immortal pyramid that he left in the hearts of succeeding generations."

Over the years that original battlefield monument, Lytle's pyramid, fell into disrepair. The cannonballs were removed one way or another until there was no pyramid left at all. However, on September 20, 2013, the 150th

The three-sided, fifteen-high pyramid of eight-inch naval shells marks the spot where Lytle fell the third and final time. Pyramids are often associated with Egypt. "I am dying, Egypt, dying..." (photograph by Randy Duncan).

anniversary of the death of William Haines Lytle, a restored Lytle monument was unveiled. Thanks to the money, time and efforts of the National Park Service, the Friends of Chickamauga and Chattanooga National Military Park (now known as National Park Partners), and the Lytle Camp of the Sons of Union Veterans, and other charitable individuals and organizations, such as the Cincinnati Civil War Round Table, the monument is once again a pyramid.

The Sons of Union Veterans of the Civil War Camp #10 is named after William Haines Lytle. A portrait of Lytle hangs in the museum at the visitor center of the Chickamauga battlefield. There is a display about Lytle at the Perryville Battlefield Museum. Lytle Park in Cincinnati contains informational plaques on the wall on the south side of the park. The Lytle Monument is the first monument you see when you pass under the railroad archway and enter the Spring Grove Cemetery from the main entrance. "Antony and Cleopatra" is still printed in anthologies. There is even a YouTube video of a young person reading that poem, using modern technology to introduce Lytle to the latest generation.

And what of the Lytle mansion? Lytle wanted the house to remain in the family. Unfortunately, at the dawn of the twentieth century, a Cincinnati politician, Michael Mullen, wanted to turn the land around the home into a park. This decision produced an outcry from the people of Cincinnati, who feared the old Lytle homestead would be torn down.[14] The *Cincinnati Enquirer* of January 30, 1904, printed a letter from Lytle's old friend Alfred Pirtle who wrote about his memories of the house. He could imagine Lytle "in deep study and reflection preparing his 'Antony and Cleopatra,'...." Pirtle had visited the house and sat at the desk where Lytle composed the poem. Then Pirtle said, "There are some things better in this life than money and making money, and one of them is to teach those who are to come after us that genius and talent leave behind monuments in the hearts and memories of their fellow citizens, and that such will always be remembered. Let the old house stand as a memorial to William Haines Lytle."

Despite the promise of Councilman Mullen, "I will endeavor to have the city preserve the Lytle homestead..." and the prophecy that "it would be a matter of universal regret in the future were we at this time to destroy this home," the city purchased the land for $242,000 and Lytle Park was dedicated on July 6, 1907. Cincinnati philanthropist Mary Emery offered $50,000 for the upkeep of the Lytle mansion.[15] All to no avail. The *Enquirer* of May 19, 1908, reported, "Oldest Brick House in City Will Be Torn Down and Site Added to Lytle Park." Mullen said, "the memory of General Lytle could be more suitably honored by means of a monument in the park."

The mansion is gone. The city did not erect a statue to Lytle in the

A mute, final tribute to the once great Lytle family, the peach tree in Lytle Park (photograph by the author).

park or anywhere else. There is, however, a bust of Mullen in Lytle Park. There is also an unintended tribute of sorts to the Lytles. Harkening back to the earliest days of the Lytle presence, when the property was called "The Peach Grove," tucked away in the southwest corner of the park, visible from the Arch Street approach, is a peach tree.

Appendix:
The Speech at Bridgeport

> Prophetic and poetic, recalling the past and looking to the future, and acknowledging Northern and Southern valor, Lytle's speech, delivered at Bridgeport on Sunday, August 9, 1863, was his final, formal presentation. These are his words as published in the Tuesday morning, August 18, 1863, edition of the *Cincinnati Commercial*.

Colonel, and Gentlemen of the Tenth Ohio Infantry—My old Friends and Comrades—I cannot tell you how deeply I am touched by this beautiful testimonial. I am very glad to learn that, although you have not for a long time been under my command, you have not forgotten me; and I feel it also an honor that you have taken the trouble to visit me in our camp in the mountains to make me this present in the midst of a campaign, and I fear, at great personal inconvenience. In all sincerity I can say to you that never did the heart of a soldier of the Old Guard beat higher—no, not even when at the hands of the "Little Corporal" himself he received the Cross of the Legion—than does mine today. Come what may to me tomorrow or in days beyond; come what may, as under the leadership of our gallant chief, the invincible Rosecrans, this Army of the Cumberland follows his happy star through the eventful drama of the war, at least for me this token, from the cherished comrades with whom I entered the service, is secure.

So long as in God's providence, my life is spared, I shall look on it, gentlemen, and be reminded of many a stirring incident, both in your experience and mine. It will recall the pale and troubled faces with which men stood in the black shadows that strove before civil war, and the horror that thrilled our breasts when the rebellion first proclaimed itself by overt acts; the revered and holy flag of the nation was fired on by parricidal hands at Charleston. It will bring back to me the fiery and tumultuous gatherings of armed men that rallied to defend the flag. I will remember, as I gaze on it, a thousand incidents connected with our camps at Harrison and Dennison. It will remind me of the long and weary marches when our solitary column threaded the mountain defiles of West Virginia, of the memorable 8th of October at Carnifex Ferry, when your ranks, plowed by shot and shell, stood fast and firm until the enemy fell back across the Gauley under cover of the night, the movement masked by darkness and the roar of the mountain stream. It will remind me of the brave Milroy; of Fitzgibbon, the color bearer; of Kavanaugh and Kennedy, of many a hero soldier whose name we will keep in memory; of that red autumnal day, at Chaplin Hills, when Jackson, Terrill, Jones and Campbell fell, their names crowned with the deathless laurel, when in your own brigade, the chivalry of Ohio and Kentucky, and Indiana and Michigan, added a new and glorious leaf to the somber annals of the Dark and Bloody Ground.

I will be reminded too, as I gaze upon its emerald and its shamrock, the significant emblems with which your taste and the craft of the artisan have enriched it, of that gallant and beautiful island of the sea, the devotion of whose children to my country and their country, has been so gloriously manifested in this hour of her bittersweet travail.

String with fresh cords the Irish harp, worn with recounting the triumphs of your race, to breathe in new and yet loftier daring during this rebellion. Let the pale cheek of Erin, as she watches across the deep, crimson with exultation at the names of Corcoran and Meagher, and the records of your own gallant regiment, the armed witness before this, your generation, to the undying fame of Richard Montgomery.

I will not deny, gentlemen, that, when on reporting to this department, I found you were to be no longer in my command, I felt that sense of loneliness and isolation natural to one whose old army associations were broken up. My present command will pardon me for saying this, I know, for, in my judgment, no man who forgets his old friends deserves to make new ones. But long since I have felt perfectly at home, and I cannot let this occasion pass without expressing to the officers and men of the First Brigade my heartfelt thanks for the warm and generous welcome they have awarded to a stranger. Gentlemen of the Tenth Ohio, you see around you your brethren in arms, the men of Sheridan's division; men from the Northwest, from the clans of the people who pitch their tents on the prairies of Illinois and Michigan and Wisconsin, and by the shores of the great lakes—veterans of Pea Ridge, Perryville, and Stone River. When the next fight comes on, may they and the old Tenth stand shoulder to shoulder, and see by whom, in glorious emulation, our battle-flags into the ranks of the enemy can be flung the farthest and followed the closest. Nor will it diminish your interest in this brigade to tell you it was once commanded by the pure and heroic Sill—Sill, whom you knew so well last year, during your campaign in Northern Alabama. Than his, the war has developed no nobler spirit. The Military Academy at West Point might point to his name, alone, and stand fast in the affections of the people. Ohio in no braver or better blood has sealed her devotion to the Union.

> Him shall no sunshine from the field of azure,
> No drumbeat from the wall—
> No morning gun, from the black fort's embrasure,
> Awaken with its call.

But his name will be embalmed in the praise of states, and this, his old brigade, at Chattanooga, or Atlanta, or in Eastern Tennessee, or wherever its proud banners flaunt the sky will cherish his memory and avenge his fall.

    But, gentlemen, I know your time is limited, and that I must not detain you too long. Rest assured that I shall follow the military career of each and all of you with the deepest solicitude. The third year of the war is upon us. How fierce has been the struggle, our vast national debt and shattered ranks bear witness. Whether the end is near or not, I cannot tell. The past months will be forever memorable for the splendid triumphs of our arms, and to the eyes of hope the sky is flushed with faint light and the morning seems near at hand. But come victory or come defeat, come triumph come disaster, this I know, that against Rebels in the field or traitors at home, despite the plots of weak-kneed and cowardly politicians of the North and the machinations of foreign despots and aristocrats, the scarred and bronzed veterans of the warlike West, the men on whose banners are inscribed Mill Springs and Donelson, Pea Ridge and Vicksburg, Shiloh, Carnifex and Stone River, will make no terms, accept no truce, indorse no treaty, until the military power of the rebellion is crushed forever, and the supremacy of the National Government acknowledged from the Potomac to the Rio Grande.

    Am I told that Union restored by force of arms is not worth fighting for? Am I told that if the states now in revolt are whipped in fair fight—beaten and humiliated—they will be unworthy and degraded members of the Union? We must have peace first, says a certain school of politicians, and then, if we can, we will argue the South into a reconstruction. In other words, these gentlemen would have the Government and the loyal masses of the country drain to the dregs the bitter cup which they would dash from the hands of traitors and Rebels. The territory you have occupied is to be abandoned, the public property, the dockyards, and fortresses you have recaptured after two years of war, are to be surrendered, the victorious armies of the Mississippi, the Cumberland, and the Potomac, followed by the jeers and scoffs of the enemy, are to sneak, with arms reversed and flags trailed in the dust, across the Northern border, and your Government—the

Government of Washington, and Jefferson, and Jackson—is to cower, dishonored and disgraced, a byword and hissing among the nations. If the rebel armies (I will not say rebel States, for it is not against the States, nor their constitutional rights, we wage war), if the rebel armies, and the oligarchs who control them, have their pride broken, and their prestige humbled, let them blame themselves. They have sown the wind, let them reap the whirlwind, till the bloody problem is finally worked out; eye to eye, foot to foot, sword to sword, bayonet to bayonet; if need be, for ten years longer, with iron hearts, and iron fleets, and iron hail, this generation of loyal men will, by God's grace, endure its heavy cross, and until the broad daylight of peace and order and victory shall come, will stand to arms.

And then for you, soldiers—soldiers, but freemen and armed citizens of the Republic—it will be for you to remember the Roman saying, "*Vel pace, vel bello, clarum fieri licet,*" or, as old Milton has paraphrased it, "Peace has her victories, no less renowned than war." It will be for you to look to it that those arbitrary war measures, justified by the awful presence of a rebellion, whose like the world never saw before, justified by the maxim that "the safety of the Republic is the supreme law," die, with the necessities which gave them birth. It will be for you to see that the powers of the Government are restricted to their lawful and appropriate channels; that each State has its full and perfect rights under the constitution, awarded to it; and, finally, through the instrumentality of the ballot box, it will be for you to put the seal of eternal political damnation on those subtle and designing demagogues, whose disaffection and disloyalty to the county have already prolonged the war, and today, more than all other agencies, feed the unholy fires of treason, riot and insurrection, Mark the prediction, that when the war is over, it will be to the men of this human army, more than to any others, that the people of the Southern States will look for a wise, generous, patriotic conservatism.

They will trust you because of your unflinching and unwavering loyalty to your great cause; they will respect you as one brave man, even though overcome, respects another with whom he has measured swords. The government of Jefferson Davis may flatter the political apostates of the North for military purposes, but I mistake the character of the Southern men, if, while they hug the treason, they do not scorn the traitor.

It will be for you, above all others, when this rebellion has spent its strength, to recall to the minds of the people, the admonition:

> "It is well to have a giant's strength,
> But oh, 'tis tyranny to use like a giant."

To heal up the sores and scars, and cover up the bloody footprints that war will leave; to bury in oblivion all animosities against your former foe; and chivalrous as you are brave, standing on forever stricken fields, memorable in history, side by side with the Virginian, the Mississippian, or Alabamian, to carve on bronze or marble the glowing epitaph that tells us of Southern as well as Northern valor.

That the day of ultimate triumph for the Union arms, sooner or later, will come, I do not doubt, for I have faith in the courage, the wisdom, and the justice of the people. It may not be for all of us here to-day to listen to the chants that greet the victor, nor to hear the bells ring out the new nuptials of the States. But those who do survive can tell, at least, to the people, how their old comrades, whether in the skirmish or the charge, before the rifle-pit or the redan, died with their harness on, in the great war for the Union and Liberty.

Chapter Notes

Abbreviations:
CMC: Cincinnati Museum Center
FHS: The Filson Historical Society
OR: *The War of the Rebellion: A Compilation of the Official Records of the Union and Confederate Armies*

Introduction

1. Walker, *Lookout: The Story of a Mountain*, 126–142; *The Chattanooga Daily Times*, November 24, 1946.
2. Zeitlin, "Poetry to Ease the Final Passage," Cornell University Press Blog. Retrieved from: https://www.cornellpress.cornell.edu/poetry-to-ease-the-final-passage/ and email exchanges with author.

Chapter 1

1. National Park Service, "The Ohio River," https://www.nps.gov/articles/the-ohio-river.htm.
2. Suess, *Lost Cincinnati*, 134; Carter, *The Lytle Family of Antebellum Cincinnati*, 61, 62.
3. Greve, *Centennial History of Cincinnati*, 501; Hall, *General William Lytle Gentleman Surveyor & Prominent Cincinnatian (1770–1831)*, 101; Carter, *The Lytle Family of Antebellum Cincinnati*, 249.
4. Carter, *The Lytle Family of Antebellum Cincinnati*, 65; Lytle Papers, Mss qL996p, Box 35, Folder 5, Letter 5 for piano forte receipt, CMC.
5. *The Cincinnati Enquirer*, March 28, 1919; Vitz, "A Brief History of Lytle Square, 1789–1964," 112.
6. Hall, *General William Lytle Gentleman Surveyor (1770–1831)*, 15; Carter, *The Lytle Family of Antebellum Cincinnati*, 380.
7. Hall, *General William Lytle Gentleman Surveyor & Prominent Cincinnatian (1770–1831)*, 15; Carter, *The Lytle Family of Antebellum Cincinnati*, 380.
8. Lytle, "Personal Narrative of William Lytle," 5–7.
9. Cramer, *The Navigator*, 37, 73.
10. Davidson, *The Tennessee Volume One*, 142; Banta, *The Ohio*, 155–159.
11. Hall, *General William Lytle Gentleman Surveyor & Prominent Cincinnatian (1770–1831)*, 19–20.
12. "Four Lytles" by Charles Livingood, Lytle Papers, Mss qL996p, Box 38, CMC; Banta, *The Ohio*, 239–246.
13. Carter, *The Lytle Family of Antebellum Cincinnati*, 347; Hall, *General William Lytle Gentleman Surveyor & Prominent Cincinnatian (1770–1831)*, 47, 49.
14. Hall, *Family Residences*, 19.
15. Hall, *Family Residences*, 19.
16. Carter, *The Lytle Family of Antebellum Cincinnati*, 101–104, 228; "Four Lytles" by Charles Livingood, Lytle Papers, Mss qL996p, Box 38, CMC.
17. Carter, *The Lytle Family of Antebellum Cincinnati*, 60.
18. Hall, *General William Lytle Gentleman Surveyor (1770–1831)*, 36–37.
19. Hall, *The Genesis of an Orchard*, 87–89; Goss, *Cincinnati: The Queen City 1788–1912 Volume 1 and 2*, 89, 442; Vitz "A Brief History of Lytle Square, 1789–1964," 113; "Historical Spots and Places," *Cincinnati Tribune*, June 2, 1896.
20. Carter, *The Lytle Family of Antebellum Cincinnati*, 64, 68.
21. Carter, *The Lytle Family of Antebellum Cincinnati*, 63.
22. Ibid., 133–143; Knepper, *The Official Ohio Lands Book*, 38.

23. Hall, *General William Lytle Gentleman Surveyor (1770–1831)*, 145.
24. Knepper, *The Official Ohio Lands Book*, 9, 19–20; Hall, *General William Lytle Gentleman Surveyor (1770–1831)*, 145.
25. *Kentucky Gazette*, Lexington, Kentucky, November 15, 1803.
26. McGrane, "Orator Bob and the Right of Instruction," 263.
27. Carter, *The Lytle Family of Antebellum Cincinnati*, 154–155.
28. Hall, *General William Lytle Gentleman Surveyor (1770–1831)*, 157; ancestry.com marriage license of William Lytle and Margaret Haines.
29. Carter, *The Lytle Family of Antebellum Cincinnati*, 361.
30. Hall, *Lytle House Time-Line*.
31. Carter, *The Lytle Family of Antebellum Cincinnati*, 16, 181, 183; Carter, ed., *For Honor, Glory and Union*, 5.
32. Carter, *The Lytle Family of Antebellum Cincinnati*, 238–239, 307–308.
33. Venable, *"I Am Dying, Egypt, Dying" and Other Poems*, 4.
34. Letter from RTL to Elizabeth, RTL poem "Elizabeth," No date, Lytle Papers, Mss qL996p, Box 21 Letter 84, CMC.
35. Hall, *General William Lytle Gentleman Surveyor (1770–1831)*, 52.
36. Carter, *The Lytle Family of Antebellum Cincinnati*, 71; McGrane, "Orator Bob and the Right of Instruction," 253.
37. Marriage license of Robert Todd Lytle and Elizabeth Haines. November 30, 1825, https://www.ancestry.com/discoveryui-content/view/313928:61378.
38. Venable, *"I Am Dying, Egypt, Dying" and Other Poems*, 6.

Chapter 2

1. Carter, *The Lytle Family of Antebellum Cincinnati*, 165–166.
2. Letter, July 25, 1828, Robert Todd Lytle to William Lytle, Lytle Papers, Mss qL996p, Box 25A, CMC.
3. Carter, *The Lytle Family of Antebellum Cincinnati*, 165–166.
4. *Charleston Mercury*, April 22, 1825.
5. Carter, *The Lytle Family of Antebellum Cincinnati*, 71.
6. McGrane, "Orator Bob and the Right of Instruction," 254.
7. Carter, *The Lytle Family of Antebellum Cincinnati*, 71, 319.
8. *Ibid.*, 66, 320.
9. Hall, *General William Lytle Gentleman Surveyor (1770–1831)*, 161; *The Weekly Raleigh Register*, May 22, 1829.
10. Carter, *The Lytle Family of Antebellum Cincinnati*, 135, 167–168, 174.
11. Carter, *The Lytle Family of Antebellum Cincinnati*, 165.
12. Carter, ed., *For Honor, Glory and Union*, 5.
13. Carter, *The Lytle Family of Antebellum Cincinnati*, 70, 119, 209, 217.
14. *Ibid.*, 87, 230.
15. Carter, *The Lytle Family of Antebellum Cincinnati*, 315.
16. Library of Congress manuscript. Andrew Jackson letters. Robert Todd Lytle to Andrew Jackson, March 19, 1831.
17. Carter, *The Lytle Family of Antebellum Cincinnati*, 168–169.
18. Carter, ed., *For Honor, Glory and Union*, 8.
19. Carter, *The Lytle Family of Antebellum Cincinnati*, 168, 236.
20. Carter, *The Lytle Family of Antebellum Cincinnati*, 75.
21. Carter, ed., *For Honor, Glory and Union*, 6.
22. Carter, ed., *The Lytle Family of Antebellum Cincinnati*, 133, 150–152, 298.
23. *Ibid.*, 150–151, 187.
24. McGrane, "Orator Bob and the Right of Instruction," 254.
25. Hall, "Moses Dawson, Chronic Belligerent," 186.
26. Wagner, ed., *The Library of Congress Civil War Desk Reference*, 124.
27. Carter, *The Lytle Family of Antebellum Cincinnati*, 40, 151–152.
28. Carter, *The Lytle Family of Antebellum Cincinnati*, 269, 312.
29. Carter, ed., *For Honor, Glory and Union*, 8–9; Carter, *The Lytle Family of Antebellum Cincinnati*, 187–188.
30. Carter, ed., *For Honor, Glory and Union*, 6; Carter, *The Lytle Family of Antebellum Cincinnati*, 170–171.
31. McGrane, "Orator Bob and the Right of Instruction," 255–272; Carter, *The Lytle Family of Antebellum Cincinnati*, 40, 77.
32. Carter, *The Lytle Family of Antebellum Cincinnati*, 152.
33. *Ibid*, 264.
34. *Ibid*.
35. Carter, ed., *For Honor, Glory and Union*, 9.

36. Carter, *The Lytle Family of Antebellum Cincinnati*, 269; Letter, Elizabeth Lytle to Joanna Reilly, n.d., Lytle Papers, Mss qL996p, Box 25A, Letter 192, CMC.

Chapter 3

1. *The Liberator*, Boston, Massachusetts, February 13, 1836.
2. Carter, *The Lytle Family of Antebellum Cincinnati*, 31, 82.
3. Ancestry.com, War of 1812 Applications Files Index; *The Rodney Telegraph*, Rodney, MS, April 25, 1837.
4. Taylor, *Frontiers of Freedom Cincinnati's Black Community*, 52.
5. Ancestry.com, War of 1812 Applications Files Index; *The Rodney Telegraph*, Rodney, MS, April 25, 1837.
6. Axtell, "What Is Still Radical in the Antislavery Legal Practice of Salmon P. Chase," 286; Finkelman, "The Strange Career of Race Discrimination in Antebellum Ohio," 398.
7. Suess, *Hidden History of Cincinnati*, 51–56.
8. Axtell, "What Is Still Radical in the Antislavery Legal Practice of Salmon P. Chase," 286; Finkelman, "The Strange Career of Race Discrimination in Antebellum Ohio," 396–398.
9. *The Rodney Telegraph*, Rodney, MS, April 25, 1837.
10. Knepper, *The Official Ohio Lands Book*, 46–47.
11. *Richmond Enquirer*, Richmond, Virginia, November 16, 1838.
12. Carter, *The Lytle Family of Antebellum Cincinnati*, 83, 153; *Rowan Family Papers* (MSS 418) (2012). Paper 2185, Special Collections Library, Western Kentucky University.
13. *Democrat and Herald*, Wilmington, Ohio, July 13, 1838; *Maumee City Express*, Maumee, Ohio, November 24, 1838.
14. Letter Sam Houston to Robert Todd Lytle, October 26, 1836, Lytle Papers, Mss qL996p, Box 25, Letter 21, CMC.
15. Carter, *The Lytle Family of Antebellum Cincinnati*, 304.
16. Carter, *The Lytle Family of Antebellum Cincinnati*, 231–232.
17. *Ibid.*, 84, 102, 269; *Gettysburg Compiler*, January 28, 1840.
18. Broadwell scrapbook, Lytle Papers, Mss qL996p, Box 40, CMC.
19. Letter, Elizabeth Lytle to an aunt, n.d., Lytle Papers, Mss qL996p, Box 25A, Letter 201, CMC.
20. Carter, *The Lytle Family of Antebellum Cincinnati*, 85.
21. *The Madisonian*, Washington, D.C., February 29, 1840.
22. Scrapbook, Lytle Papers, Mss qL996p, Box 40, CMC.
23. Carter, *The Lytle Family of Antebellum Cincinnati*, 84.
24. Carter, ed., *For Honor, Glory and Union*, 10.
25. Broadwell scrapbook, undated newspaper article from 1840, Lytle Papers, Mss qL996p, Box 40, CMC.
26. Venable, "I Am Dying, Egypt, Dying," and Other Poems, 140–142.
27. Carter, *The Lytle Family of Antebellum Cincinnati*, 117–118, 158
28. Carter, *The Lytle Family of Antebellum Cincinnati*, 189.
29. *Ibid.*, 357–358.
30. *Ibid.*, 233, 313.
31. *Ibid.*, 126
32. *Ibid.*, 324.
33. *Ibid.*, 7, 136, 234, 322.
34. Carter, ed., *For Honor, Glory and Union*, 10.
35. Carter, *The Lytle Family of Antebellum Cincinnati*, 181–182.
36. WHL page of notes, Lytle Papers, Mss qL996p, Box 41, CMC.
37. Venable, "I Am Dying, Egypt, Dying," and Other Poems, 9.
38. Broadwell scrapbook, Lytle Papers, Mss qL996p, Box 40, CMC.
39. *History of Cincinnati and Hamilton County: Their Past and Present*, 181.
40. Letter, Ida Drake to William Haines Lytle, September 17, 1845, Lytle Papers, Mss qL996p, Box 32, Letter 177, CMC.
41. Carter, *The Lytle Family of Antebellum Cincinnati*, 88.
42. *Ibid.*, 191; Carter, ed., *For Honor, Glory and Union*, 10.

Chapter 4

1. Carter, *The Lytle Family of Antebellum Cincinnati*, 122, 132, 191; Carter, ed., *For Honor Glory and Union*, 11.
2. Lytle Papers, Mss qL996p, Box 40, Folder 4, CMC.
3. Carter, *The Lytle Family of Antebellum Cincinnati*, 118.

4. Venable, *"I Am Dying, Egypt, Dying"* *and Other Poems*, 151–152.
5. Carter, *The Lytle Family of Antebellum Cincinnati*, 295–296, 351.
6. Greenberg, *A Wicked War*, 7–9.
7. Ibid., 10.
8. Ibid., 11–16.
9. Ibid., 23, 24.
10. Ibid., 60–63.
11. Ibid., 77–79.
12. Ibid., 101, 102.
13. "Rowan Faily Papers," Special Collections Library, Western Kentucky University.
14. Carter, *The Lytle Family of Antebellum Cincinnati*, 340.
15. Ibid., 143.
16. Carter, ed., *For Honor, Glory and Union*, 45; Carter, *The Lytle Family of Antebellum Cincinnati*, 88.
17. "Sunday Morning," William Haines Lytle to Uncle Elias Haines, Lytle Papers, Mss qL996p, Box 30, Letter 9, CMC.
18. Venable, *"I Am Dying, Egypt, Dying," and Other Poems*, 93.
19. Carter, ed., *For Honor, Glory and Union*, 43, 54.
20. Ibid., 44.
21. Ibid., 45.
22. Ibid., 47.
23. Lytle Papers, Mss qL996p, Box 38, Folder 1, CMC. Carter, ed., *For Honor, Glory and Union*, 45.
24. Carter, ed., *For Honor, Glory and Union*, 54, 58.
25. Carter, *The Lytle Family of Antebellum Cincinnati*, 90, 144, 153.
26. Carter, ed., *For Honor, Glory and Union*, 60–62.
27. Carter, *The Lytle Family of Antebellum Cincinnati*, 335; Carter, ed., *For Honor, Glory and Union*, 12.
28. Carter, *The Lytle Family of Antebellum Cincinnati*, 334–335.
29. Ibid., 334.
30. Lytle Papers, Mss qL996p, Box 38 Folder 1 and Box 41, CMC.
31. Carter, *The Lytle Family of Antebellum Cincinnati*, 89, 345.
32. Carter, ed., *For Honor, Glory and Union*, 12, 32n.

Chapter 5

1. Trollope, *Domestic Manners of the Americans*, 51.
2. Carter, *The Lytle Family of Antebellum Cincinnati*, 32.
3. Carter, "Cincinnatians and Cholera: Attitudes Toward the Epidemics of 1832 and 1849." 32–43.
4. Hodges, "Stephen Foster Cincinnatian and American," 96.
5. Carter, ed., *For Honor, Glory and Union*, 12.
6. Carter, *The Lytle Family of Antebellum Cincinnati*, 123, 130, 271–272, 278.
7. Carter, *The Lytle Family of Antebellum Cincinnati*, 135–136.
8. Cincinnati Directory 1850–51, 59; Nash, *Biographical Sketches of Gen. Pat Cleburne and Gen. T.C. Hindman*, 7–8.
9. Carter, *The Lytle Family of Antebellum Cincinnati*, 379; newspaper clipping courtesy of Bonnie Speeg.
10. Carter, *The Lytle Family of Antebellum Cincinnati*, 337; Carter, ed., *For Honor, Glory and Union*, 13.
11. Carter, ed., *For Honor Glory and Union*, 13–14.
12. Broadwell scrapbook articles, Lytle Papers, Mss qL996p, Box 40, CMC.
13. Broadwell scrapbook articles, Lytle Papers, Mss qL996p, Box 40, CMC.
14. Brill, "Cincinnati's 'Poet Warrior': William Haines Lytle," 195.
15. *Portsmouth Inquirer*, January 30, 1852.
16. Carter, ed., *For Honor, Glory and Union*, 14.
17. Ibid., 19.
18. Carter, *The Lytle Family of Antebellum Cincinnati*, 90.
19. Carter, ed., *For Honor, Glory and Union*, 14.
20. Ibid., 34, note 67; Carter, *The Lytle Family of Antebellum Cincinnati*, 91.
21. Charlotte Haines to William Haines Lytle, January 25, 1853, Lytle Papers, Mss qL996p, Box 32, Letter 290, CMC.
22. Josephine Lytle Foster to William Haines Lytle, n.d., Lytle Papers, Mss qL996p, Box 32, Letter 258, CMC.
23. Carter, *The Lytle Family of Antebellum Cincinnati*, 234, 359; Carter, *For Honor, Glory and Union*, 19.
24. Carter, *The Lytle Family of Antebellum Cincinnati*, 346, 360.
25. Special Collections Library, Western Kentucky University, Elizabeth Lytle to John Rowan, n.d.
26. Carter, *The Lytle Family of Antebellum Cincinnati*, 336–337.

27. Carter, ed., *For Honor, Glory and Union*, 14–15.
28. Edward Lytle to William Haines Lytle, June 28, 1853, Lytle Papers, Mss qL996p, Box 33, Letter 391, CMC.
29. Lytle Papers, Mss qL996p, Box 38 Folder 1, CMC.
30. Carter, ed., *For Honor, Glory and Union*, 16.
31. *The Cincinnati Enquirer*, March 28, 1919; Trollope, *Domestic Manners of the Americans*, 66–67.
32. Taylor, *Frontiers of Freedom Cincinnati's Black Community 1802-1868*, 13.
33. Interview with Bonnie Speeg.
34. Hodges, "Stephen Foster Cincinnatian and American," 87-95.
35. Carter, ed., *For Honor, Glory and Union*, 4, 43n3.
36. Carter, ed., *For Honor, Glory and Union*, 19; Carter, *The Lytle Family of Antebellum Cincinnati*, 98.
37. White, "The World's Oldest Steamboat Company? The U.S. Mail Line," 50–51.
38. Hall, *The Lytle/Foster/Broadwell Lot Spring Grove Cemetery*.

Chapter 6

1. Mach, "Family Ties, Party Realities, and Political Ideology," 19–24.
2. Stampp, ed., *The Causes of the Civil War*, 25.
3. Wagner, ed., *The Library of Congress Civil War Desk Reference*, 111–112; Mach, "Family Ties, Party Realities, and Political Ideology," 25.
4. Carter, ed., *For Honor, Glory and Union*, 16.
5. Greve, *Centennial History of Cincinnati*, 734.
6. Carter, *The Lytle Family of Antebellum Cincinnati*, 91, 98.
7. Lytle Papers, Mss qL996p, Box 33 Letters 463, 464, 465, CMC.
8. Lytle Papers, Mss qL996p, Box 38 Folder 1, CMC
9. Carter, ed., *For Honor, Glory and Union*, 20.
10. Elizabeth Broadwell to WH Lytle, Lytle Papers, Mss qL996p, Box 31, Letter 103, CMC.
11. Carter, ed., *For Honor, Glory and Union*, 20; Carter, *The Lytle Family of Antebellum Cincinnati*, 346.

12. Lytle Papers, Mss qL996p, Box 33, Letter 545, CMC.
13. Lytle Papers, Mss qL996p, Box 38, Folder 7, CMC.
14. Venable, *"I Am Dying, Egypt, Dying," and Other Poems*, 87.
15. Stampp, *America in 1857: A Nation on the Brink*, 4.
16. Carter, ed., *For Honor, Glory and Union*, 17.
17. Carter, *The Lytle Family of Antebellum Cincinnati*, 106–107, 376; Marriage license of Samuel J. Broadwell and Elizabeth Lytle, *ancestry.com*.
18. Carter, *The Lytle Family of Antebellum Cincinnati*, 369.
19. Stampp, *America in 1857: A Nation on the Brink*, 194–195.
20. Kremm, "The Old Order Trembles," 198–204.

Chapter 7

1. Lytle Papers, Mss qL996p, Box 38 Folder 1, CMC; *Catholic Telegraph*, June 27, 1857.
2. Carter, ed., *For Honor, Glory and Union*, 18.
3. *Ibid.*, 18.
4. Niven, *Salmon P. Chase: A Biography*, 292.
5. Carter, *The Lytle Family of Antebellum Cincinnati*, 91–92.
6. CHLA, Lytle Papers, Mss qL996p, Box 40, Broadwell scrapbook.
7. *Cadiz Sentinel*, Cadiz, Ohio, August 13, 1857.
8. Carter, *The Lytle Family of Antebellum Cincinnati*, 279, 280; Hall, Jr., *General William Lytle Gentleman Surveyor (1770–1831)*, 121, 159.
9. *Carroll Free Press*, Carroll, Ohio, November 19, 1857.
10. M.J. Worthington to William Haines Lytle, n.d. Lytle Papers, Mss qL996p, Box 34 Letter 729, CMC.
11. Carter, ed., *For Honor, Glory and Union*, 20n.
12. *Ibid.*, 20.
13. Carter, *The Lytle Family of Antebellum Cincinnati*, 353–354; Carter, ed., *For Honor, Glory, and Union*, 21.
14. July 25, 1858, Edward Lytle to William Haines Lytle, Lytle Papers, Mss qL996p, Box 33, Letter 404, CMC.

15. Tenkotte, ed., *The Encyclopedia of Northern Kentucky*, 366.
16. *Pittsburgh Daily Post*, August 13, 1897.
17. *Cincinnati Enquirer*, January 30, 1904.
18. Thomas Means to William Haines Lytle, Lytle Papers, Mss qL996p, Box 34, Letter 587, CMC.
19. Johnston, "General W.H. Lytle and His Famous Poem; 'I Am Dying Egypt Dying,'" 37.
20. Lytle Papers, Mss qL996p, Box 38, Letter 19, CMC; Suess, *Lost Cincinnati*, 14.
21. Venable, *"I Am Dying, Egypt, Dying," and Other Poems*, 71–73.

Chapter 8

1. Carter, *The Lytle Family of Antebellum Cincinnati*, 361.
2. *Ibid.*, 301
3. *Louisville Daily Courier*, July 16, 1858.
4. Carter, *The Lytle Family of Antebellum Cincinnati*, 273–275.
5. Carter, *The Lytle Family of Antebellum Cincinnati*, 274.
6. *The Library of Congress Civil War Desk Reference*, 121, 123.
7. Stampp, ed., *The Causes of The Civil War Revised Edition*, 159–160; Wagner, ed., *The Library of Congress Civil War Desk Reference*, 64–66.
8. Carter, ed., *For Honor, Glory and Union*, 17.
9. Brill, "Cincinnati's 'Poet Warrior': William Haines Lytle," 194.
10. Howe, *Historical Collections of Ohio in Two Volumes, Volume I*, 834–835.

Chapter 9

1. Carter, ed., *For Honor, Glory and Union*, 3.
2. Goss, *Cincinnati: The Queen City 1788-1912 Volume 1 and 2*, 317, 208; Carter, ed., *For Honor, Glory and Union*, 22; Starr, "Camp Dennison, 1861–1865," 168–175; Carter, *The Lytle Family of Antebellum Cincinnati*, 91.
3. Coggins, *Arms and Equipment of the Civil War*, 21; Wagner, ed., *The Library of Congress Civil War Desk Reference*, 374–376. Endres and Twohig, "With a Father's Affection: Chaplain William T. O'Higgins and the Tenth Ohio Volunteer Infantry," 115.
4. Starr, "Camp Dennison, 1861–1865," 169.
5. *Ibid.*, 169–170.
6. Endres and Twohig. "With a Father's Affection," 105.
7. Taylor, *Frontiers of Freedom Cincinnati's Black Community 1802-1868*, 24.
8. Goss, *Cincinnati: The Queen City 1788-1912 Volume 1 and 2*, 208.
9. Lytle Papers, Box 39 Folder 1, Mss qL996p, CMC.
10. Carter, ed., *For Honor, Glory and Union*, 22.
11. Endres and Twohig, "With a Father's Affection," 105.
12. Carter, ed., *For Honor, Glory and Union*, 22.
13. Venable, *"I Am Dying, Egypt, Dying" and Other Poems*, 20.
14. Broadwell scrapbook article, "Letter from Camp Dennison," Lytle Papers, Mss qL996p, Box 40, CMC.
15. Broadwell scrapbook, article, "Incidents at Camp Harrison," Lytle Papers, Mss qL996p, Boc 40, CMC.
16. "An Emeute," *The Tennessean*, Nashville, June 21, 1861; *Opening Guns: Fort Sumter to Bull Run, 1861*, Nofi, 62.
17. Carter, ed., *For Honor, Glory and Union*, 23, 68; Wagner, ed., *The Library of Congress Civil War Desk Reference*, 403.
18. Carter, ed., *For Honor, Glory and Union*, 69.
19. *Ibid.*, 75, 79.
20. *Cincinnati Daily Press*, April 19, 1861.
21. Endres and Twohig, "With a Father's Affection," 114.
22. Broadwell Scrapbook, Lytle Papers, Mss qL996p, Box 40, CMC.
23. Carter, ed., *For Honor, Glory and Union*, 70–71.
24. *Ibid.*, 72–73.
25. *Ibid.*, 77.
26. *Ibid.*, 81–82.
27. *Sept. 10th 1861, Carnifix Ferry*, West Virginia Division of Tourism and Parks, 1; Shaffer, *The Battle of Carnifex Ferry*, 3.
28. Beatty, *The Citizen-Soldier; or Memoirs of a Volunteer by John Beatty*, 12–13.
29. *Sept. 10th 1861, Carnifix Ferry*, West Virginia Division of Tourism and Parks, 3; Lowry, *September Blood*, 3, 33.
30. *Sept. 10th 1861, Carnifix Ferry*, West Virginia Division of Tourism and Parks, 4.

31. *Ibid.*, 5; Lowry, *September Blood*, 28.
32. Lowry, *September Blood*, 5; Woodworth, *Jefferson Davis and His Generals: The Failure of Confederate Command in the West*, 80.
33. Lowry, *September Blood*, 43.
34. *Ibid.*, 43–47.
35. *Ibid.*, 47.
36. *Sept. 10th 1861, Carnifix Ferry*, West Virginia Division of Tourism and Parks, 9.
37. Lowry, *September Blood*, 69.
38. *Ibid.*, 34–40.
39. *Ibid.*, 69–70.
40. OR Series 1, Volume 5, 165.

Chapter 10

1. *Sept. 10th 1861, Carnifix Ferry*, West Virginia Division of Tourism and Parks, 2.
2. Shaffer, *The Battle of Carnifex Ferry*, 2.
3. OR Series 1, Volume 5, 125, 129; Lowry, *September Blood*, 73–76.
4. Lowry, *September Blood*, 73–76; OR Series 1, Volume 5, 130.
5. Lowry, *September Blood*, 77, 80–82.
6. Lowry, *September Blood*, 80–82; OR S1 V5, 133.
7. "Battle of Carnifex Ferry," *New York Herald*, September 22, 1861.
8. OR Series 1, Volume 5, 136.
9. OR Series 1, Volume 5, 145.
10. *Monroe Sentinel*, Monroe Wisconsin, October 1, 1861.
11. Lowry, *September Blood*, 77, 80–82.
12. *Ibid.*, 80–82; OR Series 1, Volume 5, 133.
13. Lory, *September Blood*, 86–87.
14. *Soldier of Southwestern Virginia: The Civil War Letters of Captain John Preston Sheffey*, Robertson, Jr., 6, 64.
15. *Monroe Sentinel*, Monroe, Wisconsin, October 1, 1861.
16. *Soldier of Southwestern Virginia*, 6, 64.
17. OR Series 1, Volume 5, 136–137.
18. Lowry, *September Blood*, 83–87.
19. *Baltimore Sun*, September 19, 1861.
20. Lowry, *September Blood*, 86–87.
21. *Woodstock Sentinel*, Woodstock, Illinois, October 9, 1861.
22. Lowry, *September Blood*, 98–99.
23. Lowry, *September Blood*, 96, 120; OR Series 1, Volume 5, 131.
24. *Sept. 10th 1861, Carnifix Ferry*, West Virginia Division of Tourism and Parks, 11; OR Series 1, Volume 5, 128.
25. OR Series 1, Volume 5, 147–148.
26. Lowry, *September Blood*, 131–133.
27. "Battle of Carnifex Ferry," *New York Herald*, September 22, 1861.
28. Lowry, *September Blood*, 133–135, 156.
29. Broadwell scrapbook, "The Battle in Western Virginia." Lytle Papers, Mss qL996p, Box 40, CMC.
30. *Official roster of the soldiers of the State of Ohio in the War of the Rebellion, 1861-1866, Vol. 1*, Tenth Regiment Ohio Volunteer Infantry: Three Years' Service: 10th Regiment Ohio Volunteer Infantry: Field and Staff Officers, 293–308.
31. Lowry, *September Blood*, 85; OR Series 1, Volume 5, 133–135.
32. OR Series 1, Volume 5, 134–135; Lowry, *September Blood*, 85.

Chapter 11

1. *Daily Times*, Cincinnati, Tuesday Evening, September 17, 1861.
2. *Western Reserve Chronicle*, Warren, Ohio, October 16, 1861.
3. Broadwell scrapbook, *Wilkes Spirit of the Times*, Lytle Papers, Mss qL996p, CMC.
4. *Ibid*.
5. Carter, ed., *For Honor, Glory and Union*, 24.
6. Broadwell Scrapbook, *Cincinnati Daily Commercial*, November 23, 1861, Lytle Papers, Mss qL996p, Box 40, CMC.
7. Endres and Twohig, "'With a Father's Affection," 111.
8. Carter, ed., *For Honor, Glory and Union*, 87–88.
9. *Cincinnati Daily Press*, December 16, 1861.
10. FHS, Alfred Pirtle diary entry, January 2, 1862, Alfred Pirtle papers, Mss. A P672.31, Filson Historical Society.
11. Speed, *The Union Regiments of Kentucky*, 78–79.
12. FHS, William Haines Lytle to Mrs. Pirtle, February 18, 1862, Alfred Pirtle Papers, Mss. A P672.28, Filson Historical Society.
13. Carter, ed., *For Honor, Glory and Union*, 88.
14. *Ibid.*, 89–90.
15. *Ibid.*, 91; Daniel, *Days of Glory*, 39.
16. OR Series 1, Volume 52, Part 1, 204.

17. Carter, ed., *For Honor, Glory and Union*, 92.
18. *Ibid.*, 24.
19. *Ibid.*, 94, 95.
20. Venable, *"I Am Dying, Egypt, Dying" and Other Poems*, 103.
21. Carter, ed., *For Honor, Glory and Union*, 101–103.
22. *Ibid.*, 96–97.
23. *Ibid.*, 197.

Chapter 12

1. Carter, ed., *For Honor, Glory and Union*, 104.
2. FHS, Alfred Pirtle diary entry, March 1, 1862, Alfred Pirtle papers, Mss. A P672.31 Filson Historical Society.
3. Carter, ed., *For Honor, Glory and Union*, 107.
4. Carter, ed., *For Honor, Glory and Union*, 104–106.
5. Carter, ed., *For Honor, Glory and Union*, 107.
6. OR Series 1, Volume 10 Part 2, 85.
7. Beatty, *The Citizen-Soldier; or Memoirs of a Volunteer by John Beatty*, 120.
8. FHS, Alfred Pirtle diary entry, March 26, 1862, Alfred Pirtle papers, Mss. A P672.31 Filson Historical Society.
9. FHS, Alfred Pirtle diary entry, March 27, 1862, Alfred Pirtle papers, Mss. A P672.31 Filson Historical Society.
10. Venable, *"I Am Dying, Egypt, Dying" and Other Poems*, 25–26.
11. Carter, ed., *For Honor, Glory and Union*, 108.
12. Lytle, *A Wake for the Living: A Family Chronicle*, 148, 177.
13. Carter, ed., *For Honor, Glory and Union*, 108.
14. Lytle, *A Wake for the Living: A Family Chronicle*, 148, 177.
15. Carter, ed., *For Honor, Glory and Union*, 108; Hughes, *Hearthstones: The Story of Historic Rutherford County Homes*, 65.
16. Carter, ed., *For Honor, Glory and Union*, 109; "Capt. F.H. Lytle," *Confederate Veteran*, Volume 20, 1912, 131.
17. FHS, Alfred Pirtle diary entry, March 31, 1862, Alfred Pirtle papers, Mss. A P672.31 Filson Historical Society.
18. FHS, Alfred Pirtle diary entry, April 3, 1862, Alfred Pirtle papers, Mss. A P672.31 Filson Historical Society.
19. FHS, Alfred Pirtle diary entry, April 3 and 14, 1862, Alfred Pirtle papers, Mss. A P672.31 Filson Historical Society.
20. Carter, ed., *For Honor, Glory and Union*, 111.
21. Carter, ed., *For Honor, Glory and Union*, 29.
22. FHS, Alfred Pirtle diary entry, April 3 and 14, 1862, Alfred Pirtle papers, Mss. A P672.31 Filson Historical Society.
23. *Chicago Tribune*, May 2, 1862.
24. FHS, Alfred Pirtle diary entry, April 12 and 15, 1862, Alfred Pirtle papers, Mss. A P672.31 Filson Historical Society.
25. OR Series 1, Volume 10, Part 1, 877–878.
26. Carter, ed., *For Honor, Glory and Union*, 114.
27. OR Series 1, Volume 10, Part 1, 876.
28. Carter, ed., *For Honor, Glory and Union*, 115
29. Beatty, *The Citizen-Soldier; or Memoirs of a Volunteer by John Beatty*, 143.
30. OR Series 1, Volume 10, Part 2, 295.
31. Warner, *Generals in Blue*, 511.
32. Karaminski, "Civilians, Soldiers, and the Sack of Athens, Alabama," 47–51; OR, Series I, Volume 10, Part II, 212.
33. Karaminski, "Civilians, Soldiers, and the Sack of Athens, Alabama," 47–51; Warner, *Generals in Blue*, 511–512.
34. Carter, ed., *For Honor, Glory and Union*, 117.
35. Rohr, *Incidents of the War: The Civil War Journal of Mary Jane Chadick*, 44.
36. Venable, *"I Am Dying, Egypt, Dying" and Other Poems*, 104.
37. Carter, ed., *For Honor, Glory and Union*, 120–122.
38. *Ibid.*, 121–122.
39. FHS, Alfred Pirtle diary entry, June 14 and 17, 1862, Alfred Pirtle papers, Mss. A P672.31 Filson Historical Society.
40. Carter, ed., *For Honor, Glory and Union*, 123.
41. *Ibid.*, 124–127.
42. FHS, Alfred Pirtle diary entry, July 11, 1862, Alfred Pirtle papers, Mss. A P672.31 Filson Historical Society.
43. Carter, ed., *For Honor, Glory and Union*, 128.
44. FHS, Alfred Pirtle diary entry, July 15, 1862, Alfred Pirtle papers, Mss. A P672.31 Filson Historical Society.

Chapter 13

1. "Military Matters," *The Catholic Telegraph*, August 13, 1862; Carter, ed., *For Honor, Glory and Union*, 130.
2. "Military Matters," *The Catholic Telegraph*, August 13, 1862.
3. "Military Matters," *The Catholic Telegraph*, August 13, 1862.
4. FHS, Alfred Pirtle diary entry, July 26, 1862, Alfred Pirtle papers, Mss. A P672.31 Filson Historical Society.
5. "Military Matters," *The Catholic Telegraph*, August 13, 1862.
6. Carter, ed., *For Honor, Glory and Union*, 132-133.
7. Ibid., 134.
8. Ibid., 136; Carter, *The Lytle Family of Antebellum Cincinnati*, 342-343.
9. OR Series 1, Volume 16, Part 2, 442.
10. Rohr, *Incidents of the War: The Civil War Journal of Mary Jane Chadick*, 96.
11. FHS, Alfred Pirtle diary entry, August 30, 1862, Alfred Pirtle papers, Mss. A P672.31 Filson Historical Society.
12. Kleber, ed., *The Kentucky Encyclopedia*, 783.
13. Noe, *Perryville: This Grand Havoc of Battle*, 27. Woodworth, *Jefferson Davis and His Generals*, 139.
14. OR Series 1, Volume 16, Part 2, 442, 443, 450.
15. Rohr, *Incidents of the War: The Civil War Journal of Mary Jane Chadick*, 101.
16. FHS, Alfred Pirtle diary entry, August 31, 1862, Alfred Pirtle papers, Mss. A P672.31 Filson Historical Society.
17. *The Daily Milwaukee News*, October 7, 1862.
18. FHS, Alfred Pirtle diary entry, August 31, 1862, Alfred Pirtle papers, Mss. A P672.31 Filson Historical Society.
19. Carter, ed., *For Honor, Glory and Union*, 138.
20. OR Series 1, Volume 16, Part 2, 477.
21. FHS, Alfred Pirtle diary entry, September 4, 1862, Alfred Pirtle papers, Mss. A P672.31 Filson Historical Society.
22. Carter, ed., *For Honor, Glory and Union*, 138-139.
23. Cameron, *Staff Ride Handbook for the Battle of Perryville: 8 October 1862*, **88**-90.
24. Morris, *Christ Church 1817-1967 Cincinnati*, 46-47.
25. Cameron, *Staff Ride Handbook for the Battle of Perryville*, 10-11; Warner, *Generals in Blue*, 116.
26. Noe, *Perryville: This Grand Havoc of Battle*, 112.
27. OR Series 1, Volume 16, Part 1, 1024-1025.
28. Noe, *Perryville: This Grand Havoc of Battle*, 124-127.
29. Noe, *Perryville: This Grand Havoc of Battle*, 144-145.
30. Ibid., 145
31. Kleber, ed., *The Kentucky Encyclopedia*, 418-419.
32. Noe, *Perryville: This Grand Havoc of Battle*, 128-129; Kolakowski, *The Civil War at Perryville: Battling for the Bluegrass*, 83.
33. Ibid., 370-371
34. Noe, *Perryville: This Grand Havoc of Battle*, 133.
35. OR Series 1, Volume 16, Part 1, 1087.
36. Noe, *Perryville: This Grand Havoc of Battle*, 135-139.
37. Ibid., 135-139.
38. OR Series 1, Volume 16, Part 1, 1024-1025.

Chapter 14

1. Noe, *Perryville: This Grand Havoc of Battle*, 107-111.
2. Kolakowski, *The Civil War at Perryville: Battling for the Bluegrass*, 87.
3. OR Series 1, Volume 16, Part 1, 69.
4. Noe, *Perryville: This Grand Havoc of Battle*, 373-374.
5. Dyer, *A Compendium of the War of the Rebellion*, 1135, 1150, 1204, 1275-1276, 1497.
6. Noe, *Perryville: This Grand Havoc of Battle*, 160.
7. OR Series 1, Volume 16, Part 1 1085-1086.
8. OR Series 1, Volume 16, Part 1 1088, 1098-1099.
9. Noe, *Perryville: This Grand Havoc of Battle*, 147-152.
10. OR Series 1, Volume 16, Part 1, 1025, 1039.
11. Noe, *Perryville: This Grand Havoc of Battle*, 164.
12. Ibid. 164-165 OR Series 1, Volume 16, Part 1, 69.
13. Wagner, ed., *The Library of Congress Civil War Desk Reference*, 504-508.
14. Logsdon, *Eyewitnesses at the Battle of Perryville*, 13.

15. OR Series 1, Volume 16, Part 1, 1044.
16. Logsdon, *Eyewitnesses at the Battle of Perryville*, 11; Noe, *Perryville: This Grand Havoc of Battle*, 176.
17. Logsdon, *Eyewitnesses at the Battle of Perryville*, 11-13.
18. OR Series 1, Volume 16, Part 1, 67-71.
19. Holman, *Battle of Perryville Movement Maps*, 12:00 map; Noe, *Perryville: This Grand Havoc of Battle*, 180; *The Cincinnati Enquirer*, October 14, 1862; Carter, ed., *For Honor. Glory and Union*, 112.
20. Noe, *Perryville: This Grand Havoc of Battle*, 214-215.
21. *Retreat from Gettysburg: Battles and Leaders of the Civil War*, 57.
22. Noe, *Perryville: This Grand Havoc of Battle*, 272.
23. Holman, *Battle of Perryville Movement Maps*, 1:15 Map.
24. OR Series 1, Volume 16, Part 1, 67-71, 1047.
25. Holman, *Battle of Perryville Movement Maps*, 2:00 and 2:15 maps.
26. *Ibid.*, 2:30 map.
27. Noe, *Perryville: This Grand Havoc of Battle*, 221-222; Kolakowski, *The Civil War at Perryville: Battling for the Bluegrass*, 119. Logsdon, *Eyewitnesses at the Battle of Perryville*, 29.
28. Holman, *Battle of Perryville Movement Maps*, 2:45 map.
29. Noe, *Perryville: This Grand Havoc of Battle*, 216, 218.
30. Holman, *Battle of Perryville Movement Maps*, 3:00 map; Logsdon, *Eyewitnesses*, 31; OR Series 1, Volume 16, Part I, 71.
31. Holman, *Battle of Perryville Movement Maps*, 3:00 map.
32. Logsdon, *Eyewitnesses at the Battle of Perryville*, 49.
33. Noe, *Perryville: This Grand Havoc of Battle*, 238-241.
34. OR Series 1, Volume 16, Part 1, 1040.
35. Holman, *Battle of Perryville Movement Maps*, 3:30 map.
36. Noe, *Perryville: This Grand Havoc of Battle*, 225, 226, 228; OR Series 1, Volume 16, Part 1, 70.
37. Noe, *Perryville: This Grand Havoc of Battle*, 229.
38. Perryville Battlefield marker, "The 15th Kentucky Infantry (Union)."
39. Kolakowski, *The Civil War at Perryville: Battling for the Bluegrass*, 119-121; Holman, *Battle of Perryville Movement Maps*, 3:45 map.
40. *Ibid.*, 39-40, 263-264.
41. OR Series 1, Volume 52, Part 1, 51-53.
42. OR Series 1, Volume 52, Part 1, 52.
43. OR Series 1, Volume 52, Part 1, 51-53.
44. Noe, *Perryville: This Grand Havoc of Battle*, 268-269.
45. Noe, *Perryville: This Grand Havoc of Battle*, 268-269; OR Series 1, Volume 16, Part 1, 1126-1127; report of BG Bushrod R. Johnson, *The Cincinnati Enquirer*, October 14, 1862.
46. Noe, *Perryville: This Grand Havoc of Battle*, 271.
47. *Ibid.*, 276, 305; Interview with Chuck Lott, historian, Perryville Battlefield.
48. Beatty, *The Citizen-Soldier; or Memoirs of a Volunteer by John Beatty*, 180-182.
49. Logsdon, *Eyewitnesses at the Battle of Perryville*, 82.
50. *New York Herald*, October 15, 1862.
51. Noe, *Perryville This Grand Havoc of Battle*, 261.
52. *Ibid.*, 306, 314.
53. Noe, *Perryville: This Grand Havoc of Battle*, 373-374.

Chapter 15

1. OR Series 1, Volume 16, Part 1, 1031, 1088.
2. Lytle Papers, Mss qL996p, Box 38 Folders 1 and 4, CMC.
3. Johnston, "General W.H. Lytle and His Famous Poem; 'I Am Dying Egypt Dying,'" 40-41; OR Series 1, Volume 16, Part I, 71.
4. Wagner, ed., *The Library of Congress Civil War Desk Reference*, 585, 596-597.
5. OR Series 2, Volume 5, 154; OR Series 2 Volume 4, 623; Venable, *"I Am Dying, Egypt, Dying" and Other Poems*, 29.
6. Venable, *"I Am Dying, Egypt, Dying" and Other Poems*, 30.
7. October 13, 1862, to Lily Broadwell from Sed Doremus' sister, Lottie Doremus, Lytle Papers, Mss qL996p, Box 32, Letter 195, CMC.
8. Venable, *"I Am Dying, Egypt, Dying" and Other Poems*, 131.
9. Logsdon, *Eyewitnesses at the Battle of Perryville*, 120.

10. Carter, ed., *For Honor, Glory and Union*, 26.
11. OR Series, 1 Volume 16, Part 1, 71-72.
12. Johnston, "General W.H. Lytle and His Famous Poem; 'I Am Dying Egypt Dying,'" 42.
13. Carter, ed., *For Honor, Glory and Union*, 154.
14. *Ibid.*, 164, 192.
15. *Ibid.*, 239, 256.
16. *Sketches of War History 1861-1865: Papers Read Before the Ohio Commandery of the Military Order of the Loyal Legion of the United States 1883-1886*, 29; Carter, ed., *For Honor, Glory and Union*, 148.
17. Carter, ed., *For Honor, Glory and Union*, 151, note 4; Speed, *The Union Regiments of Kentucky*, 79.
18. Beatty, *The Citizen-Soldier; or Memoirs of a Volunteer by John Beatty*, 222; *The Library of Congress Civil War Desk Reference*, 383.
19. *The Library of Congress Civil War Desk Reference*, 406.
20. Lytle Papers, Mss qL996p, Box 31, Letter 107, CMC.
21. Carter, ed., *For Honor, Glory and Union*, 152.
22. Carter, *The Lytle Family of Antebellum Cincinnati*, 343-344.
23. Carter, ed., *For Honor, Glory and Union*, 154.
24. *Ibid.*, 152.
25. *Ibid.*, 153; Lytle, *A Wake for The Living: A Family Chronicle*, 177.
26. Venable, *"I Am Dying, Egypt, Dying" and Other Poems*, 106-107.
27. Carter, ed., *For Honor, Glory and Union*, 163.
28. Lytle Papers, Mss qL996p, Box 41, Item 4, CMC.
29. Carter, ed., *For Honor, Glory and Union*, 155.
30. William Haines Lytle folder, fold3.com.
31. Carter, ed., *For Honor, Glory and Union*, 158.
32. OR Series 1, Volume 30, Part 3, 271.
33. Warner, *Generals in Blue*, 437-439.
34. Dyer, *A Compendium of the War of the Rebellion*, 1061, 1083-1084, 1115, 1290, 1683.
35. Carter, ed., *For Honor, Glory and Union*, 158-159.
36. *Ibid.*, 161.
37. *Ibid.*, 158-159.
38. *Ibid.*, 173-174.
39. *Ibid.*, 175-176.
40. Powell, *The Maps of Chickamauga*, 2-3.
41. *Ibid.*, 8-9.
42. Lytle, *A Wake for the Living: A Family Chronicle*, 179.
43. Emily Perkins to Elizabeth Broadwell, Lytle Papers, Mss qL996p, Box 34, Letter 626, CMC.
44. OR Series 1, Volume 23, Part 1, 517-518.
45. *Ibid.*
46. Michigan State University Archives, Henry A. Goodale Recollection.
47. Powell, *The Maps of Chickamauga*, 10-14.
48. OR Series 1, Volume 23, Part 1, 517-518.
49. Carter, ed., *For Honor, Glory and Union*, 182.
50. *Ibid.*, 178, 185-188.

Chapter 16

1. Carter, ed., *For Honor, Glory and Union*, 189-190.
2. William Haines Lytle to J Findlay Harrison, n.d., Lytle Papers, Mss qL996p, Box 34, Letter 561, CMC.
3. OR Series 1, Volume 52, 421-423.
4. Carter, ed., *For Honor, Glory and Union*, 190-192.
5. Davidson, *The Tennessee: Volume Two The New River*, 40-48.
6. *Cincinnati Commercial*, August 18, 1863.
7. Robertson, *River of Death: The Chickamauga Campaign Volume One The Fall of Chattanooga*, 150; *Cincinnati Commercial*, August 18, 1863; FHS, Alfred Pirtle to his mother, August 10, 1863, Alfred Pirtle papers Mss. A P672.28 Filson Historical Society.
8. *Cincinnati Commercial*, August 18, 1863.
9. Carter, ed., *For Honor, Glory and Union*, 222-226; *Cincinnati Commercial*, August 18, 1863.
10. *Cincinnati Commercial*, August 18, 1863.
11. FHS, Alfred Pirtle to his mother, August 10, 1863, Alfred Pirtle papers Mss. A P672.28 Filson Historical Society.

12. Hinton, *Poems by Richard Realf*, xxi, xxvi, xxix, cvii, 149; *Parsons Daily Eclipse*, September 23, 1898; Parsons, KS, *Report of the Select Committee of the Senate Appointed to Inquire into the Late Invasion and Seizure of the Public Property at Harper's Ferry.*
13. Hinton, *Poems by Richard Realf*, 32.
14. OR Series 1, Volume 30, Part 3, 14.
15. OR Series 1, Volume 30, Part 3, 39.
16. Carter, ed., *For Honor, Glory & Union*, 195–196.
17. *Ibid.*
18. OR Series 1, Volume 30, Part 3, 102, 117, 152.
19. Robertson, *River of Death: The Chickamauga Campaign Volume One The Fall of Chattanooga*, 255.
20. Cozzens, *This Terrible Sound: The Battle of Chickamauga*, 41.
21. OR Series 1, Volume 30, Part 3, 234–235; Robertson, *River of Death: The Chickamauga Campaign Volume One The Fall of Chattanooga*, 309, 316–317.
22. Carter, ed., *For Honor, Glory and Union*, 198–200.
23. *Ibid.*
24. OR Series 1, Volume 30, Part 3, 255–256.

Chapter 17

1. OR Series 1, Volume 30, Part 3, 285.
2. FHS, Alfred Pirtle to his mother, September 2, 1863, Alfred Pirtle papers Mss. A P672.28 Filson Historical Society.
3. Pirtle, *Leaves from My Journal*, 11–12.
4. Pirtle, *Leaves from My Journal*, 3–5.
5. OR, Series 1, Volume 30, Part 3, 582.
6. Pirtle, *Leaves from My Journal*, 5–6.
7. *Ibid.*
8. Pirtle, *Leaves from My Journal*, 6–8.
9. Pirtle, *Leaves from My Journal*, 7.
10. Venable, *"I Am Dying, Egypt, Dying" and Other Poems*, 171–172
11. Pirtle, *Leaves from My Journal*, 9.
12. *Ibid.*, 10.
13. FHS, Alfred Pirtle to his sister, September 8, 1863, Alfred Pirtle papers Mss. A P672.28 Filson Historical Society.
14. Pirtle, *Leaves from My Journal*, 10.
15. Robertson, *Staff Ride Handbook for the Battle of Chickamauga*, 50–51.
16. Pirtle, *Leaves from My Journal*, 12.
17. Woodworth, *Jefferson Davis and His Generals*, 228.
18. Wagner, ed., *The Library of Congress Civil War Desk Reference*, 33.
19. *Ibid.*, 229.
20. Cozzens, *This Terrible Sound*, 59–60.
21. Pirtle, *Leaves from My Journal*, 13–15.
22. Walker, *Lookout: The Story of a Mountain*, 82.
23. OR Series 1, Volume 30, Part 3, 1003–1004.
24. Pirtle, *Leaves from My Journal*, 16.
25. OR Series 1, Volume 30, Part 3, 606.
26. OR Series 1, Volume 30, Part 3, 1007–1008.
27. Pirtle, *Leaves from My Journal*, 15–18.
28. OR Series 1, Volume 30, Part 3, 648, 675.
29. Pirtle, *Leaves from My Journal*, 19.
30. Pirtle, *Leaves from My Journal*, 19–20.
31. OR Series 1, Volume 30, Part 3, 676, 678.
32. Pirtle, *Leaves from My Journal*, 18–21.
33. *Ibid.*, 21; Robertson, *Staff Ride Handbook for the Battle of Chickamauga*, 173.
34. Broadwell scrapbook, letter, Rye Beach September 2, 1863, Lytle Papers, Mss qL996p, Box 40, CMC.
35. Pirtle, *Leaves from My Journal*, 22–23.
36. Alfred Pirtle to Lily Foster Livingood, December 25, 1923, Lytle Papers, Mss qL996p, Box 34 Letter 638, CMC.
37. FHS, Alfred Pirtle Papers, *Lytle's Last Sacrifice*, Mss. A P672, Filson Historical Society.
38. Pirtle, *Leaves from My Journal*, 23.
39. FHS, Alfred Pirtle Papers, *Lytle's Last Sacrifice*, Mss. A P672, Filson Historical Society.

Chapter 18

1. Cozzens, *This Terrible Sound: The Battle of Chickamauga*, 71–74.
2. Robertson. *Staff Ride Handbook for the Battle of Chickamauga*, 50–52.
3. Robertson. *Staff Ride Handbook for the Battle of Chickamauga*, 52, 53.
4. Robertson, *Staff Ride Handbook for the Battle of Chickamauga*, 52, 53; Powell,

The Chickamauga Campaign Glory or the Grave, xiv; Cozzens, *This Terrible Sound*, 131.
  5. FHS, Alfred Pirtle to his sister, September 19, 1863, Alfred Pirtle papers Mss. A P672.28 Filson Historical Society.
  6. Pirtle, *Leaves from My Journal*, 24.
  7. Powell, *The Maps of Chickamauga*, 126.
  8. Pirtle, *Leaves from My Journal*, 24–25.
  9. OR Series 1, Volume 30, Part 1, 587.
  10. Pirtle, *Leaves from My Journal*, 24–26; OR Series 1, Volume 30, Part I, 583. FHS, Alfred Pirtle to his mother, October 1, 1863, Alfred Pirtle papers Mss. A P672.28 Filson Historical Society.
  11. Robertson, *Staff Ride Handbook for the Battle of Chickamauga*, 52, 53; OR, Series 1, Volume 30, Part 3, 740.
  12. OR Series 1, Volume 30, Part 2, 287; Cozzens, *This Terrible Sound*, 299.
  13. OR Series 1, Volume 30, Part 1, 136.

Chapter 19

  1. Pirtle, *Leaves from My Journal*, 34.
  2. Cozzens, *This Terrible Sound: The Battle of Chickamauga*, 288; Carter, ed., *For Honor, Glory and Union*, 27.
  3. Powell, *The Chickamauga Campaign Glory or the Grave*, 276.
  4. OR Series 1, Volume 30, Part I, 583; Pirtle, *Leaves from My Journal*, 26; Michigan State University Archives, *Henry A. Goodale Recollection*.
  5. Powell, *The Chickamauga Campaign Glory or the Grave*, 51; Robertson, *Staff Ride Handbook for the Battle of Chickamauga, 18–20 September 1863*, 173; Tucker, *Chickamauga: Bloody Battle in the West*, 203.
  6. Robertson, *Staff Ride Handbook for the Battle of Chickamauga*, 52, 53.
  7. Woodworth, *Jefferson Davis and His Generals*, 235–236.
  8. Powell, *The Chickamauga Campaign Glory or the Grave*, 51; Bennett and Haigh, *History of the Thirty-Sixth Regiment Illinois Volunteers During the War of the Rebellion*, 465–466.
  9. Pirtle, *Leaves from My Journal*, 29.
  10. OR Series 1, Volume 30, Part 1, 43.
  11. FHS, Alfred Pirtle papers, *Lytle's Last Sacrifice*, 7, Filson Historical Society.
  12. Pirtle, *Leaves from My Journal*, 28–29.
  13. Ibid., 30–31.
  14. Bennett and Haigh, *History of the Thirty-Sixth Regiment Illinois Volunteers During the War of the Rebellion*, 466.
  15. Powell, *The Maps of Chickamauga*, 147.
  16. Cist, *The Army of The Cumberland*, 205.
  17. FHS, Alfred Pirtle to his mother, October 1, 1863, Alfred Pirtle papers Mss. A P672.28 Filson Historical Society.
  18. OR Series 1, Volume 30, Part II, 489.
  19. Walker, *Lookout: The Story of a Mountain*, 86.
  20. Powell, *The Chickamauga Campaign Glory or the Grave*, 199–203 and Cozzens, *This Terrible Sound*, 361.
  21. Powell, *The Chickamauga Campaign Glory or the Grave*, 166.
  22. Pirtle, *Leaves from My Journal*, 31.
  23. FHS, Alfred Pirtle to his mother, October 1, 1863, Alfred Pirtle papers Mss. A P672.28 Filson Historical Society.
  24. Pirtle, *Leaves from My Journal*, 31; OR Series 1, Volume 30, Part 1, 583, 585–586; Bennett and Haigh, *History of the Thirty-Sixth Regiment Illinois Volunteers During the War of the Rebellion*, 468.
  25. Ross, *Lincoln's Veteran Volunteers Win the War*, 139; Bennett and Haigh, *History of the Thirty-Sixth Regiment Illinois Volunteers During the War of the Rebellion*, 467.
  26. Powell, *The Chickamauga Campaign Glory or the Grave*, 280. Bennett and Haigh, *History of the Thirty-Sixth Regiment Illinois Volunteers During the War of the Rebellion*, 467–468.
  27. OR Series 1, Volume 30, Part 2, 15.
  28. OR Series 1, Volume 30, Part 2, 303, 330.
  29. Powell, *The Maps of Chickamauga*, 180–181; Powell, *The Chickamauga Campaign Glory or the Grave*, 277.
  30. Pirtle, *Leaves from My Journal*, 32–33.
  31. FHS, Alfred Pirtle to his mother, October 1, 1863, Alfred Pirtle papers Mss. A P672.28 Filson Historical Society; Pirtle, *Leaves from My Journal*, 32.
  32. Cozzens, *This Terrible Sound*, 384.
  33. Powell, *The Chickamauga Campaign Glory or the Grave*, 292–293.
  34. Ibid., 281–282, 291.
  35. Beaudot, *The 24th Wisconsin Infantry in the Civil War: The Biography of a*

Regiment, 233; Ross, *Lincoln's Veteran Volunteers Win the War,* 139–140.
36. *Ibid.,* 138–141. Powell, *The Chickamauga Campaign Glory or the Grave,* 285.
37. Beaudot, *The 24th Wisconsin Infantry in the Civil War,* 235.
38. OR Series 1, Volume 30, Part 1, 585–586.
39. Ross, *Lincoln's Veteran Volunteers Win the War,* 138–141.
40. Tucker, *Chickamauga, Bloody Battle in the West,* 293.
41. OR Series 1, Volume 30, Part 1, 588–589.
42. Powell, *The Chickamauga Campaign Glory or the Grave,* 284.
43. *Ibid.,* 286–287.
44. Cozzens, *This Terrible Sound: The Battle of Chickamauga,* 385–386; OR Series 1, Volume 30, Part 2, 331.
45. Powell, *The Chickamauga Campaign Glory or the Grave,* 292–293.
46. *Ibid.,* 292–293.
47. Venable, *"I Am Dying, Egypt, Dying" and Other Poems,* 38–40; Carter, *For Honor, Glory & Union,* 27.
48. Pirtle, *Leaves from My Journal,* 35.
49. *Ibid.,* 34–36.
50. Lytle Papers, Mss qL996p, Box 32 Letter 283, CMC.
51. Venable, *"I Am Dying, Egypt, Dying" and Other Poems,* 41–42; Lytle Papers, Mss qL996p, Box 34, Letter 614, CMC.
52. Bennett and Haigh, *History of the Thirty-Sixth Regiment Illinois Volunteers During the War of the Rebellion,* 469.
53. Lytle Papers, Mss qL996p, Box 32 Letter 283, CMC.
54. Venable, *"I Am Dying Egypt, Dying," and Other Poems,* 45.
55. Pirtle, *Leaves from My Journal,* 36; Howard Greene to Nathaniel Foster November 1, 1863, Lytle Papers, Mss qL996p, Box 34, Letter 773, CMC.
56. Baumgartner, *Echoes of Battle,* 116.
57. FHS, Alfred Pirtle to his mother, October 1, 1863, Alfred Pirtle papers Mss. A P672.28 Filson Historical Society.
58. Pirtle, *Leaves from My Journal,* 34–36.
59. FHS, Alfred Pirtle to his mother, October 1, 1863, Alfred Pirtle papers Mss. A P672.28 FHS, Alfred Pirtle Papers, *Lytle's Last Sacrifice,* Mss. A P672, Filson Historical Society.
60. Brock, "'I Am Dying, Egypt, Dying' and Its Author," 87.

61. Anderson, "Gens. Anderson and Lytle—A Remembrance," *Confederate Veteran,* Volume 12, 1904, 442.
62. Brock, "'I Am Dying, Egypt, Dying' and Its Author," 86–87.
63. Johnston, "General W.H. Lytle and His Famous Poem; 'I Am Dying Egypt Dying,'" 42; "General Lytle's Death," *The Cincinnati Enquirer* February 25, 1882.
64. Brock, "'I Am Dying, Egypt, Dying' and Its Author," 87.
65. *Nashville Daily Union,* February 3, 1864
66. Otey, Mercer, "Story of Our Great War" *Confederate Veteran.* Volume 8, 1900. 343.
67. Archer, B.L. "Incidents of Gen. Lytle's Burial." *Confederate Veteran.* Volume 9, 1901. 413.

Chapter 20

1. Powell, *The Maps of Chickamauga,* 270.
2. Pirtle, *Leaves from My Journal,* 36.
3. FHS, Alfred Pirtle to his father, September 23, 1863, Alfred Pirtle papers, Mss. A P672.28 Filson Historical Society.
4. *Ibid.*; FHS, Alfred Pirtle to his father, September 26, 1863, Alfred Pirtle papers, Mss. A P672.28 Filson Historical Society.
5. FHS, Alfred Pirtle to his sister, September 27, 1863, Alfred Pirtle papers, Mss. A P672.28 Filson Historical Society.
6. Michigan State University Archives, Henry A. Goodale Recollection.
7. Pirtle, *Leaves from My Journal,* 38.
8. Carter, ed., *For Honor, Glory and Union,* 37, note 119.
9. OR Series 1, Volume 30, Part 1, 585.
10. *Ibid.,* 582.
11. *Ibid.,* 82.
12. FHS, Alfred Pirtle to his mother, October 1, 1863, Alfred Pirtle papers, Mss. A P672.28 Filson Historical Society.
13. FHS, Alfred Pirtle to his mother, October 6, 1863, Alfred Pirtle papers, Mss. A P672.28 Filson Historical Society.
14. *Cincinnati Daily Commercial,* October 9, 1863.
15. OR Series 1, Volume 30, Part 4, 280.
16. *Ibid.*
17. Lytle Papers, Mss qL996p, Box 34, L702a, CMC.
18. Owen, *In Camp and Battle with the Washington Artillery of New Orleans,* 287.

19. *Rutland Daily Herald*, September 23, 1879.
20. OR, Series 1, Volume 30, Part 4, 321.
21. Josephine Foster scrapbook, Lytle Papers, Mss qL996p, Box 45, CMC.
22. FHS, Pirtle Papers, *Leaves from My Journal*, 37, Mss. A P672, Filson Historical Society; Colonel Ward to Caroline Owen, February 25, 1865, Lytle Papers, Mss qL996p, Box 34, Letter 768, CMC.
23. Pirtle, *Leaves from My Journal*, 38.
24. *Official roster of the Soldiers of the State of Ohio in the War of the Rebellion, 1861-1866, Vol. 1.* Tenth Regiment Ohio Volunteer Infantry: Three Years' Service: 10th Regiment Ohio Volunteer Infantry: Field and Staff Officers, 314.
25. *Louisville Courier Journal*, January 14, 1895.
26. *The Catholic Telegraph*, October 14, 1863.
27. Pirtle, *Leaves from My Journal*, 38.

Chapter 21

1. FHS, Alfred Pirtle Papers, *Lytle's Last Sacrifice*, Mss. A P672, Filson Historical Society; Pirtle, *Leaves from My Journal*, 38.
2. Scrapbook, Lytle Papers, Mss qL996p, Box 41, CMC.
3. Pirtle, *Leaves from My Journal*, 38–40; Broadwell Scrapbook, Lytle Papers, Mss qL996p, Box 40, CMC.
4. Pirtle, *Leaves from My Journal*, 38–40.
5. *Ibid.*, 44.
6. *Ibid.*, 45.
7. *Ibid.*, 46; FHS, Alfred Pirtle papers, *Lytle's Last Sacrifice*, Mss. A P672, Filson Historical Society.
8. FHS, Alfred Pirtle Papers, *Lytle's Last Sacrifice*, Mss. A P672, Filson Historical Society; *Cincinnati Enquirer*, October 22, 1863.
9. Pirtle, *Leaves from My Journal*, 46–47.
10. Josephine Foster scrapbook, Lytle Papers, Mss qL996p, Box 45, CMC.
11. Cramer, *The Navigator*, 30.
12. Josephine Foster scrapbook, Lytle Papers, Mss qL996p, Box 45, CMC.
13. *Cincinnati Enquirer*, October 16, 1863.
14. FHS, Alfred Pirtle Papers, *Lytle's Last Sacrifice*, Mss. A P672, Filson Historical Society; Carter, ed., *For Honor, Glory and Union*, 204.
15. *Cincinnati Daily Gazette*, October 22, 1863.
16. Alfred Pirtle to Lily Foster Livingood, December 25, 1923, Lytle Papers, Mss qL996p, Box 34 Letter 638, CMC.

Chapter 22

1. Alfred Pirtle to Lily Broadwell, November 4, 1863, Lytle Papers, Mss qL996p Box 34, Letter 636, CMC.
2. *Cincinnati Gazette*, October 23, 1863.
3. *Ibid.*; Venable, "I Am Dying, Egypt, Dying" and Other Poems, 51.
4. *Cincinnati Daily Commercial*, October 23, 1863.
5. *Cincinnati Enquirer*, October 23, 1863.
6. *Cincinnati Commercial*, October 23, 1863; *Cincinnati Daily Gazette*, October 23, 1863.
7. *Cincinnati Commercial*, October 23, 1863.
8. N.H. to Ezekiel Haines, Lytle Papers, Mss qL996p, Box 34 Letter 696, CMC.
9. *Cincinnati Daily Gazette*, October 23, 1863.
10. *Cincinnati Daily Gazette*, October 23, 1863; FHS, Alfred Pirtle papers, *Lytle's Last Sacrifice*.

Epilogue

1. Hall, Jr., *The Lytle/Foster/Broadwell Lot Spring Grove Cemetery.*
2. Emily Perkins to Elizabeth Broadwell, Lytle Papers, Mss qL996p, Box 34, Letter 626, CMC.
3. Speer, *Sketches of Prominent Tennesseans*, 233; *Chattanooga Daily Times*, September 15, 1926; Lytle, *A Wake for the Living: A Family Chronicle*, 255.
4. *Cincinnati Enquirer*, January 11, 1890.
5. *Cincinnati Enquirer*, December 22, 1898. Carter, *The Lytle Family of Antebellum Cincinnati*, 377.
6. Hamilton M. Weedon to William Lytle Foster, April 20, 1903, Lytle Papers, Mss qL996p, Box 34 Letter 724, CMC.
7. *Nashville Banner*, September 5, 1950.
8. "Antony and Cleopatra," *Confederate Veteran*, Volume 5, 1897, 88.
9. *History of Cincinnati and Hamilton County: Their Past and Present*, 182; Goss, *Cincinnati The Queen City 1788-1912 Volume 1 and 2*, 153–154.

10. *Linn County Republic*, Linn County, Kansas, February 22, 1907; *The Inter Ocean*, Chicago, Illinois, June 10, 1892.

11. Guthrie, Ann, Guthrie-Genalogy.com; *Chattanooga Daily Times*, September 18, 1895; *The Chattanooga News*, August 30, 1909.

12. Sanborn, *Memories and Anecdotes*, 127–128; Kansfield, *Letters to Hazel*, 21–23; *Butte Miner*, June 11, 1902; The Woman's Union Missionary Society of America, *Fifty-Fourth Annual Report*, New York, January 1915.

13. Johnston, ed., *Memorial History of Louisville from Its First Settlement to the Year 1896 Volume 1*, 460; Kleber, *The Encyclopedia of Louisville*, 706.

14. Suess, *Lost Cincinnati*, 134–135.

15. *Ibid.*, 134–135.

Bibliography

Primary Sources

Ancestry.com. Ohio, U.S., County Marriage Records, 1774–1993. (2024). Marriage licenses of Robert Todd and Elizabeth Lytle, Nathaniel and Josephine Foster, and Samuel and Elizabeth Broadwell. Retrieved from https://www.ancestry.com/discoveryui-content/view/313928:61378.

Beatty, John. *The Citizen-Soldier; or Memoirs of a Volunteer by John Beatty*. Cincinnati: Wilstach, Baldwin, & Co. Publishers. 1879.

Cincinnati Museum Center. *The Lytle Family Papers*. Cincinnati, Ohio.

Cramer, Zadok. *The Navigator; Containing Directions for Navigating the Monongahela, Allegheny, Ohio and Mississippi Rivers*. Pittsburgh: Robert Ferguson & Co. Printer. 1814.

Elliott, Sam Davis. *Doctor Quintard, Chaplain C.S.A. and Second Bishop of Tennessee: The Memoir and Civil War Diary of Charles Todd Quintard*. Baton Rouge. Louisiana State University Press. 2003.

The Filson Historical Society. *Alfred Pirtle Papers, 1847–1924*. Special Collections. Louisville, Kentucky.

Johnston, J. Stoddard. "General W.H. Lytle and His Famous Poem; 'I Am Dying Egypt Dying.'" *Register of Kentucky State Historical Society*, Vol. 12, No. 34 (January 1914): 37–44.

Library of Congress Manuscript. Andrew Jackson Letters. Robert Todd Lytle to Andrew Jackson, March 19, 1831. Retrieved from https://www.loc.gov/item/maj012202/.

Library of Congress Manuscript. Andrew Jackson Letters. Robert Todd Lytle to Andrew Jackson, April 2, 1835. Retrieved from: https://www.loc.gov/item/maj014164/.

Library of Congress Manuscript. Andrew Jackson Letters. William Lytle to Andrew Jackson, May 17, 1829. Retrieved from https://www.loc.gov/resource/maj.01073_0052_0053/?sp=1.

Lytle, William. "Personal Narrative of William Lytle." *The Quarterly Publication of the Historical and Philosophical Society of Ohio*, Vol. 1, No. 1 (1906).

Michigan State University Archives. *Henry A. Goodale Recollection*. East Lansing, MI. 2003.

Owen, William Miller. *In Camp and Battle with the Washington Artillery of New Orleans*. Boston: Ticknor & Company. 1885.

Pirtle, Alfred. *Leaves from My Journal*. Author's collection.

Report of the Select Committee of the Senate Appointed to Inquire into the Late Invasion and Seizure of the Public Property at Harper's Ferry, Report No. 278, Senate, 36th Cong., 1st Sess., 1860 (commonly known as the Mason Report). (90–112).

Robertson, James I., Jr., editor. *Soldier of Southwestern Virginia: The Civil War Letters of Captain John Preston Sheffey*. Baton Rouge. Louisiana State University Press. 2004.

Rohr, Nancy. *Incidents of the War: The Civil War Journal of Mary Jane Chadick*. Huntsville, AL: SilverThreads Publishing. 2005.

Special Collections Library, Western Kentucky University.

Secondary Sources

Alderson, William T., and Robert M. McBride, editors. *Landmarks of Tennessee History.* Nashville: Tennessee Historical Society. 1965.
The American Heritage Book of the Presidents and Famous Americans Volume 5. By the editors of American Heritage. New York. Dell Publishing Co. 1967.
Anderson, Mrs. Patton. "Gens. Anderson and Lytle—A Remembrance." *Confederate Veteran,* Vol. 12 (1904): 442.
"Antony and Cleopatra." *Confederate Veteran,* Vol. 5 (1897): 88.
Archer, B.L. "Incidents of Gen. Lytle's Burial." *Confederate Veteran,* Vol. 9 (1901). 413.
Axtell, Matthew A. "What Is Still Radical in the Antislavery Legal Practice of Salmon P. Chase." *Hastings Race & Poverty Law Journal,* Vol. 11, No. 2 (Summer 2014).
Baber, George. "Colonel J. Stoddard Johnston. A Great Kentuckian Who Was Distinguished as a Soldier, Scholar and Journalist." *Register of Kentucky State Historical Society,* Vol. 14, No. 40 (January 1916): 7, 9–13.
Banta, R.E., *The Ohio.* Lexington. The University Press of Kentucky. 1998 Edition.
Barnett, James. "Forty for the Union: Civil War Generals Buried in Spring Grove Cemetery." *Cincinnati Historical Society Bulletin,* Vol. 30 (Summer 1972): 90–121.
Baughin, William A. "Bullets and Ballots: The Election Day Riots of 1855." *Bulletin of the Historical and Philosophical Society of Ohio,* Vol. 21, No. 4 (October 1963): 267–272.
Baumgartner, Richard A., and Larry M. Strayer. *Echoes of Battle: The Struggle for Chattanooga.* Huntington, WV: Blue Acorn Press. 1996.
Beaudot, Wm. J.K. *The 24th Wisconsin Infantry in the Civil War: The Biography of a Regiment.* Mechanicsburg, PA. Stackpole Books. 2003.
Beckman, Wendy Hart. *Founders and Famous Families: Cincinnati.* Covington, KY: Clerisy Press. 2014.
Bennett, L.G., and Wm. H. Haigh. *History of the Thirty-Sixth Regiment Illinois Volunteers During the War of the Rebellion.* Aurora, IL: Knickerbocker & Hoddler Printers and Binders. 1876.
Brill, Ruth. "Cincinnati's 'Poet Warrior': William Haines Lytle." *Bulletin of the Historical and Philosophical Society of Ohio,* Vol. 21 (July 1963): 188–201.
Brock. R.A. "'I Am Dying, Egypt, Dying' and Its Author." *Southern Historical Society Papers,* Vol. XXII. (1894).
Brown, John Howard, editor. *Lamb's Biographical Dictionary of the United States, Volume V, Leaming-Newton.* Boston: Federal Book Co. of Boston. 1903.
Browning, Charles Henry. *Americans of Royal Descent: A Collection of Genealogies of American Families Whose Lineage Is Traced to the Legitimate Issue of Kings.* Philadelphia: Porter and Coats. 1891.
Cameron, Dr. Robert S. *Staff Ride Handbook for the Battle of Perryville: 8 October 1862.* Fort Leavenworth, KS: Combat Studies Institute Press. n.d. U.S. Army Armor Center, Fort Knox, Kentucky.
"Capt. F.H. Lytle." *Confederate Veteran,* Vol. 20 (1912).
Carter, Ruth C. "Cincinnatians and Cholera: Attitudes Toward the Epidemics of 1832 and 1849." *Queen City Heritage,* Vol. 50 (Fall 1992): 32–48.
Carter, Ruth C., editor. *For Honor Glory and Union: The Mexican and Civil War Letters of Brig. Gen. William Haines Lytle.* Lexington, KY: The University Press of Kentucky. 1999.
Carter, Ruth C. *The Lytle Family of Antebellum Cincinnati: Everyday Life, Kin, and Values of Elites in the Urban West.* PhD dissertation. University of Pittsburgh. 1993. University Microfilms International. Order Number 9406420. Unpublished.
Cayton, Andrew R.L. "Artery and Border: The Ambiguous Development of the Ohio Valley in the Early Republic." *Ohio Valley History,* Vol. 1, No. 1 (Winter 2001).
Charlton [Charlotte Pendleton]. *Songs of the Year and Other Poems.* Cincinnati: Robert Clarke and Company. 1875.
Chase, Salmon P. *Speech of Salmon R. Chase in the Case of the Colored Woman, Matilda: Who Was Brought Before the Court of Common Pleas of Hamilton County, Ohio, by Write*

of Heabeus Corpus. Cincinnati: Pugh & Dodd. 1837. Retrieved from https://www.loc.gov/item.10034635/.
Cincinnati City Directory of 1819. Cincinnati Public Library.
Cist, Henry M. *The Army of the Cumberland*. Wilmington, NC: Broadfoot Publishing Company. 1989.
Clary, David A. *Eagles and Empire: The United States, Mexico, and the Struggle for a Continent*. New York. Bantam Books. 2009.
Clay-Clopton, Virginia. *A Belle of the Fifties: Memoirs of Mrs. Clay, of Alabama Covering Social and Political Life in Washington and the South, 1853–66*. New York: Doubleday, Page & Co. 1905.
Coggeshall, William T. *The Poets and Poetry of the West*. New York: Follett, Foster and Company. 1864.
Coggins, Jack. *Arms and Equipment of the Civil War*. New York: Barnes and Noble Books. 1999.
Connelly, Thomas Lawrence. *Autumn of Glory: The Army of Tennessee, 1862–1865*. Baton Rouge: Louisiana State University Press. 1991 printing.
Cozzens, Peter. *No Better Place to Die: The Battle of Stones River*. Urbana: University of Illinois Press. 1991.
Cozzens, Peter. *This Terrible Sound: The Battle of Chickamauga*. Urbana: University of Illinois Press. 1992.
Cushing, Daniel. "An Accurate Return of the Lots of Men Ordered to Be Raised by the United States in the First Regiment, Second Brigade, First Division, Ohio Militia, Nov. 23, 1809." *Quarterly Publication of the Historical and Philosophical Society of Ohio*, Vol. 15 (January-June 1920): 42.
Daniel, Larry J. *Days of Glory: The Army of the Cumberland, 1861–1865*. Baton Rouge: Louisiana State University Press. 2004.
Daniel, Susan G., compiler. *Rutherford County Tennessee Pioneers Born Before 1800*. Murfreesboro, TN: Rutherford County Historical Society. 2003.
Davidson, Donald. *The Tennessee: Volume Two, The New River: Civil War to TVA*. Nashville: J.S. Sanders & Company. 1992 Printing.
Denney, Ellen Wilson. "Surveyor Speculation in the Virginia Military Tract: The Territorial Period." *Cincinnati Historical Society Bulletin*, Vol. 34 (Fall 1976): 174–188.
Dyer, Frederick H. *A Compendium of the War of the Rebellion*. Des Moines, IA. The Dyer Publishing Company. 1908.
Elliott, Sam Davis. *Doctor Quintard, Chaplain C.S.A. and Second Bishop of Tennessee: The Memoir and Civil War Diary of Charles Todd Quintard*. Baton Rouge, Louisiana. Louisiana State University Press. 2003.
Endres, David J., and Jerrold P. Twohig. "'With a Father's Affection': Chaplain William T. O'Higgins and the Tenth Ohio Volunteer Infantry." *U.S. Catholic Historian*, Vol. 31, No. 1 (2013): 97–127.
Everts, Louis, H. *History of Clermont County, Ohio, with Illustrations and Biographical Sketches of Prominent Men and Pioneers*. Philadelphia. J.B. Lippincott & Co. 1880.
Finkelman, Paul. "The Strange Career of Race Discrimination in Antebellum Ohio." *Case Western Law Review*, Vol. 55, Issue 2 (2004).
Flagel, Thomas R. *The History Buff's Guide to the Civil War*. Naperville, IL: Cumberland House. 2010.
From Sumter to Shiloh: Battles and Leaders of the Civil War. New York: Castle Books (Published by arrangement with A.S. Barnes and Co., Inc.). 1956.
Goss, Rev. Charles Frederic. *Cincinnati: The Queen City, 1788–1912, Volume 1 and 2*. Chicago: The S.J. Clarke Publishing Company. 1912.
Greenberg, Amy S. *A Wicked War: Polk, Clay, Lincoln, and the 1846 U.S. Invasion of Mexico*. New York: Vintage Books. 2012.
Greve, Charles Theodore. *Centennial History of Cincinnati*. Chicago: Biographical Publishing Company. 1904.
Guthrie, Ann. Guthrie Genealogy. Guthrie Ancestry and Genetic Genealogy. Retrieved from https://guthrie-genealogy.com/guthrie-family-groups/gfg2a/j-joseph-guthrie-julia-mccarthy/. March 27, 2020.

Hall, Virginius C. "The Genesis of an Orchard." *Bulletin of the Historical and Philosophical Society of Ohio*, Vol. 7 (April 1949): 87–89.
Hall, Virginius C. "Journal of Isaac Hite, 1773." *Bulletin of the Historical and Philosophical Society of Ohio*, Vol. 12 (October 1954): 262–281.
Hall, Virginius C. "Moses Dawson, Chronic Belligerent." *Bulletin of the Historical and Philosophical Society of Ohio*, Vol. 15 (July 1957): 175–189.
Hall, Virginius Cornick, Jr. *Family Residences*. Fort Thomas, KY: MicroPress. 2018.
Hall, Virginius Cornick, Jr. *General William Lytle Gentleman Surveyor and Prominent Cincinnatian (1770–1831)*. Fort Thomas, KY: MicroPress, Printed by Living Magazines, Inc. 2018.
Hall, Virginius Cornick, Jr. *The Lytle/Foster/Broadwell Lot Spring Grove Cemetery*. Unpublished. n.d.
Hall, Virginius Cornick, Jr. *Lytle House Time-Line*. Unpublished. n.d.
Hinton, Richard J. *Poems by Richard Realf: Poet ... Soldier ... Workman*. New York: Funk and Wagnalls. 1898.
History of Cincinnati and Hamilton County; Their Past and Present. Cincinnati: S.B. Nelson & Co. Publishers. 1894.
Hodges, Fletcher, Jr. "Stephen Foster Cincinnatian and American." *Bulletin of the Philosophical and Historical Society of Ohio*, Vol. 8, No. 2 (April 1950).
Holman, Kurt. *Battle of Perryville: Movement Maps Showing the Fighting Ground of the Union Left and Center 12:00 PM to 8:00 PM*. Friends of Perryville Battlefield. As of Monday, May 9, 2016.
Howe, Henry. *Historical Collections of Ohio in Two Volumes, an Encyclopedia of the State: The Ohio Centennial Edition Volume I*. Cincinnati: Published by The State of Ohio. C.J. Krehbiel & Co. 1907.
Hughes, Mary B. *Hearthstones: The Story of Historic Rutherford County Homes*. Murfreesboro, TN: Mid-South Publishing Co. 1942.
Hunt, Roger D. *Colonels in Blue: Indiana, Kentucky, and Tennessee*. Jefferson, NC: McFarland 2014.
James, Edward T., editor. *Noted American Women: A Biographical Dictionary*. Cambridge, MA: Radcliffe College. 1971.
Johnston, J. Stoddard, editor. *Memorial History of Louisville: From Its First Settlement to the Year 1896, Volume 1*. Chicago: American Biographical Publishing Company. n.d.
Kansfield, Mary K. *Letters to Hazel: Ministry Within the Woman's Board of Foreign Missions of the Reformed Church in America*. Grand Rapids, MI: Wm. B. Eerdman's Publishing Company. 2004.
Karamanski, Theodore J. "Civilians, Soldiers, and the Sack of Athens, Alabama." Illinois Periodicals Online. Retrieved from https://www.lib.niu.edu/1997/iht429748.html.
Kesterman, Richard R. "Six Views of Lytle Square." *Ohio Valley History*, Vol. 11, No. 4 (Winter 2011).
Kleber, John E., editor. *The Encyclopedia of Louisville*. Lexington. The University Press of Kentucky. 2001.
Kleber, John E., editor. *The Kentucky Encyclopedia*. Lexington: The University Press of Kentucky. 1992.
Knepper, Dr. George W. *The Official Ohio Lands Book*. Columbus, OH: The Auditor of State, East Broad Street. 2002.
Kolakowski, Christopher L. *The Civil War at Perryville: Battling for the Bluegrass*. Charleston, SC: The History Press. 2009.
Kremm, Thomas W. "The Old Order Trembles." *Cincinnati Historical Society Bulletin*, Vol. 36, No. 3 (Fall 1978): 193–215.
Life and Light for Woman. Woman's Board of Missions. Volume 32. 1902. Frank Wood, Printer. 1902.
List of Staff Officers of the Confederate States Army, 1861–1865. Washington, D.C.: Government Printing Office. 1891.
Logsdon, David R. *Eyewitnesses at the Battle of Perryville*. Nashville: Kettle Mills Press. 2007.

Lowry, Terry. *September Blood.* Special Sesquicentennial Reprint. Charleston, WV: Quarrier Press. 2011.
Lytle, Andrew. *A Wake for the Living: A Family Chronicle.* New York: Crown Publishers. 1975.
Mach, Thomas S. "Family Ties, Party Realities, and Political Ideology: George Hunt Pendleton and Partisanship in Antebellum Cincinnati." *Ohio Valley History*, Vol. 3, No. 2 (Summer 2003).
Malone, Dumas, editor. *Dictionary of American Biography: Volume 11, Larned–MacCracken.* New York: Charles Scribner's Sons. 1933.
Mansfield, E.D. *Personal Memories: Social, Political and Literary, with Sketches of Many Notable People, 1803–1843.* Cincinnati: Robert Clarke and Co. 1879.
McDonough, James Lee. *War in Kentucky: From Shiloh to Perryville.* Knoxville: The University of Tennessee Press. 1994.
McGrane, Reginald C. "Orator Bob and the Right of Instruction." *Bulletin of the Historical and Philosophical Society of Ohio*, Vol. 11 (October 1953): 250–273.
Morford, Jana C. "Preserving a 'Special Place': The Lytle Park Neighborhood, 1948–1976." *Queen City Heritage*, Vol. 44 (Fall 1986): 2–22.
Morris, Wesley J., *Christ Church 1817–1967 Cincinnati*, The Episcopal Society of Christ Church. Cincinnati: Cincinnati Lithographing/Ohio Press. 1967.
Moseley, Edward H., and Paul C. Clark, Jr. *The A–Z of the United States–Mexican War.* Lanham, MD: Scarecrow Press. 1997.
Nash, Charles Edward. *Biographical Sketches of Gen. Pat Cleburne and Gen. T.C. Hindman.* Little Rock, AR. Tunnah & Pittard Printers. 1898.
National Park Service. "The Ohio River." Retrieved from: https://www.nps.gov/articles/the-ohio-river.htm.
Nelson, William. *Genealogy of the Doremus Family in America.* Patterson, NJ: The Press Printing and Publishing Company. 1897.
Neville, Morgan. "Morgan Neville to James Findlay, Jan. 10, 1831." *Quarterly Publication of the Historical and Philosophical Society of Ohio*, Vol. 2 (January-March 1907): 28.
Niven, John. *Salmon P. Chase: A Biography.* New York: Oxford University Press. 1995.
Niven, John, editor. *The Salmon P. Chase Papers Volume I Journals 1829–1872.* Kent, OH: Kent State University Press. 1993.
Noe, Kenneth W. *Perryville: This Grand Havoc of Battle.* Lexington: The University Press of Kentucky. Paperback Edition. 2011.
Nofi, Albert A., editor. *Opening Guns: Fort Sumter to Bull Run, 1861.* New York: Gallery Books. 1988.
Official Roster of the Soldiers of the State of Ohio in the War of the Rebellion, 1861–1866, Vol. 1. Tenth Regiment Ohio Volunteer Infantry: Three Years' Service: 10th Regiment Ohio Volunteer Infantry: Field and Staff Officers. Compiled under direction of the roster commission. Published by authority of the general assembly. Akron, OH. The Werner Company. 1893.
Ohio Encyclopedia, 2008–2009 Edition, Volume 1. St. Clair Shores, MI. Somerset Publishers. 2008.
Otey, Mercer. "Story of Our Great War." *Confederate Veteran*, Vol. 8 (1900): 343.
Partlow, Thomas E., compiler. *Rutherford County, Tennessee Chancery Court Minutes 1845–1867.* Greenville, SC: Southern Historical Press. 1999.
Pessen, Edward. "How Different from Each Other Were the Antebellum North and South?" *The American Historical Review*, Vol. 85, No. 5 (1980): 1119–1149.
Pierson, Rev. Arthur T., D.D., editor. *The Missionary Review of the World. Volume 25.* January–December 1902. New York: Funk and Wagnalls. 1902.
Pierson, Delavan, editor. *The Missionary Review of the World, Volume 28.* January–December 1915. New York: Funk and Wagnalls Company. 1915.
Platt, George Lewis. *The Platt Lineage: A Genealogical Research and Record.* New York: Thomas Wittaker. 1891.
Powell, David A. *The Chickamauga Campaign: A Mad Irregular Battle: From the Crossing of the Tennessee River Through the Second Day, August 22–September 19, 1863.* El Dorado Hills, CA: Savas Beatie. 2014. Overdrive edition.

Powell, David A. *The Chickamauga Campaign Glory or the Grave: The Breakthrough, the Union Collapse, and the Defense of Horseshoe Ridge, September 20, 1863.* El Dorado Hills, CA: Savas Beatie. 2017.
Powell, David A., and David A. Friedrichs. *The Maps of Chickamauga: An Atlas of the Chickamauga Campaign, Including the Tullahoma Operations, June 22–September 23, 1863.* El Dorado Hills, CA: Savas Beatie. 2015.
The Progressive Men of the Commonwealth of Pennsylvania. Compiled and Edited by Colonel Charles Blanchard. Pennsylvania: A.W. Bowen and Company. 1900.
Prouty, Fred M. and Gary L. Barker. *A Survey of Civil War Period Military Sites in West Tennessee.* Tennessee Department of Environment and Conservation Division of Archaeology, Report of Investigations Number 11. Nashville, TN. 1996.
Ramage, James. "Liberty on the Border: A Civil War Exhibit." *Ohio Valley History*, Vol. 3, No. 2 (Summer 2003): 47–50.
Reid, Whitelaw. *Ohio in the War: History of Ohio During the War, and the Lives of Her Generals Volume 1.* Cincinnati: The Robert Clarke Company. 1895.
Retreat from Gettysburg: Battles and Leaders of the Civil War. New York: Castle Books. (Published by special arrangement with A.S. Barnes and Co., Inc.). 1958.
Robertson, Dr. William Glenn, Lt. Col. Edward P. Shanahan, Lt. Col. John I. Boxberger, and Major George E. Knapp. *Staff Ride Handbook for the Battle of Chickamauga 18–20 September 1863.* Ft. Leavenworth, KS. Combat Studies Institute. 1992.
Robertson, William Glenn. *River of Death: The Chickamauga Campaign Volume One, The Fall of Chattanooga.* Chapel Hill: The University of North Carolina Press. 2018.
Ross, D. Reid. *Lincoln's Veteran Volunteers Win the War: The Hudson Valley's Ross Brothers and the Union's Fight for Emancipation.* Albany: State University of New York. 2008.
Rowe, John. J. "Money and Banks in Cincinnati Pre-War." *Bulletin of the Historical and Philosophical Society of Ohio*, Vol. 6, No. 3 (1948).
Rutherford County Archives Marriage Index. Marriages 1804–1888. Retrieved from: http://asp.rutherfordcountytn.gov/apps/archivesmarriageindex/marriage1804-1888.aspx.
Sanborn, Kate. *Memories and Anecdotes.* New York. G.P. Putnam's Sons. The Knickerbocker Press. 1915.
Schilling, David Carl. "Relation of Southern Ohio to the South During the Decade Preceding the Civil War." *Quarterly Publication of the Historical and Philosophical Society of Ohio*, Vol. VIII, No. 1 (January-March 1913).
Sept. 10th, 1861, Carnifix Ferry. West Virginia Division of Tourism and Parks. n.d.
Shaffer, Dallas B. *The Battle of Carnifex Ferry.* Carnifex Ferry Battlefield State Park. Charleston, WV: West Virginia Division of Natural Resources. n.d.
Sherwood, Henry Noble. "The Movement in Ohio to Deport the Negro." *Quarterly Publication of the Historical and Philosophical Society of Ohio*, Vol. 7 (June and September 1912): 53–78.
Sketches of War History 1861–1865: Papers Read Before the Ohio Commandery of the Military Order of the Loyal Legion of the United States 1883–1886. Published by The Commandery Volume I. Cincinnati: Robert Clarke and Company. 1888.
Smith, Derek. *The Gallant Dead: Union and Confederate Generals Killed in the Civil War.* Mechanicsburg, PA. Stackpole Books. 2005.
Smith, Ophia D. "The Early Theater of Cincinnati." *Bulletin of the Historical and Philosophical Society of Ohio*, Vol. 13, No. 4 (October 1955): 230–253.
Speed, Captain Thomas, Col. R.M. Kelly, and Maj. Alfred Pirtle. *The Union Regiments of Kentucky.* Louisville, KY: Courier-Journal Job Printing Company. 1897.
Speer, William S. *Sketches of Prominent Tennesseans.* Baltimore: Reprinted Genealogical Publishing Co. 2003.
Stampp, Kenneth, editor. *The Causes of The Civil War, Revised Edition.* New York: Simon & Schuster. 1986. First Touchstone Edition.
Stampp, Kenneth M. *America in 1857: A Nation on the Brink.* New York: Oxford University Press. 1990.
Starr, Stephen Z. "Camp Dennison, 1861–1865." *Bulletin of the Historical and Philosophical Society of Ohio*, Vol. 19 (July 1961): 166–190.

Stephens, Robert O. *The Family Saga in the South. Generations and Destinies.* Baton Rouge: Louisiana State University Press. 1995.
Stern, Robert D. "One Lytle Place." *Queen City Heritage*, Vol. 41 (Summer 1983): 34.
Suess, Jeff. *Hidden History of Cincinnati.* Charleston. SC. The History Press. 2016.
Suess, Jeff. *Lost Cincinnati.* Charleston, SC: The History Press. 2015.
Sword, Wiley. *Shiloh: Bloody April.* Dayton, OH: Morningside Bookshop. 1988.
Taylor, Nikki M., *Frontiers of Freedom Cincinnati's Black Community 1802-1868.* Athens: Ohio University Press. 2005.
Tenkotte, Paul A., and James C. Claypool, editors. *The Encyclopedia of Northern Kentucky.* Lexington. The University Press of Kentucky. 2009.
"Tribute to a Federal Officer." *Confederate Veteran*, Vol. 5 (1897): 249.
Trollope, Mrs. Frances. *Domestic Manners of the Americans.* New York. Whittaker, Treacher & Co. 1832.
Tucker, Glenn. *Chickamauga: Bloody Battle in the West.* Dayton, OH: Morningside House. 1992.
Tucker, Gregory. "Civil War Seduction Linked to Carnation Evaporated Milk." Murfreesboro Post, April 25, 2017.
United States War Dept. *The War of the Rebellion: A Compilation of the Official Records of the Union and Confederate Armies.* Washington, D.C. 1880-1901.
Venable, William Henry. *"I Am Dying, Egypt, Dying" and Other Poems of William Haines Lytle.* Edited with Memoir. Cincinnati: Stewart and Kidd Company. 1913.
Vitz, Carl. "A Brief History of Lytle Square, 1789-1964." *Cincinnati Historical Society Bulletin*, Vol. 22 (April 1964): 110-122.
Vitz, Carl. "The Cincinnati Water Front, 1848." *Bulletin of the Historical and Philosophical Society of Ohio*, Vol. 6 (April 1948): 28-39.
Wagner, Margaret E., Gary W. Gallagher, and Paul Finkelbaum, editors. *The Library of Congress Civil War Desk Reference.* New York: Simon & Schuster. 2002.
Walker, Robert Sparks. *Lookout The Story of a Mountain.* Chattanooga, TN: George C. Hudson & Co. 1952. Second edition.
Walter, John. *The Sniper Encyclopedia: An A-Z Guide to World Sniping.* Haverton, PA. Casemate Publishers. 2019.
Warner, Ezra J. *Generals in Blue: Lives of the Union Commanders.* Baton Rouge: Louisiana State University Press. 1964.
Warner, Ezra J. *Generals in Gray: Lives of the Confederate Commanders.* Baton Rouge: Louisiana State University Press. 1983 printing.
Wells, Carol. *Pioneers Of Rutherford County, Tennessee: Abstract of County Court Records 1804-1810.* Nacogdoches, TX: Ericson Books. n.d.
Whealen, John J. "The Jackson-Dawson Correspondence." *Bulletin of the Historical and Philosophical Society of Ohio*, Vol. 16 (January 1958): 2-30.
White, John H., Jr. "The World's Oldest Steamboat Company? The U.S. Mail Line." *Queen City Heritage* (Summer/Fall 1999): 50-68.
Whitley, Edyth Rucker, compiler. *Marriages of Rutherford County, Tennessee 1804-1872.* Baltimore: Genealogical Publishing Co., Inc. 1981.
Wiley, Bell Irvin. *The Life of Billy Yank: The Common Soldier of the Union.* Baton Rouge: Louisiana State University Press. 1990 printing.
Wiley, Samuel T., and W. Scott Garner, editors. *Biographical and Portrait Cyclopedia of Blair County Pennsylvania.* Philadelphia, PA. Gresham Publishing Company. 1892.
Winkle, Kenneth J. *The Politics of Community Migration and Politics in Antebellum Ohio.* Cambridge. Cambridge University Press. 1988.
Winkler, John F. *Wabash 1791: St. Clair's Defeat.* Oxford, England. Osprey Publishing. 2011.
The Woman's Union Missionary Society of America. *Fifty-Fourth Annual Report.* New York. January 1915.
Woodworth, Steven E. *Jefferson Davis and His Generals: The Failure of Confederate Command in the West.* Lawrence: University of Kansas. 1990.
Zeitlin, Steve. "Poetry to Ease the Final Passage." Cornell University Press Blog. Retrieved from: https://www.cornellpress.cornell.edu/poetry-to-ease-the-final-passage/ .

Bibliography

Newspapers from newspapers.com

Altoona Tribune (Altoona, Pennsylvania)
Baltimore Sun
Cadiz Sentinel (Cadiz, Ohio)
Carroll Free Press (Carroll, Ohio)
The Catholic Telegraph (Cincinnati)
Charleston Mercury
Chattanooga Daily Times
The Chattanooga News
Chicago Tribune
Cincinnati Commercial
Cincinnati Daily Press
Cincinnati Enquirer
Cincinnati Gazette
The Daily Milwaukee News
Daily Times (Cincinnati)
Democrat and Herald (Wilmington, Ohio)
Democratic Free Press
The Fremont Weekly Journal
Gallipolis Journal (Gallipolis, Ohio)
Gettysburg Compiler
Kentucky Gazette (Louisville)
Lancaster Gazette
The Liberator
The Liberator (Boston)
Louisville Courier
The Madisonian (Washington, D.C.)
Monroe Sentinel (Monroe, Wisconsin)
Nashville Banner
Nashville Daily Union
Nashville Whig
The National Gazette
National Gazette (Philadelphia)
New York Herald
New York Tribune
Ohio Statesman
Pittsburgh Daily Post
Pomeroy Weekly Telegraph
Portsmouth Inquirer
Richmond Enquirer
The Rodney Telegraph (Rodney, Mississippi)
Rutland Daily Herald
Semi-Weekly Times Democrat (New Orleans)
The Summit County Beacon (Akron, Ohio)
The Tennessean
Western Reserve Chronicle (Warren, Ohio)
Wilkes Spirit of the Times (New York)
Woodstock Sentinel (Woodstock, Illinois)
Wyandott Pioneer (Upper Sandusky, Ohio)

INDEX

Numbers in ***bold italics*** indicate pages with illustrations

acoustic shadow 96
Adams, Daniel 98, 101–102
Alabama troops: 19th 147; 22nd 146; 33rd 97
Alexander, E. Porter 126
Allison, Richard 12
Anderson, John 69
Anderson, Patton 117, 119, ***128***, 139, 142, 145, 149–150
Anderson, Robert 54
"Antony and Cleopatra" 49–50, 53, 152, 165, 168
Archer, B.L. 147
Arkansas troops: 15th 101
Athens, AL (Turchin's raid) 81–82
Ayers, Josephine 158

Bank of the United States 13–14, 16, 19
Banton, N.S. 116
Bardstown, KY 15, 75, 89–91, 97
Baum, Frederick 152
Beatty, John 59, 77, 81–82, 93, 100, 103
Beauregard, Pierre Goustave Toutant 76
Beckham, Julia Wickliffe 76
Beckham, William 76
Benham, Henry W. 61–62, 66, 70
Benjamin, Judah 69
Birney, James Gillespie 23
Blanchard, Mary 39
Blanchard, William Lytle 20, 54, 79
Boal, Charles 117, 123, ***124***, 127, 142
Boone, Daniel 11
Bottom, Henry P. 96
Bottom House 96, 98, 100
Bradley, Luther 136
Bragg, Braxton 88–89, 91–92, 94, 96, 103, 105–107, 112–113, 126–127, 132, 134–135, 151
Brannan, John Milton 132, 137–138
Breckinridge, John Cabell 52

Bridgeport, AL 115–116, 121, 124, 128, 139, 145, 150, 155, 171
Broadwell, Samuel J. 44, 71, 87, 129, 156, 162
Brooks, Preston 52
Brown, John 52, 119
Brown, John Calvin 97, 99–100
Buchanan, James 43–44, 60–61
Buchanan, Rowan 47
Buckner, Simon Bolivar 73, 106, 126
Buell, Don Carlos 73–74, 82, 87, 90–92, 96, 100, 105, 107–109
Burke, Joseph W. 76, 79, 93, 112
Burnet House (Hotel) 35, 54, 108
Burnside, Ambrose Pierce 112, 126
Butler, David 152
Butler, William Orlando 32–33
Byron, Lady 119
Byron, Lord 27–28

Calhoun, John Caldwell 40, 53
Camp Dennison 54–***55***, 57, 62, 86, 93, 149
Camp Gauley 61, 69
Camp Jackson 93
Camp Morton 75
Camp Van Buren 78
Campbell, William 100, 124
Carlisle, Isabel 72
Carnifex Ferry, and battle of 59–60, 62, 64–70
Casement, John Steven 61
Chadbourne, Alexander S. 137
Chadick, Mary 87, 89
Chalfant, Therese 37, 42, 53
Chaplin Hills *see* Perryville, Battle of
Chase, Salmon Porter 22–23, 45–46
Chattanooga, TN 5, 88, 115–116, 120, 126, 128, 132, 135, 146, 148–151, 153–154, 166
Chickamauga, battle of 135–147
cholera 35, 88

201

Index

Christ Church Cathedral 90, 158–*159*
Cincinnati, OH 2, 5–6, 9, 12, 16, 18, 20–23, 25–26, 29, 31, 33, 35–40, 42–43, 46, 51, 54–59, 71–72, 75, 77, 79–80, 86–87, 90, 93, 106, 108–109, 112, 118, 125, 146, 154–156, 159, 164–165, 168
Cincinnati College 6, 12, 14, 29
Clark, George Rogers 11
Clay, Henry 5, 9, 13, 31
Cleburne, Patrick 36, 88, 98, 100–102
Clermont County 12, 46
Coggeshall, William T. 49
Coltart, Robert W. 87
consumption 12, 17, 25, 27, 37
Cowan, TN 114, 120
Cox, Jacob 57, 62, 69
Cramer, Zadok 10, 155
Crittenden, George Bibb 79
Crittenden, Thomas Leonidas 90–91, 126
Cunningham, John 152

Danville, KY 10, 91, 93
Dargan, Lucas McIntosh 6–7
Darr, Calvin 70
Darr, Frank 105
Davies, Samuel W. 12
Davis, Jefferson 124
Davis, Jefferson Columbus 90, 137–138
Dawson, Moses 19
Deas, Zachariah C. 139, 142
Dennison, William 54, 56
Dodge, Joseph 127
Dolan, Thomas 152
Donohue, Joseph 152, 155
Doremus, Charlotte ("Lottie") 106
Doremus, Sarah Du Bois ("Sed") 42, 83, 106–107, 112, 120, 157, 166
Douglas, Stephen Arnold 40–41, 52
Dragging Canoe 10
Drake, Ida 29

Eaton, Charles W. 116, 123–*124*
Eells, Samuel 23
Englehart, Frederick 152
Ewing, Hugh B. 68

Faugh-a-Ballaugh 57, 59–*60*, 66–67
Federal Hill ("My Old Kentucky Home") 15, 39, 75
Finigan, Patrick 153
Fisher, Horace N. 100
Fitzgibbon, Michael 66, 70
Floyd, John Buchanan 60–63, 69
Forman, James Brown 100
Forrest, Nathan Bedford 89, 112, 133
Fort Donelson 69, 79, 115
Fort Hamilton 10
Fort Henry 115
Fort Pitt 10
Fort Sumter 54
Fosdick, William F. 47, 59, 77
Foster, Dunning 38
Foster, Nathaniel 37, 106, 129, 155–156, 162
Foster, Stephen Collins 39
Frazer, C.W. 100
French and Indian War 9–10

Gallagher, Thomas 57
Garfield, James Abram 138, 158
Gates, Thruston P. 138
German, Thomas 69
Gilbert, Charles Champion 90–91, 96, 100
Gilmour, Richard 57
Glenn, Edward 144
Goodale, Henry A. 113, 149
Grant, U.S. 112, 115, 126
Green, John H. 68, 70
Greene, Howard D. 137, 142, 144
Grover, James A. 116, 123–*124*, 148, 150
Guthrie, Joseph 79, 113, 116, 135, 149, 166

Haines, Charlotte 18, 31, 35, 37, 42
Haines, Daniel 51
Haines, Elias Henry 14, 18, 26, 30, 32–33, 35, 139, 160
Haines, Ezekial Smith ("Smith") 14, 18, 25, 31, 35, 160
Halleck, Henry 134
Hamer, Thomas 19
Hammond, Charles 19
Hardee, William Joseph 91
Harmony Hill 12
Harpe Brothers 11
Harris, Leonard 94
Harris, S.D. 38, 45
Harrison, Carter Bassett 164
Harrison, James Findlay ("Fin") 27, 31, 114–117, 120, 123–*124*, 144–145, 149, 150, 166
Harrison, William Henry 31
Hawes, Richard 91
Hawkins, A.T. 97
Hayes, Rutherford Birchard 62
Hayes, Samuel K. 106
Heartland Offensive 88
Henderson, Richard 10
Herrera, Jose 31
Heth, Henry 61
Hickey, James T. 64, 66
Hindman, Thomas Carmichael 132, 139
Hoffman, William 108
Hood, John Bell 111, 126
Houlihan, William 58

Index

Houston, Sam 25
Hudson, John 64, 152
Humphrey, George 93
Hunter, David 144
Huntsville, AL 81, 83, 86–89, 93, 120

Illinois troops: 19th 81; 36th 111, 136–143, 148; 88th 111, 137–140, 142, 148
Indiana troops: 5th Battery Indiana Light Artillery (Peter Simonson's) 96; 11th Battery Artillery 133, 137–139; 38th 98, 101; 42nd 77, 93–95, 98–99, 101, 103; 88th 93–94, 96, 99, 101, 103
Innes, William 120
Irwin, Mary Jane 39
Irwin, William S. 39, 47
Iverson, Alfred 52

Jackson, Andrew 5, 9, 16, 18, 20, 31, 40
Jackson, N.P. 123
Jenkins, E.P. 155
Johnson, Bushrod Rust 98, 100–102
Johnston, Harris H. 146
Johnston, Josiah Stoddard 49, 105, 108, 146
Jones, James G. 93
Jones, Thomas Marshall 97, 100
Jones, William 125
Jouett, George Payne 100, 124

Kansas-Nebraska Act 40
Kavanaugh, Patrick 69
Kennedy, John 69
Kenton, Simon 5, 11
Kentucky troops: 15th 77, 93, 96, 99, 100, 102–103
King, Edward Augustine 125
Kirsel, John 69
Korff, Herman J. 68

Laiboldt, Bernard 115, 130, 136, 138–140
Landrum, George 95
Larrabee, Charles H. 121
Lawrence, Larkin 22–23
Lawrence, Matilda 22–23
Lee, Robert E. 61, 69, 126
Liddell, St. John 94
Lincoln, Abraham 52, 54, 82, 110, 114
Longstreet, James 126, 134–135, 137, 139
Loomis, Cyrus 93, 97–98
Louisville, KY 2, 14, 25, 27, 32, 39, 41, 72–74, 77, 88–90, 108, 121, 130, 146, 155, 166–167
Lowe, John 68, 71
Lucas, Robert 20
Lytle, Agnes ("Ann," great-aunt) 10, 15
Lytle, Andrew Nelson 113

Lytle, Edward Hiley (uncle) 12, 37–38, 46
Lytle, Eliza Ann (aunt) 12, 37
Lytle, Elizabeth ("Lily," sister) 20, **28**, 33–35, 42, 44, 46, 58, 71, 74, 77, 79, 83, 87, 91, 109, 120–121, 128–129, 156, 162, **164**
Lytle, Elizabeth Haines (mother) 14, 16–**17**, 18–21, 25, 27, 37, 162
Lytle, Frank Henderson 79
Lytle, John (uncle) 12, 25
Lytle, Josephine ("Josie," sister) 18, **28**, 33–35, 79, 106, 109, 120–121, 128–129, 164–165
Lytle, Margaret Smith Haines (grandmother) 14, 16–17, 21, 27, **28**, 31–33, 36, 162
Lytle, Margaritta (sister) 17–18
Lytle, Mary (great-aunt) 10
Lytle, Mary Steele (great-grandmother) 10
Lytle, Robert Todd (father) 5, 12, 14–26, **34**, 162
Lytle, Sophie Dashiell Ridgely 78, 109, 112–113, 162, 164
Lytle, William (grandfather) 5, 9–13, **14**, 16, 17, 31, 45–46, 57, 162
Lytle, William (great-grandfather) 9, 10
Lytle, William Franklin Pitt ("Billy Creek") 78–79, 109
Lytle, William Haines: alcohol use of 5, 18, 46, 74, 77, 95; bad behavior 37–38, 46–47; battle wounds received 67, 71, 101, 142–143; Buell Court of Inquiry 108–109; childhood 9, 15–19; education 26–27, 30; law career 34, 37–38, 41; music, love of 34, 75, 80, 112, 158; physical description 53, 105; pictures **28, 40, 60, 111, 124, 129, 136**; poems (*Antony and Cleopatra* 49–50; *The Farewell* 30; *Fragment* ("Night garlanded…") 43; *Impromptu* 51; *In Camp* 75; *Lines on My Thirty-Sixth Birthday* 107; *The Soldier's Death* 26; *Tis Not the Time* 82–83; *Untitled* ("Go It Boots!") 42–43; *The Volunteers* 32; *When the Long Shadows* 110); political career 36–37, 41, 45–46; presentation of the cross by Tenth Ohio 117–120; promotions, military 32–33, 42, 45, 77, 83, 87, 110–111; romantic interests (*see* Chalfant, Therese; Doremus, Sarah Du Bois ("Sed"); Macalester, Eliza ["Lily Mac"]); social activities 37, 39, 41, 76, 84–85, 119; Southerners, thoughts on 44–45, 53, 114; speeches 28–29, 43–46, 57, 72, 78, 86–87, 117–119, 124; travels 35, 39, 51
Lytle, William Henry (uncle) 12, 162

Index

Lytle mansion 9, 14–15, *24*, 31, 47, *48*
Lytletown 12

Macalaster, Eliza ("Lily Mac") 37, 42, 120
Maltese cross (gift of Tenth Ohio to Lytle) *117*
Manigault, Arthur 132, 139–140
Mason, Samuel 11
Massie, Nathaniel 12
McCarty, John W. 158, 160
McClellan, George B. 56, 58–59, 61–62
McCook, Alexander McDowell *90*, 92, 94–95, 100, 112, 126–127, 133, 135–136, 138
McCook, Daniel, Jr. 94, 99
McCook, Robert 47
McCreery, William H. 137, 141, 144
McIlvaine, Charles Petit 90, 154
McKinley, William 62, 68
McLaws, Lafayette 126
McPherson, James 111
Means, Thomas 49
Medary, Charles 69
Michigan troops: 1st Battery Michigan Light Artillery 93–96; 21st 111, 113–114, 136–139, 141–143, 148
Miller, Silas 137, 143, 149
Mirer, Ernest 152
Mississippi troops: 7th 119; 9th 119; 10th 119; 32nd 97; 33rd 97; 41st 119; 44th 119
Mitchel, Ormsby Macknight 74, 78, 81, 83
Monte Sano (mountain) 83–*84*
Moore, R.M. 79
Moorehouse, William 69
Morgan, John Hunt 81
Morris, Robert 10
Mullen, Michael 168–169
Munfordville, KY 89
Murfreesboro, TN 78–79, 89, 108–109, 112–113, 162, 164
Murphy, George S. 69

Nashville, TN 77–78, 88–89, 108
Negley, James 138
Nelson, William ("Bull") 90
New Orleans, LA 25, 32, 47, 110
Nightingale 155
Nott, Deas 146

O'Connor, Daniel 69
O'Higgins, Father William 80, 154
Ohio River 9–12, 15, 23, 32, 38–40, 71, 77, 115
Ohio troops: 2nd 95; 3rd 77, 93, 96, 98–100, 103; 4th (Kennett's cavalry) 88; 7th 59; 7th (Militia) 156; 10th 56, 59, 61, 64–71, 77–78, 86, 88, 93, 95–98, 100–103, 108–109, 112, 117–118, 137, 153–154; 12th 66, 68; 13th 57–58, 62, 65–66; 23rd 62 33rd 96–97
Owen, Miller 67

Paredes, Mariano 31
parole and exchange 78, 105–106
Parsons, E.B. 143
Patterson, Henry 62
Patteson, Mary 62
Patteson, Okey Leonidas 62
Patton, George S. 61
Payne, Henry B. 46
the Peach Grove 12, 169
Pendleton, George H. 37, 47
Perkins, Emily 162, 164
Perryville, battle of 93–104
Peters, James 69
Pierce, Franklin 19, 33, 37, 43
Pierce, John S. 152
Pirtle, Alfred 6, 47, 72, *73*–78, 83–84, 89, 108, 116, 119, 123–128, 130, 133, 136–138, 140, 142, 144, 148, 153–156, 166–168
Pirtle, Henry 73
Pittsburgh, PA 10, 38, 51–52, 61
Polk, James Knox 20, 31
Polk, Leonidas 90–92, 94, 132, 135, 158
Polk, Sarah 20
Pope, Curran 93, 100, 124
Port Clinton, OH 12, 45
Post, P. Sidney 127–128
Powers, Hiram 34, 36
Preston, William 146
Pugh, George 47
Purcell, Father Edward 71

Quintard, Charles Todd 96

Read, Buchanan 47
Realf, Richard 119, 151
Reilly, Joanna Haines 14, 21, 27, 35–36, 87, 91, 109
Reynolds, Joseph 138
Richmond, KY., Battle of 88
Robb, James 96
Roberts, Albert ("John Happy") 165
Rooney, Harry 69
Rosecrans, William Starke 54, 59, 61–62, 65, 68, 108–109, 112–113, 116–117, 120–121, 126–127, 132, 134–135, 138, 140, 144, 148–*149*, 150–151, 166
Rousseau, Lovell Harrison 88, 95–97, 101
Rowan, Agnes "Ann" Lytle 31, 35
Rowan, John 13, 15, 27, 35
Rowan, John, Jr. 76
Rowan, Josephine 76
Rowan, Rebecca 76

Index

Rowan, William Lytle 54
Russell, John Calvin 94
Russell House 94–95, 98, 101–102

St. Clair, Arthur 5
St. Clair, Arthur, Jr. 12
Sandusky, OH 26, 35, 39, 46, 59, 79
Scary Creek, Battle of 61
Schoepf, Albin F. 100
Schofield, John 111
Shankin, James 98, 107
Sheffey, John Preston 67
Shelbyville, TN 79–80, 82, 87, 89, 112–113
Sheridan, Philip 94, 99, 111, 114–115, 119, 125, 127–128, 133, 135–136, 138, 146, 149, 162
Shramm, Herman 36
Shuck, Louis 69
Sill, Joshua 90–91, 111–112
Silver Lake 71
Smith, Edmund Kirby 88, 91, 95
Sorrel, Moxley 134
South Carolina troops: 10th/19th 142
Spencer, E.M. 86–87
Spring Grove Cemetery 39, 160, 162–163, 165, 168
Springer, Jennie 76
Stall, Eliza Noel 12, 14, 162
Stall, Frances 12
Stall, Mary 12
Stanley, David Sloane 126–127
Stanton, Edwin McMasters 106
Starkweather, John Converse 94
Stevenson, AL 115–116, 122, 154
Stones River, Battle of 100, 108, 110, 112
Storer, Bellamy 19
Stowe, Harriet Beecher 35
Sullivan, William ("Billy") 137, 153
Sumner, Charles 52
Sutermeister, Arnold 137
Sutter, Frank 153

Talmadge, Eugene 5
Taylor, John C. 142
Taylor, Zachary 31
Tennessee River 3, 115–116, 121, 123, 154
Tennessee Troops: 18th 79

Thomas, George Henry 126–127, 132, 138, 146
Thomason, E.W. 146–147, 151–152
Thompson, L.P. 152
Todd, Allen 34
Toledo War 23
Toulmin, Harry 142
Trollope, Francis 35
Trowbridge, W.E. 149
Turchin, John Basil 81–82
Turnbull, John 116–117, 120, 123–*124*, 137, 139–140
Tyler, E.B. 59, 61
Tyler, John 31

Venable, William Henry 165
Virginia troops: 22nd 61–63; 36th 61–63; 45th 62–63; 50th 62–63; 51st 62–63; Henry Guy's Goochland Artillery 62–63; Thomas E. Jackson's Horse Artillery 62–63

Wakefield, Alice Rowan 31
Walker, Robert Sparks 5, 167
Wallace, Lew 106
Walworth, Nathan 136
Ward, William M. 117, 152, 154
Washington, George 20–21
Webster, Daniel 9, 20
Weedon, Doctor Hamilton Moore 165
Welker, Martin 46
West, Douglass 145–146
West, Theodore S. 137
Wheeler, Joseph 79, 112
Wickliffe, Charles Anderson 76
Wilder, John Thornton 89
Williamsburg 12
Wilson, John 58
Wilson, Joshua Lacy (J.L.) 15
Wisconsin troops: 24th 111–112, 120, 133, 136–139, 141–143, 148
Wise, Henry A. 60–61, 63, 69
Wood, Sterling Alexander Martin (S.A.M.) 96–97
Wood, Thomas 75, 97, 137–138

Young America 32, 44

www.ingramcontent.com/pod-product-compliance
Lightning Source LLC
Chambersburg PA
CBHW032044300426
44117CB00009B/1182